Hume Nisbet

A colonial tramp - Travels and adventures in Australia and New Guinea

Vol. II

Hume Nisbet

A colonial tramp - Travels and adventures in Australia and New Guinea
Vol. II

ISBN/EAN: 9783337150297

Printed in Europe, USA, Canada, Australia, Japan

Cover: Foto ©Andreas Hilbeck / pixelio.de

More available books at **www.hansebooks.com**

A COLONIAL TRAMP

Travels and Adventures in Australia and New Guinea

BY

HUME NISBET

AUTHOR OF 'THE LAND OF THE HIBISCUS BLOSSOM' 'EIGHT BELLS'
'MEMORIES OF THE MONTHS' ETC.

IN TWO VOLUMES—VOL. II.

London
WARD & DOWNEY
12 YORK STREET, COVENT GARDEN
1891

CONTENTS

OF

THE SECOND VOLUME

CHAPTER XXIX
AT SEA

En route to Brisbane—The Daring Captain—Smoke-room Yarns—'How we were Saved,' and Dick's 'Tale of a Shark' . . 1

CHAPTER XXX
INSECT LIFE

Coast Scenery from Sydney to Brisbane—Moreton Bay and Brisbane River—Impression of Long Ago regarding Foreign Countries—Habits of Insects—Mosquitoes, Scorpions, Centipedes, Fleas, Ants—A Great Battle on a Limited Field . 13

CHAPTER XXXI
BRISBANE

Early Days of Brisbane—A Gold-digging Episode . . 25

CHAPTER XXXII
BRISBANE—*continued*

A Gold-digging Episode—*continued* . . . 34

CHAPTER XXXIII
AUSTRALIANS

Brisbane of To-day—Governors Macquarie and Brisbane—Why all True Australians must be strictly Conservative—A Pious Land Speculator—About some Bazaar Horses—From Bowen Terrace 48

CHAPTER XXXIV
MARYBOROUGH

Sugar Plantations and Kanakas—Black-birding—The 'Young Dick'—An Idea for the Planters The Kanaka Melodies of the Future 60

CHAPTER XXXV
ROCKHAMPTON

Some Shady Passengers—The Lion Comique and Lionesses—Burnett Heads—Keppel Bay and the Fitzroy River A Night at Rockhampton—The Fasting Insect—Rockhampton as it is and as it ought to be 68

CHAPTER XXXVI
MOUNT MORGAN

The Queensland Throne of Greasy Mammon the Great . . 79

CHAPTER XXXVII
COAST SCENERY

Suburbs of Rockhampton—Olsen's Caves—Towards Townsville—Whitsunday Passage—Bowen—Two Nice Young Passengers—A Breakdown at Bowling Green Cleveland Bay and Townsville 91

CHAPTER XXXVIII
HIGHER THAN NIAGARA

The Future Capital of Northern Queensland—Why the Town of Cairns should be Chosen—The Barron River and Falls—Mr. Monk's Idea, and Description by Mr. A. Meston . 100

CHAPTER XXXIX
TO CAPE YORK

Mr. McNaulty of Thursday Island and the Everlasting Ego—The Alexandrine Ranges—Cook Town—Albany Pass, and the Land's End 109

CHAPTER XL
AT THURSDAY ISLAND

Mr. Kerry's Account of a New Guinea Massacre . . . 116

CHAPTER XLI
SAVAGES

At Thursday Island—Kanakas—Superstitions of Savages—Will-power—Cannibalism 127

CHAPTER XLII
CAUSES OF MASSACRES

Savage Customs and Superstitions—Laws of Tapu . . 144

CHAPTER XLIII
NEW GUINEA

A General Survey of New Guinea—Its Possibilities, &c. . . 160

CHAPTER XLIV
THE LAND QUESTION

A General Survey of New Guinea—*continued* . . 169

CHAPTER XLV
THE PAPUAN AT HOME

A General Survey of New Guinea—*continued* . . 179

CHAPTER XLVI
UP MILNE GULF

New Guinea—East Cape—From Samarai to Milne Gulf—Natives on the Rampage—An Errand of Peace—Scenery Going up . 187

CHAPTER XLVII
NEW GUINEA

The Return Journey—Teste Island and Mr. Kessick—Surrounding Islands—Lakatoes and South Cape . . . 205

CHAPTER XLVIII
MISSIONARIES AND TRADERS

The Rev. James Chalmers and his Work—Samarai—Jerry's Swim—Kerepuna—Dressed and Undressed Savages—Currie, Guise, and the *Pall Mall Gazette* 215

CHAPTER XLIX
KEREPUNA

A Big Man—Mourners—Hula—Coast Scenery—Port Moresby—Ellevara and Hanuabada 225

CHAPTER L
PORT MORESBY

A Parting at Port Moresby—Mr. Lawes and Father Vergus, the French Missionary—Laws of Permit—Andrew Goldie and his Journal—A Pretty Sunday-school Story . . . 237

CHAPTER LI
FAREWELL TO NEW GUINEA

The Islands of Torres Straits—Thursday Island, and once more towards Brisbane 250

CHAPTER LII
ABOUT A VEXING QUESTION

To Men and Women who may wish to Emigrate—Where they should go—South and Western Australia—Queensland . 260

CHAPTER LIII
TASMANIA

Prison and Prisoners—Hobart—To Launceston—Mount Bischoff Tin Mine—A Launceston Sage—To Sea . . . 270

CHAPTER LIV
THE AUSTRALIAN ALPS

Featherton, Baldy—Razor Back—The Dargo—Omeo—Kosciusko—The Murray Gates—Drive to Bairnsdale—and End 280

ILLUSTRATIONS
TO THE
SECOND VOLUME

PLATES

SYDNEY HARBOUR FROM NEAR SOUTH HEAD	*Frontispiece*
BRISBANE FROM THE RIVER	*page* 16
THE BUSHRANGER	,, 40
THE BARRON FALLS	,, 96
PETER BOTTE	,, 104
ALEXANDRINE RANGE	,, 112
CAPE MELVILLE	,, 120
THE LIGHTSHIP	,, 128
A NEW-GUINEA DANDY	,, 136
A PAPUAN QUEEN	,, 144
COAST SCENERY	,, 152
MISSION HOUSE, PORT MORESBY	,, 168
PORT MORESBY BY MOONLIGHT	,, 176
HEATH ISLAND, EAST CAPE	,, 184
AROMA, NEW GUINEA	,, 200
CATAMARANS AND LAKATOES	,, 208
BELL AND CLIFFY ISLANDS	,, 216

TAPU HOUSE AND HUTS	page 224
THE GARDENS OF HULA	„ 232
KAPA-KAPA, NEW GUINEA . . .	„ 240
MORNI-CHERNÉ	„ 248
FROM MURRAY ISLAND, TORRES STRAITS . . .	„ 256
MOUNT YULE . . .	„ 264
WHITE TERRACE, NEW ZEALAND . . .	„ 272
VICTORIAN ALPS, MOUNT KOSCIUSKO .	„ 280

IN TEXT

	PAGE
QUEENSLAND NATIVE WEAPONS . .	52
A QUEENSLAND ABORIGINAL .	85
A QUEENSLAND GIN . . .	87

A COLONIAL TRAMP

CHAPTER XXIX

AT SEA

En Route to Brisbane—The Daring Captain—Smoke-room Yarns—
'How we were Saved,' and Dick's 'Tale of a Shark.'

A DAY or two before I left for Brisbane the whole of the Colonies were ringing with the news of a most awful wreck which had occurred between Melbourne and Sydney. One of the coasting steamers had gone ashore and foundered, losing most of the passengers, so that people were chary about putting to sea.

Yet I knew that the old adage was a true one: One is never so safe at sea as just after a wreck. The coasting skippers like to beat the record in their runnings, and so have a tendency to cut sharply round corners, and this is where the danger lies. Familiarity has made them grow contemptuous of the rocks in the way, and so they sometimes strike and go down, and there is no coast so relentless to wrecked sailors as the Australian coast is, except it be the cliff-coast of New Zealand.

Two rival steamers were leaving for Brisbane when I got to the Wharf. The captain of one belonged to the slow-and-sure school, and the other was managed by the most dare-devil captain of all those who run inside Sydney Heads; he always got up to Brisbane a few hours before his rival, and hitherto had always carried his passengers safely. So I decided upon the swiftest and, as it proved, the most comfortable ship.

After dinner, while I was walking along the deck smoking, this daring captain joined me in a cigar. During the conversation I remarked, casually:

'I heard that you were the most reckless skipper round Australia. That is why I took my passage aboard.'

The captain took out his cigar and looked me over savagely. 'What the —— do you mean, sir?'

'Well, you see I want to get to Brisbane—or heaven—as soon as possible,' I replied quietly.

'Look here,' said he, grasping my arm and pointing to a yellow light away on the left, 'do you see that light in there?'

'Yes, captain.'

'That's the other ship which left along with us—the slow one—two miles nearer the coast than we are. What do you say to that for safety, eh?'

'That I have wronged you, captain, and apologise.'

We shook hands over it. He did not say, and I did not let him know I was aware, that at the time we were boldly cutting in a straight line from promontory to promontory, and that the steady and sure captain was keeping his usual safe distance all the way round, hugging the shore for fear of the storm which was brewing outside. There was no use going into such details.

'And I'll tell you what, we'll be in Brisbane eight hours before him in spite of his reckless folly.'

I didn't doubt it in the least, so shortly afterwards we adjourned to the smoke-room, where several of the passengers had gathered to play cards and tell yarns.

One old man, who was the owner of a pearl-fishing station in the Torres, got on to telling of an adventure which he had with the natives of New Guinea, and as I intended going there I pricked up my ears to listen.

They called him the Captain, as he owned several fishing sloops in those parts. He was half-way through with his yarn, but, as I could gather, he had been wrecked near Cloudy Bay on a coral reef, with only time for himself and men to get ashore by swimming. As we entered he was saying:

'Yes, mates, I have been into many a hair-raising scrape in my life before and since, but this appeared to be the very worst; here we stood, five men and a boy, on the sands of New Guinea, with our cutter forty fathoms under water, her bottom ground to matchwood on the cruel reefs, and ourselves without a weapon of defence, in the midst of the most savage tribes of man-eaters which the habitable globe could produce, weapon-less, foodless, and with only what we had upon us when the cutter went down, waiting for the day to dawn to be discovered and trussed up like a row of winged ducks.

'It had all happened in a moment: rough water outside, we thinking to get past the reef into a haven of rest, a sudden shock and crunching like rats' teeth, time only to jump overboard and swim ashore as best we could, while our little "Sarah" went down like a thunderbolt, and left us helpless.

'We were at the mouth of Cloudy Bay, which, if any of you knows the geography of those parts, meant slow roasting alive as soon as the natives woke up in the morning and got a peep at us.

'A splendid country as far as scenery went, but, Lord bless you! what was scenery to us, watching through the long night, wet, miserable, and without even a quid of tobacco to stay the pangs of hunger, knowing as we all did what was before us as soon as daylight came to show up those beautiful mountains, valleys and forests behind us, as we stood shivering on the sands.

'"God help us," I muttered, as I saw the daylight at last steal ghost-like over the blue-grey hilltops, and then turned seaward in the vain hope of a distant sail—nothing, only the snow-white surf breaking over the murderous coral reef, and the tumbling black line of water beyond.

'Yet, within the reef I did see something—a case of some sort slowly drifting with the inflowing tide to shore. In a moment every man was active, wading and swimming out to secure the treasure. We had it ashore in no time, and prised it open with our fingers and nails, thinking it might be meat, or tobacco.

'I appreciate the comforts of a nice bath and good soap to wash with as well as any man, but to find, instead of tucker or tobacco, a case of *Pears' Soap*, on a cannibal land, as we then were, was a disappointment which language fails to express, although we all at the moment used it pretty strong.

'"Close round the case, boys; they are coming," I shouted, as I saw the sun lift itself over the peaks, and in front of us about fifty mop-headed savages armed with bows, arrows, and spears, rushing round the promontory pell-mell upon us.

'On they came at a run until about fifteen yards distant; then, seeing us all standing quietly waiting upon them, they paused, and after a minute or two of palaver amongst themselves sent out their chief to talk to us.

'Seeing this I grabbed up an armful of the soap tablets and advanced from my men to meet him. He was a savage-looking fellow, stark naked excepting for some shark's teeth round his neck, but as he noticed the load I carried I saw his eyes lighten up at the amber-like cakes which the sun was now shining upon; thus I felt a little hopeful. This was a novelty in the land, and novelties, when they do take the popular fancy, mean success both in savage and civilised communities.

'Going straight up to this noble man-eater I held out a cake for his acceptance. He took it, smelt it, and afterwards tasted it, but did not seem to take to it in that fashion, for he turned upon me with a heavy scowl.

'Then I hastened, by pantomimic action, to show how it was used amongst us. Ah, that took, for if the Papuan is fond of anything, it is of washing and bathing himself. Seeing a little fresh-water stream running near by, I led the chieftain by the arm over to it, first washing my own hands to show him the way, and then giving him the tablet to use himself.

'What a scrubbing took place for the next ten minutes amongst these copper-skins, and how they glistened in the sun afterwards! Bows, arrows, and spears were pitched headlong down, while they lathered one another, and tossed fresh water over their bodies.

'We were saved, and made medicine-men of the tribe on the spot, while the Dubo house was decorated with the pictorial advertisements of this great firm, and ourselves treated to the very best in the village. Two weeks afterwards, when we were rescued by Her Majesty's cruising war-sloop, we left behind us at least one tribe in New Guinea who had taken with the first leap the last step of civilisation. They were happy in the possession of Pears' Soap, and disconsolate that the stock was getting low, for they used nearly the same words, when they bade us farewell and implored us to return with more, that the accomplished Jersey Lily writes: "It had become a necessity which they could not live without." '

There was a slight pause after the Torres Straits skipper had finished—not one of incredulity, as no one, to look upon that open, sun-tanned, grey-whiskered, and scanty-tressed countenance, could have dared to doubt the accuracy of his legend. It was a respectful pause, such as we are used to in church after the parson has uttered the final 'Amen.'

Then someone broke the ice by making a remark upon the voracity of sharks, and wondering how they ever got ashore in such a shark-infested sea. A few related hair-breadth escapes which they had had from the monsters, when finally one young fellow called Dick said: 'There's a mighty difference between a deep-sea shark and a ground-shark. Did you ever try to catch a regular bluenose?'

We all remarked that we hadn't, and then he began his narrative.

Story of a Shark.

'We had reached the Line after a fair share of roughing it at Cape Horn—running short of water through our condensing machine breaking down, an accident which might have been exceedingly disagreeable but for the amusement we contrived to *extract* from it, our skipper being fond of experimenting and obstinate in his convictions. However, that threads me on to another hank, which will serve again.

'We had got into the doldrums, and filled our casks with the everlasting rains, and now lay rocking and sweltering on an ultramarine plain, under an ultramarine sky, with the sun straight overhead, and only the shadow of our soles on the heated deck underneath.

'There was nothing to be done except wash our shirts, pour water over the crackling boards, and lie half-dressed under awnings on the poop, but even there to sit long was to stick fast to the melting pitch that oozed upwards from every gaping seam.

'The skipper had gone down to sleep it out, the little French officer, my fellow-passenger, had retired to his cigarette and diluted claret, when one of the men proposed a swim, to which all hands eagerly agreed, there being no one to forbid it.

'Off went our shirts and ducks, and in another moment we were all floundering in the deepest of known waters.

'The boldest amongst us went aloft to one of the yards, and took the plunge from there. As I watched them cleave the breast of that intense ocean, it seemed as if they had disappeared into liquid cobalt, and the length of time which elapsed before they appeared to view again showed the fearsome depth they had dived into.

'I am not a bold swimmer, so that I made use of the rope which hung over the ship's side, and let myself down very gently. What a sensation it was to turn my back to the vessel, and, letting go the rope, consign myself to immensity! Blue above, blue beneath, blue on every side. It felt as if with that rope I had let go my hold of life, and was floating on a blue immensity.

'I struck out, but could not drive away the awesome fear. Blue sparkles flew from my limbs; blue got into my very brain; until just as I felt the desire to throw up my arms in horror and sink in it, the skipper's angry voice came booming from behind, ordering us all on deck at once. A scramble at the rope's end, and we stood before him like discovered schoolboys, dripping, and making shame-faced lunges for our clothes.

'"Did any one ever hear the like of this—floundering in an ocean swarming with sharks! See yonder! Where would some of you have been but for my timely appearance?"

'He pointed over the side to where a pair of black spots appeared to be floating, and immediately forgot to rage as the sportsman's instinct leapt into action.

'"Quick, steward! A lump of pork, and the longest line we have aboard."

'We got the big whale-hook baited with about ten pounds of raw pork, and, taking our positions on the poop, let it over, and prepared to watch.

'Then a very pretty little play began: the black fins never moved from where they lay, but from the locality darted forward a small green-and-white barred fish like a mackerel, right up to the pork, seeming to smell it all over, and with critical scrutiny examine it.

'"All right," concluded the pilot, as he darted back to inform his chief. No good. For a female she was wonderfully cautious, but then she was a matron, as we saw afterwards, so had a right to be careful.

'Again the pilot swam round the bait, and reckoned it up on all sides as perfectly safe; indeed, brought the two baby sharks, of whom he evidently was nurse, to have a look as well, and confirm his opinion.

'Back trotted the two young things with their active attendant, and, adding their juvenile voices to that of the more experienced critic and guide, evidently overruled even maternal caution, for the fins began to sail closer.

'On they glided, with the pilot leading the way, and the youngsters in the rear, until from our elevated position we could see the gigantic outline of the monster fully revealed in the sunlit depth below us.

'She was a blue-nose, one of the largest and most savage of the shark species, evidently roused up from her deep repose by the smell of sailor, and not quite satisfied with the substituted salt pork. I shuddered as I thought of my swim, and vowed "never again" to take an equatorial ocean bath.

'But still, it didn't seem good enough. Mrs. Shark either had been at this sort of game before, or else expected a bigger feed, for after a sniff or two she drew off.

'"Go it, mum," seemed to observe the pilot fish; "it is all right; better than nothing." "Yes, mammy, or let us have a try." "No!" she seemed to say in disgust, "that's not the kind of grub I smelt ten minutes ago. I feel inclined to wait." "Take it while you wait," observed the pilot fish persuasively, going round it once more. "It's really good, and I'll get what you leave."

'"Well, since it's all we're likely to get, here goes," and with a long-suffering air Madam drew languidly near, and, turning slowly round, revealed her snowy bosom and horse-shoe-shaped archway of a mouth.

'The half-circle unclosed, and we shivered at the rows of jagged teeth, interlacing after the most approved form of cross-cut saws, which the action revealed.

'Nearer, in no hurry seemingly, and just as it was about to close, did some warning strike her sharkly mind, as she again drew back? If so, she shook off the presentiment, for next time she came rapidly, gaped, and closed with a jerk.

'"Look out for the line. Stand all clear," yelled the skipper, as he prepared to tug.

'Jerk! and a piece of Madam's jaw came out with the pork. It had been a haul too soon.

'Now began the sport, for Madam showed her temper. Some fish, I suppose most fish, treated in this rough way would have bolted, and never looked behind them. Not so this specimen of the blue waters. With a splash she went back a few yards, and leaping forward with a savage twist turned swiftly round, bolted pork and hook in an angry moment, and then went straight down like a thunderbolt.

'Well for us that we had leapt back out of reach of the line; well for the man telling it out that there was no hank anywhere; well that the line was an extra long one, and that the water was plentiful to throw on to the gunwale, for how that fish went for it! What a depth the ocean must be at the Equator! I leaned over and watched that line bolting down, the centre of a spiral column of crystals, never slackening speed until within a fathom or two of its end.

'There was a moment's pause, and it grew suddenly slack, and we began to haul aboard.

'"Look out against her next bolt," cried the skipper, as he himself stood out of the way.

'Up she darted, half out of the water, snapping at the iron chain in her mouth, and then away once more, this time along the surface.

'And so she flashed along, her black upper fins working about, now half out, now wholly under water, with the pilot in her rear and the two youngsters hopping about, the pilot looking horribly distressed, like an old retainer who had accidentally poisoned the family, and the young ones knowing something was up, and wondering what it could be.

'To the very end of her tether the old dame spun, then brought up with a jerk, and turned shipward to find out the cause and avenge the insult.

'And so again we hauled and wound up the windlass turn by turn, until we had brought her alongside.'

'And then you lifted her, I suppose,' interrupted the

listeners, impatient at the length of the yarn and anxious to end it. 'Your story, old man, is about as long as the line you let out to catch the fish. Wind it up, Dick, my boy, wind it up.'

'There's little more to tell you. As we hauled her out of the water the pork once more appeared, with a fresh supply of shark attached to the hook, and the shark, with a snort, flopped back again.'

Dick clearly had lost all enthusiasm in the narrative after this pull up, for he spoke dejectedly and with an effort.

'Then she got off, after all?'

'No! Opposition acted on her as on all her sex. She got desperate to be caught, snapped at the bait viciously for the third time, and, I believe, rather than be thwarted, fixed in the hook of her own accord, for when we hauled in the next time she came along with the pork intact.'

'You'd have considerable trouble getting her up?'

'Yes, some. One of the seamen, a half-caste American Indian, with a war-whoop that would have done him credit on a prairie or at a Buffalo Bill show, forked out his jack-knife, and sprang overboard with a piece of rope in his hands, and the knife between his teeth, when to the music of her lashing tail he carved out a dead-eye in her hide, and fixed his rope.'

Dick was getting more helpless in his style. Clearly his interest had departed in the story.

'The pilot waited until the last with his charges, and then, when he had seen his much-loved mistress hoisted fairly over the ship's side, with tears streaming down his venerable cheeks, he mournfully tucked the babies under his fins, and vanished in purple froth.'

'I suppose you cut her up?'

'That's right; we cut her up, punched a marline-spike

down her throat to keep her gnawing, hacked off her lashing tail, and dodged generally out of the gory tracks.'

'Did you find anything inside her?'

'Find?' echoed Dick, absently. 'Oh yes! Lots of relics: a wedding-ring, two brooches, part of a decomposed letter from a missing boatswain of the skipper's, informing his wife at home of the thundering walloping in store for her when this utilised husband only got home again; a chew of tobacco, from the size and quality estimated likewise to have belonged to that blasphemous but untimely-taken-away boatswain; some bone buttons, and a bundle of tracts.'

Dick drawled out these details in monotonous tones. Was it through lack of interest, or else was he beginning to embellish his formerly unvarnished tale?

'Yes, we cut her up, made necklaces out of her gleaming teeth, and——'

Dick here brightened up a little.

'The best bit of the whole was that when I told that story to a London audience, and mentioned how the beast's severed heart leapt about the deck like a lively frog for six or seven hours after, until the sun went down, a wiseacre of a clergyman who was present solemnly told me that he might swallow the rings and buttons, even go the length of making a single pill out of that bundle of tracts, but when it came to the beating heart—No! Principle compelled him, as a humble minister of the Gospel, to decline that with thanks.'

CHAPTER XXX

INSECT LIFE

Coast Scenery from Sydney to Brisbane—Moreton Bay and Brisbane River—Impression of Long Ago regarding Foreign Countries Habits of Insects—Mosquitoes, Scorpions, Centipedes, Fleas, Ants—A Great Battle on a Limited Field.

WE certainly did not loiter on the way between Sydney and Brisbane under the management of our energetic captain; never had the engines so much work to do, or the piston so many strokes to make up and down. If he was keeping farther out to sea than was his usual custom, he meant to make up the extra distance by extra speed, for we literally boiled along the blue opposing waves.

Past Newcastle, the chief shipping-port of New South Wales, with its fixed white lighthouse of Nobby, which we can see plainly as we pass, it being night time.

Sometimes we lose sight of land altogether as we cross a bay, but we always make up again close enough to the points to let me get good sketching. Past Port Stephens, Sugarloaf Point, Cape Hawke, Crowdy Head, Port Macquarie—one of the most picturesque seaports all along the coast, and centre of a large planting district, the outcome of the productive lands about the Macleay, Hastings, and Clarence Rivers.

Point Korogoro looms up boldly as we shave it, then Trial Bay, where they are making great harbour works, and which is intended to be the main centre of the New England District.

We next sight Smoky Cape, Solitary Island, with its lighthouse, Fish Island with the white waves breaking against its barren sides, Trial Bay, with the very small white granite station of Arakoon, Capes Byron and Danger. We are now in the vast colony of Queensland, and in the region of the great squatting paradise, the Darling Downs.

Past Beenleigh, Stradbroke Island, Cleveland, Moreton Island, and into Moreton Bay, and near to our journey's end. We have beaten time by six hours, and the rival company by twelve, and the captain is once more jubilant.

Stradbroke Island is the second largest in the Colony; it is thirty-three miles long by six broad. Moreton Island comes next, and is twenty miles by six.

Moreton Bay, or Harbour, is forty miles long by seventeen miles wide, and receives the water of six navigable rivers—the Narang, Pimpana, Logan, Brisbane, Pine, and Caboolture; it is formed by the Islands of Birbie, Moreton and Stradbroke, as well as the mainland, and gives a safe anchorage in any part of it to all sizes of vessels.

I have seen some curiously-shaped mountains, but nothing so strange as the shape of the Glass House Mountains as they are seen from Moreton Bay. It was Captain Cook who named these, from their likeness to glass-houses. I did not quite see the resemblance myself, as the two outermost ones looked more like gigantic ant-hills or African huts, while the centre one was like a carved elephant's tusk placed upright; they are on the mainland, and not far from the sea coast.

A pleasant bay this is to sail into, and filled with old associations, with a busy and fertile river, the Brisbane, up which we steam for the twenty-five miles between the bay and the capital—low, muddy banks when the tide is in, with reeds beyond watermark. Vessels of all sizes lie about, or sail up and down, clouds overhead breaking up the sky, and settlers' huts, Chinese and European, dotting the shores behind, with the gum tree forming a picturesque background.

Years ago these Glass House Peaks were the first Australian landmarks which met my eyes after four months' of uninterrupted ocean line, and the shores of Brisbane my first experience of a foreign land.

When we read about a country which we have never seen, we are very apt to form our own ideal of that country. And, as a rule, in that ideal land the sun generally smiles upon the fruit trees and the flower-bespangled plains, and Nature puts on her most seductive costume.

Snakes do not sojourn there, nor centipedes; the fireflies may twinkle about, but the mosquitoes only hum.

A hot country is quite pleasant to think about on a cold night, is it not?

After we had lost sight of old England's shores, and while we forged along the deep blue ocean under a soft blue velvety sky, or lay on deck watching myriads of strange stars blazing up above, or leaned over the taffrail and followed with our eyes the line of silver light that flashed from our ship's side and sparkled away into the blackness of that boundless waste, we wrought out mental pictures of the land before us, sketched them in vaguely, spent time over them course by course until they were finished to the last touch—and they were always bright and cheery, I can tell you.

I don't think I ever put a rain-cloud in one of these mental pictures, the sky was always blue and fair; there were palm trees always waving their feathery tops, and bananas always wagging their loaded tails.

I wasn't quite so sure what bananas were, nor how

high the pine-apple trees grew out there, but I knew that they were good eating, and I had seen a date, and tasted the milk of the cocoa-nut, and so I felt pretty well content.

I never saw any dust there except gold dust, and that lay about by the sackful, so I had no cause to complain of being choked.

So I drew, and so the vessel drew every day nearer its port; months became weeks, weeks grew into days, days shrivelled into hours, and hours brought us to Moreton Bay, with its sharks. The tug carried us up the river Brisbane, where we tasted our first fresh bread and colonial mutton, and cracked our first fancy about gentle heat. We landed at Brisbane Quay, to be greeted by thousands of touters, tens of thousands of ragged hungry hangers-on, and hundreds of thousands of famished mosquitoes.

These latter came on in legions—ten thousand legions to the man; they came in hosts, in clouds, with columns of burning dust, without a speck of gold about it to console us; palm trees were from home, pellucid streams a dead fallacy, fireflies too uncertain to be considered, and bananas a tattered failure.

Nothing was like what we had dreamt it; only the snakes and the centipedes and mosquitoes came above the mark.

This was the reaction of course, the first stroke between the eyes that drove away idle fancy before the stern face of reality. Afterwards, when the dream had become subordinate, and we could look upon things dispassionately, we found ways of treating with even mosquitoes, and means of evading the sand clouds.

Queensland, when we landed, was suffering sadly from an emigration surfeit. People without any capital, many without proper trades, had immigrated by thousands, expecting to find a warm welcome and an easy berth provided for them the moment they set foot ashore, the consequence

BRISBANE FROM THE RIVER.

of their own and the emigration company's want of foresight being that before very long they were homeless and bootless loafers, without either much hope or much desire left in them to better their condition.

Talking about warm welcomes, I experienced a most strikingly warm one on the day of my arrival. I saw on the wharf as we moored alongside hordes of barefooted loafers, male and female, and seeing only an occasional pairs of boots here and there, I fancied they were the exception, and that the rule of that country was ease before elegance, and so inclination backing up the force of example, I just paused to take off my boots and socks from my swelling feet, and the first object which I landed upon, with my bare soles, was an iron plate which had been laid down a few moments before, red hot, on that wharf to cool.

It may appear strange to those accustomed to red-hot plates, and I hope I did not act injudiciously; yet I must tell you that I did not linger upon that plate, neither did I strike up the dignified position one might expect from an exile greeting his adopted land for the first time. I did say a few words, however, which I need not now repeat, as I left my roasted soles behind me, and sought out a quiet position by the river to cool my feet in for the rest of the day. Ah! that was a warm welcome.

Brisbane at this time was a gay place, consisting mostly of wood houses which their owners raised up with the help of some neighbours on a moonlight night, painted and papered next day, and held their first party in the night after. You might pass a bare paddock some evening, when a cart of wood and some piles were being unloaded, and repass the same paddock next morning to find a house erected, verandah and fence complete, and the proprietor gravely mixing up his white lead to begin the next stage, decoration.

Or, if the first position did not please the owner, it was no uncommon sight to see him and family take up their house and walk to the next block, or half-dozen streets off, as the new locality might have been decided on. That is one advantage of a wooden house.

Brisbane on a sunny day—and that was every day for at any rate nine months in the year—was a cheery place to live in, despite its excessive heat, its snakes ashore, and sharks afloat; of course you could not venture to sit down on a grass plot, if you were lucky enough to find one, without first beating the ground with your cane for fear of sleeping snakes; and if you felt a creeping sensation under your ducks, it became a matter of speculation as you carefully rolled up the canvas as to whether it would be a soldier ant, a tiger mosquito, a centipede, or a scorpion; sometimes, to be sure, it turned out to be only a colony of fleas; but again it might be either of the others.

Fleas are not very respectable members to introduce to the notice of a polite audience, but still, as an undoubted fact, even in this country, where the sight of one solitary straggler is a blush-raising evidence of their being, I feel constrained to give them the place which their colonial importance entitles them to in my experiences. Fleas abroad are by no means objects to be ashamed of as they are with us; indeed, it would be very little use to feel there as we do here, seeing that they are everywhere, and on everything animate and inanimate. I have seen the white dresses of ladies embroidered round the skirt with about three inches of what appeared to be black lace, but which really were countless hoards of wrangling insects; gentlemen with deep black borders round their white linen trousers, so thickly were they clustered that you could only at rare moments catch a glimpse of white between—moments when a few weakly or immature members were knocked off the course by the old stagers. And yet, crowded though they were, they were so modest in their pretensions that I have been worse worried with one home-bred marauder than I ever was with the countless hordes abroad. Perhaps they were, like human office-seekers, so many candidates after each place that they lost all the time abusing one another, and so forgot what they were fighting about. I sometimes think that is how we got off so easily.

Now mosquitoes are very different in their mode of treating a victim, especially if they can get hold of a nice fat juicy new chum; you can always tell new chums the moment they land by their fresh and rosy complexion, and if you fail to recognise a new chum on the first day of his arrival, I defy any one, with half an eye, to be able to mistake him the day *after* his arrival. Talk about fresh complexions, or raw beefsteaks, or a prize-fighter after twenty-eight rounds; these are only mild symbols compared with the new chum after he has had his first night with the mosquitoes. You search in vain for nose, lips, or eyes; if lucky—that is, if let off easy—you may trace where the ears once were, or might make a rough conjecture as to the probable position of a chin, but the rest of that puffed-out scarlet outline is a blank space; from a slight pucker there comes a muffled voice, but even the blasphemy you ought to expect, seeing the condition of the object before you, and knowing what he was capable of in this line yesterday, becomes lost as it struggles out in a melancholy monotone.

I learned to smoke battling with mosquitoes. I used to concoct the vilest abominations, and, setting fire to them, revelled, even while I choked in the reeking of that awful incense to keep them at bay. I used to oil myself from crown to toe before retiring, like an Indian housebreaker; and when olive oil could not keep them off I used to try candle grease, until life became a burden, all to have the quiet hour of peace which I never had until I had patiently borne the infliction, and paid the taxes with my blood.

The humming demons! I used to sit up at night with the candle burning outside the mosquito-netting, and listen to their tantalising songs as they hovered all round; sit up smoking, in spite of heartburn and squeamishness, watching the old reckless ones dash themselves frantically against the barrier; the watchful ones soaring round, on the look-out for a rent or portion not firmly fastened in, through which they might enter and devour; or the thoughtful matrons providing for their young by pushing them through the holes they were too big themselves to enter — signs of insect intelligence and devotion which never touched me half so much as they might have done had the food provided for those graceful and melodious young things been another person instead of myself.

It is rather difficult, you must all admit, to give that grave and philosophical attention, or calculate with the deliberation required to satisfy scientists, the exact virulence of a wasp's poison if the sting has been just inserted in your own body. We might even give the matter more fair play if the objects of our calculation were the wasp and a very dear relative, but it is difficult to calculate calmly between the wasp and ourselves.

We have some very clever insects in this country, I will admit, but they are complete duffers compared with the insects abroad—the ants in all their many varieties. I remember once sitting down on a tree-trunk in the bush to ruminate, and as I pondered I was beating the ground idly with my cane, not looking much at what I was disturbing, when after a time, happening to glance in that direction, I saw that I had cut a poor soldier ant in two—there he lay, writhing, with his red jacket on one side of my stick and his black trousers on the other.

I felt sorry for this idle destruction, and stopped at once the pitiful game, and, looking remorsefully in the direction of that slaughtered life—a life perhaps more useful at that moment than mine had hitherto been—I perceived that I had done much more damage with that senseless beating of my stick. I had broken up the deposits of years, perhaps of centuries—mosses, and lichen, and fine tissues of roots. I had desecrated homesteads, for I saw hundreds of families rushing away from the earthquake without even taking time to gather up their relics or belongings; and I knew that I had wrought destruction and caused consternation far beyond where my imperfect eyes could pierce.

I was exercising myself with these reflections and humiliations, as we might all do every instant of our clumsy lives if we only took time to consider, when I saw a friend of my military victim march up. Stopping at the black half, now still, he examined it carefully round and round; next came under scrutiny the red half; then an examination of both; a near inspection separately, and then a distant survey of both and the space between; a long pause as he apparently pondered upon the cause, then a dash at my stick, as if the inspiration had struck him suddenly that this was it; up the inanimate stick his bright eye wandered to the active hand that had used it; and then off, with resolution in his tread, he passed out of my sight.

'Is he frightened,' I wondered, 'that he made away like that?'

The day was inviting to loaf, and so I loafed and watched my dead soldier. Presently came along a little black ant and also examined the corpse, but more with the air of a speculator than one afflicted; he caught hold of first one piece and tried to drag it away, and finding it too much of a load he tried the next; both, however, were too heavy for him, so he too departed with an air of business.

By-and-by from where the soldier had disappeared there came along a couple of redcoats; straight up they came to where the body lay, and after a repetition of the former examination, they consulted and went off in different directions.

Next came back the black ant with six more, and began to drag off the spoil in unison, three to each half; but after a time I saw they were tired, for three left the red-coated half, and, joining the others, bore away the other half easily.

While they were gone, I saw from the different directions which the two soldiers had gone a crowd of soldier ants appear, each band being led on by one soldier ant who walked in front. Up they marched in beautiful order, and, joining together by the red half of their dead comrade, began their court-martial. I thought, as I watched them, that there was a movement of surprise when they could only see one portion of the dead ant, and that this seemed to alter some former determinations which they had agreed upon; for, after looking at the stick, they all drew back and worked about amongst themselves as if excited and talking.

While they were thus engaged, the six black fellows returned for their spoil, and, seeing the enemy in force, they retreated with speed.

This was seen by the soldiers, and two made off after them, to be again driven back by a crowd of black ants, who came on as if by magic from every quarter in countless hosts.

Now began a war between the black ants and the soldier ants. The soldier ants were bigger and stronger, but the black ants were about a hundred to one; and while the soldiers knocked them down by the dozen, they swarmed up again on their backs and all over them, until I hardly saw any red at all.

It was a great battle I can tell you, although all going on at my feet : squares were formed, and battalions drawn off, but numbers won the day. The soldier ants like the gallant French people, and the black hordes who swarmed over every place seemed to me like the Prussian legions who were at that time lying before Paris.

I saw who was going to win, and forgot, in my sympathy for the big fools, the destruction I had already wrought upon one of them ; for lifting up my stick, I moved it amongst them, breaking up all their battle lines, and sending the black myriads scurrying away in all directions.

When peace was once more restored, the remnant of the soldiers—for they did not seem so frightened by the stick—gathered once more together to consult ; and it wasn't the number they had lost which seemed to concern them so much as the half of the soldier which I had killed. That was the reason of their coming together, and it had to be settled first.

While I looked they came to a determination, and made a rush up my stick, up inside my trousers, up inside my sleeves ; their purpose was revenge, and I quickly had my punishment—for soldier ants can bite, I assure you—and in a few moments I was jumping about half-mad from the attack of that regiment of redcoats. And while I jumped about shaking them from me and killing them in self-defence this time, the wise little black ants, too mercantile to bother about profitless vengeance, again assembled by the thousands, and occupied themselves in bearing off, for burial or for food, the dead carcases of fallen friends and foes.

I have seen a dead dog thrown down one day in the

sun, and a day or so after have picked up the skeleton glittering white, without the faintest vestige of marrow or flesh upon it. A tramp goes along a road, and turns into the bush, and losing himself within a very short distance, is known only by his shirt and trousers in less than a month after, when some stockrider's nervous horse shies aside from the shining skull. Ants very soon polish bones in the colonies.

CHAPTER XXXI

BRISBANE

Early Days of Brisbane—A Gold-Digging Episode.

BRISBANE, with its wooden houses all painted white, and the trellised verandahs round about them, some with grape vines and Passion fruit clustering up, and the dripping, tattered fringe of a banana tree growing round the end, is picturesque after the first shock is over—the first shock of eternal glare, dry dust and white or red sand—fields of caked earth instead of grass, for that is all fired up by the sun ; and all vegetation is useless unless watered by the owners. It is a gay city, in spite of the ragged loafing emigrants who stalk about by the hundred in rags that would make even a Belfast beggar blush, and that is going a long way down the social scale of tatters.

Here women meet you during the day in the daintiest of dimity and muslins that are cooling to look upon, and sail along the silvered pavements on a moonlight night—and such immense globes of gold those southern moons are !—with variegated silks that shimmer and rustle with prismatic thrills that strike upon the senses like chords of music.

It is a sight to remember on a moonlight night—the great spiders' webs, those tarantulas about the size of saucers, with the long hairy claws, spinning thick lines from passage to passage, and even at times across the lanes, from verandah to verandah, with those vast geometrical problems hung up between the passers-by and that golden disc, catching the heavy dew, and upon which are shed gleaming fly-wings, stars shooting down sparks of musselshell tones; spider-webs which catch the passers-by who may have stepped aside from the beaten track with tenacious and dank but tender welts across the eyelids—welts that strike deeper than the skin, although so lightly dealt, for the chill of expectancy, shot from the surprise, rushes down to the heart, and checks, for a moment, its beats. Those vast geometrical shapes that were repeated in silver and sable on the pavement; the blackness from the verandah roof, with the white glare on the end beyond; the lamps under their coloured shades inside furnished rooms, or well-filled shops—butchers' shops with their rich tones, grocers' shops with their glittering, fruit stalls with their variations of delight!

The men smoking in their white trousers and broad straw hats, and puggarees falling to the neck, and inside billiard-rooms young men working hard with their chalked cues over green tables, or marking scores on black screens with white stops, or wiping the large sweat-beads from their foreheads against their rolled-back, cream-tinted flannel sleeves.

Spiders in Australia are by no means the harmless workers of web-craft that they are here. Black spiders and the mighty tarantulas bite, and bite dangerously—I have known a man to be laid up for six months in hospital through the bite of a spider; for that matter I have seen people taken to the hospital from the effects of mosquito biting; but cases of this kind, like cases of snake, centipede, and scorpion biting, are very rare, considering the number, variety of the species, and the chances they constantly have of exercising their venom.

In lifting a stone which has lain for some time on the ground you may dislodge a whole menagerie of varied and ugly specimens of poisonous biters: the puny little scorpion, who turns up its tail and pierces both ends; the centipede, with about an inch of green-yellow at the end and the rest of its six or ten inches of length of the most revolting pallid dun. I always hated the look of these more than the snakes; perhaps it was from their unsympathetic colour, or the afterthought of my first night's experience in Queensland.

There had been a tropic shower—quite an event at that season—and Brisbane looked its very freshest, as I opened the windows of my bedroom, and drank in the fragrance from the fruit trees, the pine-apples, and the trumpet lilies, wafted in on the night air, rain-cooled, ozone-freighted. Coming, as it did, from the direction of Moreton Bay, I forgot the dust of the mid-day; even the recollection of that red-hot plate was deadened into a dull numbness. It was all delightful, all my fancy had hoped it would be, and so, as yet mosquito-innocent, I gave a sigh of intense contentment, and, blowing out my candle, turned into bed.

For fully ten minutes I lay, looking through the netting round my bed, through the black framework of the window, like elaborated carved work, where the vine leaves broke the straight edging of the squares, and showed me the opal lustre above the distant bush-outline which preceded the rising of the moon. A deep grey cloud or two hung above that lustre like gigantic flying foxes with outspread wings, dark against the blue of the sky beyond, where stars were hung like electric lamps, towards that opal lustre at the horizon.

And through all this tropic loveliness came the sea-air, softly breathing past the pine-apple beds and the orange orchards and the trumpet lily trees, heavily laden, since it first caught up the ocean brine-aroma, with the refinement of those varied scents.

Outside I heard the croaking chorus of a community of frogs, the old king leading off with his bass, and the others going up the scale according to sex and age until it wound up with the shrill treble of the youngest chorister; a song without a termination, bass, tenor, alto, and soprano, only broken at intervals by the jeering burst of mockery from the laughing jackass in the distant bush, as it caught up its victim snake, and, darting swiftly above the highest gum tree, shrieked out with wild laughter to see it sink prone through the air and break its back against a bare branch as it fell to earth.

I heard the locusts ticking and chirruping, and the vine leaves softly rustle, and through all the melody the everlasting humming of those tiny tormentors of whose existence I was yet to learn. This humming was soothing to my ignorance, and I was just inhaling all the delicacies and confusing all the melodies, and passing away from it all into sleep, when a heavy soft thud from the rafters broke my mosquito netting and hit the coverlet above my shoulder, driving, in one sudden bang, sleep from my eyes, music from my ears, perfume from my nostrils, and filling all my senses instead with intense horror.

It was too heavy for anything my imagination could conceive except a serpent. The soft thud was too horribly suggestive of snakedom for me to be calm. I had no matches to strike a light, even if I dared move, which I candidly confess I dared not. I could only yell out; this I did, incoherently connecting snakes with fire and murder and a few other popular war-cries, which speedily brought to my rescue the landlady and lodgers, male and female, in their varied conditions of night attire.

It was only an old venomous centipede, about ten inches

long, which had been the cause of all this disturbance—drawn out of its nest in the shingles by the hour's heavy rain, and coming down to my bed for more comfort, so the landlady lightly told me, as she daintily picked it up with the snuffers, and coolly held it over the candle till it frizzled and fried and writhed, and polluted the air with its smoke, while I lay shivering with disgust and horror, watching it being reduced by that practical lady into a brown cinder.

I got used to these interruptions in time, as I got used to sandflies and fleas, mosquitoes and muddy drinking water; meat that was three parts maggots; cockroaches by the shovelful, and blow-flies in shoals. I got used even to snakes; learnt to lie down quite comfortably and go quietly to sleep, even although I might be told that the night before I had slept with a black snake (certain death if it had bitten) under my pillow, as was once the case with me. I got used to watching my feet as I walked, and grew to think as little of the swift rustle and sudden glitter of a retreating snake as I might think of a playful lizard in the sun, or the walloping of a clumsy iguana amongst the rocks; used to whisking my horsetail in the evening, and smoking out enemies in the night; used even to the black fins of the sharks, who watched us like hungry dogs over a bone when we bathed in the bay; used to everything, the heat and the cold, and even to gold coming up along with earth in buckets. I didn't get so much chance of being used to that, though, as I did to the buckets coming up with earth without the gold.

I wish that I had time to tell you all the interesting incidents which I know connected with gold-seeking. Of course we are all gold-seeking every hour of our lives excepting Sundays, and even then many of us are gold thinking (more is the pity); for if we consider the question in any of its aspects, it seems a very pitiful game to spend so much time and thought and energy over. In its virgin state gold is a soft, unusable, dirty-tinted metal, fit for nothing that we may put it to except it be as a a very indifferent writing medium. It makes, in its original state, a poor pencil, and that is all. We cannot make a pot of it, or a weapon of defence, and it is only sometimes that it will mark on paper, a bit of blacklead being a hundred times to be preferred to a bit of gold ore for that purpose.

What pictures I have seen on the diggings—doctors, schoolmasters, lawyers, ministers, all trades and castes, digging and sweating, and smoking and swearing—winning a nugget by hours of labour below ground, and losing it on the surface at Nap or poker in a few moments!

Wives waiting hungrily on telegraphic messages, forgetting all about the husbands in the intensity of their eagerness to hear their 'luck'; and the husbands also forgetting, in the moment of luck, all the purpose of their coming, and washing their faces in champagne, or lighting their pipes with bank-notes, drinking and gambling not allowing them to spend the money fast enough.

I fear that I cannot tell you much about the good of gold, although I could tell you stories by the dozen of the influence for evil which it had on the seeker.

Life at the diggings is a fever, a riot, the Rake's Progress intensified and concentrated from six parts into one; plenty of excitement and tearing about, plenty of speculation and betting on results, oceans of ' stringy-bark ' and adulterated brandy; a fast four days in the week and a burst on the sixth, heart-diseases and palpitations, and over it all an infatuation that is almost incurable. The ' digger ' cannot go back to calm life any more—respectability, and what's short of it, are no longer tolerable after ' damper,' red flannel, and Panama hat; if he is a worker he goes down below, like the whale, to work, and only comes up like the whale to 'blow.' If he is of the tribe of Israel, a speculator, he stops on the surface, starts a store or a drinking 'shanty'—a weighing shop or a betting 'booth'—and gets back to the cities wealthy, healthy, and wise.

The Chinese are the only people who, by honest labour, save money at the diggings; they neither eat nor drink too much, and so are always active and wary to take advantage of a chance, and that is the true secret of luck.

I knew a motherly woman once in Brisbane who rose early and worked all day to keep her children and her house nice. Her husband was a mason; made good wages when at work—twelve shillings for eight hours' work—so that they were comfortable, for people do not require to spend much on dress or food; and if they live quietly—that is, without drink or cards—the necessaries are a mere trifle; freehold property, ground cheap, and fashion not much of a consideration.

I have seen her children running about in the warm sun in their night-dresses, free of encumbrances in the shape of braces, stays, and petticoats, happy in their easy folds, able to enjoy the use of their limbs. They scrambled from the bath to the sand-heap, gaining health without ceremony as children ought to do, with nothing on to injure if they tumbled, nothing fine on to keep their mothers in a fume of excitement lest they spoil the velveteen or the starch with the rumpling freedom of careless childhood.

How it does pain me to see a dressed-out child; how it must pain the parents, and how it must afflict the child.

He or she wants to be down in the sand, or dust, or mud; there is no attraction, in the gratification of juvenile vanity, like to the intense delight of a dirty puddle, or a nice muddy paste to make pies with. To be able to go over the ankles and splash! splash! splash; what can come up to it—to squat down in the mud and knead away at all sorts of shapes! To be able to fling up the sand or dust, and fill one's pockets with it, and cram it down the necks of boy and girl friends! To pick up all sorts of muck —old boots, dirty rags, torn pictures out of buckets, broken bottles and saucers, treasure-trove all to childhood, which is barred by that horrid nightmare, dress and respectability.

You need only look at the little boy or girl who can tumble without any fear of breaking their mother's heart, the little boy or girl with a half-dirty nightdress in a warm enough country, to find the perfect symbol of free-and-easy enjoyment.

Well, this friend of mine was a mother of that sort; she went about herself easy and free, looking after the comfort of her husband and her children, and taking her own ease between times when she could, for a mother cannot have her sixteen hours off work and eight hours on. She must rest by snatches.

She was very scrupulous about dirt: if water was to be had at all, from water-butt or sunk well, she got it and used it. Her husband never was without a clean shirt or fresh pair of overalls; never had occasion to growl, as he plunged into trousers or shirt of a morning, at the want of a button; spiders had no comfort in that establishment; and if a cockroach or two did hunt the back kitchen behind the stove, it was in a skulking sort of manner they ventured out, as if the dread was on them that they would never get back again.

Her husband never had to look for a basin, or have an empty bucket crammed into his fist the moment he showed his hot, sand-grimed face at five o'clock. She was one of those wise women who know that men are animals to be a little studied the first moment they put in an appearance; that men like to find things at home ready and waiting for them when they come back from what they call work (of course it is mere work-flirtation compared with the perpetual and jarring labour of the woman, but that is not the point). She knew, from experience, that men hate to be bothered with children the first moment of their coming home; that they are brutal enough to expect an easy welcome and ready smile, in spite of the troubles the women are longing to pour into their ears.

CHAPTER XXXII

BRISBANE (continued)

A Gold-Digging Episode—*continued.*

THIS friend of mine knew all these matters, and acted accordingly; she knew that she must bottle up her confidences of wrong and trouble and affliction until she had listened to all he had to tell her, until he was fed and washed, and had his hair brushed, and his pipe filled and lighted, and his shirt-sleeves rolled up to the elbows, and then, remembering that there was something else wanted to complete the perfect comfort and felicity of the hour, asked of his own accord to have the children produced.

She knew that men, like cats, hate to see water splashing about floors; dinner-dishes lying steeping inside basins in odd corners : and although demanding, as a strict marital right, clean linen, &c., that they will not tolerate the sight of the cleaning; that the sight of a shirt or a pair of socks hanging up on a clothes-line is like a nightmare to them, whether inside or outside of the house; that the steam from a wash-tub, the bubbling from a washing-pot, the froth of soapsuds, and the other signs of desolation which betoken that most awful test of matrimonial felicity, washing-day—dirty-faced, whimpering children, red-armed, flush-browed matron, and discomfort unutterable all round, are abominations from which even a male angel will fly howling to the nearest public-house bar.

She knew this, I suppose, the first year of marriage, when she had nothing else to do except study the habits of the wild animal she had captured, and she took care that he came home to nothing distasteful to him. A dry floor met his eyes; a comfortable-looking wife in fresh print, easy-fitting as became the office of a mother-nurse, greeted him with a placid air, as if the machinery of her daily routine went smoothly, like well-oiled wheels. A table was set and ready for him, and a savoury smell from he cooking-shed behind stole through his nostrils to his heart; the youngsters were outside rolling about in their undress uniform; at the shed door he knew he would find a bucket filled with water, and soap and towels, and on the mantel there was no danger of the pipe-shank being broken. These were imperative duties, and she had the sense to know it.

This friend of mine was a perfect model of a good wife and mother at the time I speak of, stout and healthy, with a shape like the female saints of Peter Paul Rubens; she did not bother about bracing in her waist, because it was too hot, and because her husband was better pleased with her as she was, and he was the only person whom she cared to please in the world. She wore a loose wrapper that touched her as little as possible anywhere, kept her cool, and allowed the figure to fold and curve, as Nature intended it to.

She at that time did not bother her head as to what people round about her thought or said; she was not very sociable with her neighbours, as she had such a lot to get through before five o'clock; so they did not often trouble her with their company, for gossips do not care to sit down and chatter to a woman who is bustling about her house all the time and replying only in monosyllables. She was very careful about her children being thoroughly washed with soap and hot water at night; very scrupulous not to let laziness, or pleasure, or fatigue interfere with that duty; careful not to demand assistance from her husband (unless he proffered of his own accord, which, seeing that she never asked, he generally did); careful never to miss a single item of it, no matter how tired out she herself felt.

She was also very particular to give them all a good cold douche of water in the morning, before they set out on their day's journeyings; very particular that they all got their hominy and goat's milk, the colonial substitute for our porridge and milk, which everyone ought to take in the morning; they all had their own goats there.

She was very careful that the hominy and all the dishes were well served, and that they had each meal regularly to a moment, and timed herself so that this regularity did not interfere with the hours that her husband was present; so that her duty towards her children never interfered with her duty towards the man who brought in the money which gave them all those comforts.

She soon learned that butter and fatty dishes made her children feverish, and disturbed her own and her husband's rest in the night-time, gave them white faces and hollow eyes in the morning, and brought on all sorts of troubles incidental to childhood, forcing her to get in the doctor and buy physic, and waste more time than she could afford; so being a woman after the ideal type in the Book of Proverbs, she reasoned the whole problem out, and, testing it by experiments, came to the wise conclusion that, the further doctors were kept from a workman's house the better for all parties, the less medicine a child swallowed the healthier it grew, and that the most effectual methods of keeping the doctor and his drugs out of the house altogether were to study her own health, not to stint cold water and thorough cleanliness, be regular in all the food, and feed her children as much as possible on hominy or porridge, rice, sagos, and all sorts of grains, potatoes and salt when they craved for a change, and flagged on the grains and fruit (of which they had plenty, almost for the picking up—oranges, apricots, peaches, pomegranates, lemons, limes, grapes, figs, bananas, and pine-apples).

She found out what agreed best with them, and kept all the other things out of sight, teaching her children, as we might teach them a prayer, to say 'No, thank you' to rich cakes, currant loaves, and butter pieces. A mutton-chop or a bit of beef represented one of the cardinal vices to those juveniles; if they saw their parents eating them they gazed with great open eyes of wonderment, anticipating horror; as we would look on a man laying a box of dynamite under the foundation of a house preparatory to firing it, so they looked on expecting a catastrophe to follow.

Of course this friend of mine might have reasoned the matter out a little further, including her husband and herself in her conclusions, but as it happened from the results on her family, she did very well indeed. A gossiping neighbour seldom showed up, and when she did she did not stay long: her women-friends thought her a perfect frow and fright with her free, loose wrapper on; her children disgraces to a respectable community for not being be-stayed and be-petticoated enough; the doctor's bill disgustingly paltry, since he had generally to be called in only once a year, and the account squared up with the extravagancies of the Sarah Gamp.

The result of her system was that the olive branches sprouted fast and flourished apace, the undertaker having *grave* cause to pull a long face when he passed that cottage, for not a single little coffin had ever to be ordered for all that increasing crowd coming on so fast; the little crowd, a tumbling, writhing, screaming multitude of red cheeks, fat bare arms and legs—in fact, a most disreputable exhibition of human nature and robust health.

I cannot say that my Brisbane friend trained her children very well according to the orthodox and popular ideas of training. They were not very refined; they fought and quarrelled amongst themselves wildly, and had their mother tearing out after them like a maniac a dozen times a day; but the husband never saw this, the truce had been proclaimed before five o'clock, and if any one had told him that his children were wild or unlamblike, or that his smooth-voiced wife could yell out like an Apache over a scalp-lock, he would have scouted the idea as a vile calumny. I don't think she had any clear ideas upon theological matters, or that the spiritual state troubled her as much as it might have done; at any rate, she did not go to church as often as her gossiping neighbours went, and was singularly silent respecting religious tenets and speculations; but she taught her children the Lord's Prayer and 'Gentle Jesus,' and took a special delight in seeing them give up their toys and pieces to the little beggars and black fellows who passed the door, and she never allowed them to torture any living thing—if it was venomous, she killed it outright as a duty; if it was not, they were taught to walk round it if outside, and let it go on its own way unmolested, or carry it out and let it go unhurt if it had got where it had no business to be. She was a very curious compound, this friend of mine, having her own ideas upon more matters than you would think a woman ought to have: she herself belonged to the Baptis denomination, yet I never heard her say anything against infant baptism; indeed, she seemed to find truth in al that was self-sacrificing and aspiring to virtue. She was very strong and decided upon charity; she believed in it unquestioningly and implicitly, believed in it in its broadest and widest sense. Her youngest child was taught to *give* without reasoning out where it went to or if it was deserved, taught to give without expectation or regret.

Mercy, also, was another of her most obstinate qualities —not only that human mercy which Portia describes in the trial-scene of the 'Merchant of Venice,' when she says: 'The quality of mercy is not strained. It droppeth as the gentle rain from heaven upon the place beneath. It is twice blessed. It blesseth him that gives and him that takes'—but the mercy of that great and gracious Indian prince, Gautama, the founder of the Buddhist religion, which embraces in its godlike and boundless reverences all things, animate and inanimate, throughout Nature. 'All things that have life, be they feeble or strong, minute or vast—setting the good-will that is boundless, unmeasurable, impartial, unmixed with enmity—prevail throughout the world, above, below, around' (Buddha).

Her children had a host of faults and bad habits. They were half-savage in their robustness, but they were not selfish with their toys or their delicacies, and they never did a cruelty wantonly beyond fighting amongst themselves. They did not quite reverence the milk-providers of the family—the goats. But then, Nanny always can take care of herself, and will not permit any more liberties than she is inclined for. I have seen goats and youngsters arguing out a disputed part of the paddock, but these disputes generally ended in a wild display of bare limbs, a chorus of bellowing, and the goats standing triumphant mistresses of the position.

And this was the kind of daily life of my friends, the mason and his wife, when I first knew them in Brisbane. They had everything that they wanted, and put money away in the bank every Saturday night. A smoke satisfied him, or perhaps a glass of grog on the Saturday night after their money was banked. This, and maybe a quart of beer for their Sunday dinner, was all the extravagance they allowed themselves to indulge in. Neither of them read much. A peep at the 'weekly' satisfied them. On Sundays he went to church, holding a post there as deacon; and so, in this way, she managed to get the hours to herself that the children and cooking required, and in this way he escaped seeing any of the discomforts or confusion.

But in the middle of it all, just as if some demon had feared a second edition of Paradise, and wanted to get his infernal hoof into it, the Queensland gold-fever broke out; some prospecting fiends had discovered gold out from Rockhampton, and a wild rush took place; workmen left their work, shopkeepers sold out their businesses for anything they could realise, lawyers flung down their briefs, doctors galloped away from their dispensaries and patients, even clergymen tore off their bands, and joined in the mad stampede.

My friends tried to resist the devil as long as they could—home comforts against the chance of fortune, steady employment against 'luck.' Every day more glowing accounts of finds came down to Brisbane; all his mates, nearly, had forsaken the stone-cutting, and some of them were doing well, and urged him very much to join them. I think she held back the longest, but she had caught the infection as well as her husband and everyone else, and so at last she drew out a year's savings, packed up his traps, and, with a fond hopeful hug, bade him go in and win.

It was a wild time; old men and young women spent all the day and half the night rushing about the Stock Exchange, speculating and betting on the result of next morning's news; quarrelling and wrangling inside public-house bars, where telegrams were received and given out;

THE BUSHRANGER

drinking, of course, for you cannot go into a public-house and expect attention to your wants unless you 'shout,' that is, drink and stand drinks all round.

Some trained pigeons, and sent messages that way to those mostly interested, keeping back the public telegrams until the birds had time to go home. There were painful incidents and amusing incidents constantly occurring every hour. One reckless wife, who, on the strength of the telegram of one day 'We've struck it heavy,' from her husband, laid in a stock of dresses and jewellery, carpets, furniture, and utensils enough to satisfy a duchess, was observed the Saturday after smashing her cleaned out, home-coming master from the house-door, which she had taken on credit, with a span new frying-pan, he rushing along for his very life in his ragged pants and shirt, and she in full war costume, satins and jewellery complete, laying on to him with the new frying-pan, and shrieking out in her maniac fury: 'You've struck it, have you, struck it heavy, eh?'

The telegram had been a false hope, the find which he thought a rich vein of gold being only a few small nuggets and a vain delusion.

The whole life and principles of my friend seemed to alter under the influence of this absorbing passion. Her placid composure left her: she could not work or be content with the letters she received from her husband; she seemed to have a hunger and thirst on her to hear all the general news, to hear if others were succeeding better than he; she became restless and more impatient with her children, glad to get them washed and dressed and off to school as quickly as possible. The neighbours had no cause now to complain that the children were running wild, for they were packed off every day as soon as she could pack them.

She also went two or three times a day to the popular public-house for news, getting acquainted with the wives and fathers of other absent diggers, who also haunted the bar for news, getting acquainted with crowds of people, and standing or taking drinks, as the turn might be. He was doing very well, on the whole, up there, sometimes sending down cash, sometimes getting cash sent up to keep things going; but his letters were always hopeful, for he had a pair of first-rate mining partners, and their claim promised, from the earth-colour and other indications, to be good.

The children were getting to be better behaved and more orderly in their habits, and most certainly becoming more attentive to their lessons, and really good readers. They had every prospect of getting prizes and certificates now, and that was always something, even although they did sometimes have to hurry off to school with only a drink of milk and a slice of bread, instead of the well-boiled hominy of the olden days, and returned sometimes to find their mother out getting news of father, and no dinner ready for them.

My friend also was decidedly getting more careless in her habits, growing redder in the face, more unyielding in her figure; her wrapper was not so tidy either, and sometimes I have heard that she came home and went off to bed herself, falling dead asleep immediately, and leaving her eldest girl of about nine years to put all the other children to bed, and at those times they had to go to bed unwashed and supperless. Still the news was hopeful always, and all going on as they could desire, both up at the diggings and in the school.

About this time, that is, about two months and a half after he had left her, her first trouble came on them; the youngsters all took the whooping-cough, and had to be kept at home; she tried her hardest to nurse them, but it seemed harder work than before, with her restlessness and impatience to be out hearing the news. At times, when she could no longer bear staying at home, she would get in a neighbour to take her place for a few moments, while she ran down to see what was going on.

On one of those occasions she heard that her husband had hit it richly; it was a vague rumour, but on the strength of it she had to stand brandy all round; no small matter, let me tell you, when drinks are sixpence each, and perhaps forty or fifty people are assembled at a time. But as it was the etiquette of the place, she had to conform to it; more people came in, and more 'shouting' went on, the news becoming more definite; some said they were sure of it, and loaded her with congratulations, and so she had to stay longer and drink more than she wanted to.

When she got home she found the neighbour absent, and her children all alone and very ill. That night she woke up with a start, to find the youngest child choking with the croup.

Next morning a glowing letter confirmed the vague reports of the night before. Her husband had, indeed, struck a heavy lode. It was gold, every shovelful. She got the letter at the moment she was wailing hopelessly over the dead body of her youngest child—the youngest and the cleverest of all the family. And so the undertaker would have got a job at last, only that he was not there to take it in, he also having gone to the diggings; and therefore a new chum, who had bought the melancholy business, stock and all, got the miserable commission. Her husband had the best claim on the diggings. The vein seemed inexhaustible, and the gold of the best quality. He was too busy, and too fearful lest someone might have taken advantage of his absence, to leave his post in order to comfort his wife; besides, he could not have got down in time to bury their bonny bairn. However, it was a grand funeral. He sent down a cheque right off for five thousand pounds, to set up a house and help to pay the expenses, and hundreds of admiring and sympathetic friends gathered round to follow the little one to his last home, and wallow afterwards in champagne and brandy.

That stroke of fate—the loss of this almighty treasure, the child, and the finding of the substitute for it, gold, gold—sent the last of the angels out of that whilom paradise. The strong qualities, mercy and charity, unbalanced in my friend's mind by other necessary qualities, and turned into the wrong groove by chance, or luck, or the curse of gold—devil enough to ruin any Eden—sent her and her husband, who leaned upon her strong will, straight down, like balloons which have lost their gas. Money came pouring in to her, and friends and admirers crowded about her perpetually. She didn't set up a very grand establishment, for the people abroad do not, as a rule, think much about how their houses look if they are comfortable. She got a couple of girls to look after her children and house, and then left them to their own devices, while she administered to her large court of hangers-on.

She didn't dress very stylishly; too long accustomed to the free-and-easy wrappers, she kept to them still; of course they were always spotless and clean when she put them on of a morning, however much they might be rumpled and wine-stained at night.

All day long she lounged in the public-house bar where the telegrams were worked, receiving messages from the camp and dictating replies; drink passed round as freely as water, for she paid all, her generosity getting outcome in this way. No beggars or loafers were turned away empty-handed, but meat and drink were sent about galore.

So her fame spread, and she had hosts at her command. How they flattered her and her husband, and drank themselves blind, and sent her staggering home each afternoon elevated into the seventh heaven!

It was a gay and festive court while it lasted; the publican enlarged his premises on her account, and treated her with the reverential respect due to a Princess-royal. The pastor came to remonstrate, but as in her days of wisdom, so in her days of folly, she listened to him with respectful silence, and went on as she had done before. By-and-by her husband came swaggering down with brannew clothes, and be-ringed and be-chained as only a successful digger can present himself, and so, king and queen together, they reigned in that bar-court, and listened to the vile adulation, and spent money like air, and drank themselves bloated and hoarse. What oceans of champagne floated out from that bar! cartloads of gold-labelled bottles, full in the morning, were lowered into the cellar, and hoisted outside empty at night.

And that gold vein held out as richly as ever; in five months they had drawn out over fifty thousand pounds, and were now negotiating about a company to work it.

A bustling time, and the children were getting on at school, although the parents seldom saw them, for the house was a home no longer, and the mother was becoming a frowsy, fat, unyielding mass of blotched sottishness, and the father had become a hoven up, empty-headed, self-indulgent, contemptible fool.

Fifty thousand pounds gained, and ten human souls ruined for this life!

There is little more to tell you of these gold victims. The merry court soon ended, not for want of money—for more, and more, and more came in, piling up like a plague; all Brisbane could not have drunk it away—but for want of kidneys and liver. The woman went out first, took dropsy and passed away in no time, and the maudlin fool of a husband, after the death of his wife, took solely to raw spirits and burnt himself up in a couple of months; bad brandy takes a shorter time in the colonies to kill a man than with us here.

I was there the night she died. My friend, whom I had honoured in her days of simplicity, who had been led so far off her feet in the hours of her mad extravagance! She had been tapped some time before, and this was her first appearance for weeks, so we all clustered round her and her husband, to inquire after and *drink* to her health.

She did not look so very bad, although white and puffy and weak-limbed, yet she drank with the rest and spoke pleasantly enough to us all, and felt she was getting better. Then a nice supper was served up in first-rate style, and everyone that liked sat down, and when the table was crammed by the guests, plates and knives and forks were handed round the room and outside on the verandah, even to the street; a German band came on spec. and gave us music after their style from the moonlit street outside, while we ate and drank. By-and-by some sponge got up and made a speech in honour of the occasion of her resumption of empire, &c., laudatory of course, to which the poor generous-hearted victim dragged herself to her feet to reply.

How well I remember her as she stood in her white wrapper, amid all that crystal of glasses and chandeliers, with the wax candles casting down their lights on that pale puffed-out motherly face, and contending with the white light of the full moon which flooded in at the open windows, broken below by the crowd of faces that filled up the verandah; the brassy sounds of the German band outside mixing along with the silver tinkling from a musical box placed up on the shelf beside the cigar-boxes and cordial bottles; the blotched, expressionless face and podgy figure of that vulgarly-dressed poor drunkard-consort by her side; and the character depicted on the varied faces which were looking or leering, or sneering up at her, as she swayed to and fro, her champagne-glass loosely held in her deformed and trembling fingers!

What a contrast to the woman I used to know only a year before; the woman who had made a man out of the animal her husband. She was going to say something in reply to that sponge, but she was not very ready-tongued at the best, and we waited while she tried to gather her scattered senses and collect appropriate words.

Three moments, perhaps, passed in expectancy, as she stood with her unwieldy figure bulging out from that loose white wrapper and her dough-tinted face bathed in the mixed lustre of candles and moonlight.

Then she found the words she had wanted, and she began—'I think, John, we made a great mistake——'

She got no further; the champagne-glass slid from her relaxing swollen fingers, and fell with a melodious crash on her half-empty plate, and the next instant she was on the floor—dead!

CHAPTER XXXIII

AUSTRALIANS

Brisbane of To-day—Governors Macquarie and Brisbane—Why all true Australians must be strictly Conservative—A Pious Land Speculator—About some Bazaar Horses—From Bowen Terrace.

BRISBANE on September 7, 1890, reached its thirty-first birthday since it was incorporated as a city. Before that it was a penal settlement from as early as 1824, but until 1842 it made no progress; at this date it was opened to free settlers, and at once began to make strides.

Sir Thomas Macdougal Brisbane was the Governor who succeeded Macquarie in New South Wales, and who commenced to build Brisbane town. He was of a scientific turn, and the historians say he was of an amiable character, introducing many wise reforms, especially in penal matters; also at his own expense he secured the first good breed of horses for the colonies. He promoted and encouraged the cultivation of the sugar-cane, vine, tobacco and cotton, established the freedom of the press and trial by jury, and consigned the prisoners to free settlers and squatters, thus showing the colonists how to utilise convict labour for their own good, while greatly lessening the expenses of government. And yet he was unpopular, and in spite of all the benefits he' conferred his reign was a short one.

Why? The answer is simple. No king or aristocrat can ever become a leader of the people. The man who will win their sympathy must rise from their own ranks, as an aristocratic friend of mine, who fain would keep to the ancient prejudices, while striving to be a democrat, once complained bitterly of his non-success to touch the hearts of the people he appealed to. 'I feel for them, I love their cause, why will they not listen to me?' 'Because you are not of them and can never suffer or feel like them; sing to your own order, and expose their rottenness and follies, and you will succeed, but leave us alone to those who come from us.'

Macquarie went, in a rough overbearing way, to work as a master with his men, and never troubled himself to win them, so long as they did his work; he was active and bustling, and gave them no leisure to grumble. Brisbane attempted to win their sympathies without comprehending them in the slightest degree; he gave them opportunities to think, for he was scientific as well as aristocratic in his tastes, so he was before his time in the first place with the rough pioneers, and a decade behind his time in a land where the community were beginning to expand their lungs with the breath of freedom. I mean strictly Conservative liberty of course.

They had all drawn in a full breath of the freedom-developing ozone of Australia, convicts and settlers alike. The home-sickness had worn off, and they were beginning to comprehend and appreciate the superior advantages which this new land offered to them and their children over what the mother-country did or could do, no matter what reforms took place there; and this was what made the pickpocket and housebreaker forget their old crafts and take so naturally to honesty and perseverance. This balmy atmosphere, filled with hope, wafted away the blood-lust of the murderer, and made him become mild and peaceful. The grand old Conservative instinct, which is in the whole of us, to be owners and possessors of the land, came upon them like a universal infection, and that made them all in Australia loyal subjects, which had forced them to turn thieves and outlaws in the land of their birth—a land which belonged only to the order of Sir Thomas Brisbane, and to which they had no sort of birthright at all, except as housebreakers, poachers, and pickpockets—free renters of the jails and poor-houses.

There would be no more use trying to make democrats of Australians than there would be to make a Conservative of any man of sense in England who is not a freehold landlord for ever and ever. As human beings we are all landlords by instinct, and all conservative, only we must go to Australia to develop the instinct, unless some of our fore-mothers were lucky and attractive enough to lure for us, from their owners the kings, what God should have given to them without conditions, for their children and children's children.

The Brisbane of to-day is divided into four portions— North Brisbane, South Brisbane, Kangaroo Point, and Fortitude Valley. It has a population of upwards of 40,000, has over seventy miles of streets and over 1,920 acres of well-built stone houses, for the wooden ones have all mostly disappeared. I was witness, the first time I was there, of a fire which started in Queen Street and demolished nearly half the town in a night.

Down by one of the flats (they are all drained and built upon now) used to be lovely green fields in the dry season and swamps in the wet. There was an amusing affair happened in this part, where a young man of an enterprising turn of mind, who was one of the converted, attempted to serve God and Mammon at the same time, and very nearly succeeded.

He had bought a lump of this swamp for almost nothing at the Government auction sales, at the time it was at its worst state, to the great amusement of all his acquaintances. As the dry season set in he divided it into small allotments for building purposes, and advertised them for sale. In a little while all the country round Brisbane excepting these swamps was as dry as a brickfield, without a blade of grass to be seen, excepting here, where it grew green, cool, and inviting to those who did not know the cause of it. But to those who did it was a matter of open derision that any man in his senses would ever dream of building a house here; still this sedate young Christian said nothing except offering up fervent prayers at the Wednesday night prayer-meeting, and instead of explaining his hopes, went regularly to church, keeping his own counsel and his weather-eye open.

At last the chance he was waiting for came. A shipload of thirsting new chums arrived during the height of the dry season, and, looking round the parched land for ground, greedily pitched upon these green allotments as the only thing which reminded them of home.

He sold all his land in a few days, making about fifteen hundred per cent. on his original outlay. It was then that his brethren hauled him over the coals, much to his virtuous indignation, for, as he truthfully enough said, ' Jacob was not above increasing his flocks in any legitimate way, even if out of the ordinary, and he could not see where the blame came in how he increased his store, so long as it was done legally.'

Thus they wrangled week after week, while he stuck to his bargain. He would have won his point also, like honest Jacob, if the rains had not come on while they were still arguing the morality of the question, and nearly drowned some of the purchasers on their own freeholds. They, however, when the swindle was forced upon their understandings by Nature, rose in rebellion to a man, and, taking the side of the deacons and elders, made the pious young man disgorge the money which they had paid him. He had resisted all moral appeals of his Church brethren, but

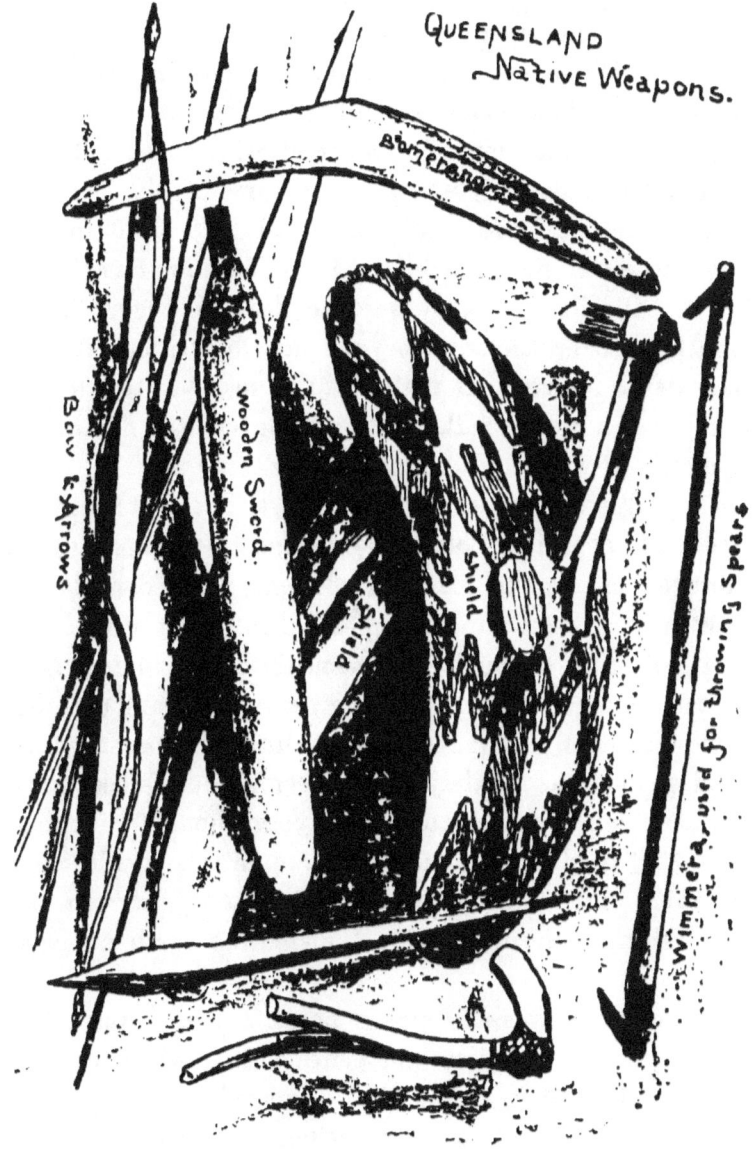

when it came to be a question of lynching, he relented and caved in.

It all depends upon the way a man treats God and Mammon how he succeeds in this life and the next; if the pressure he puts upon them is equal it comes out all right.

As in Melbourne, I got confused about the streets of Brisbane. It had been rebuilt since I last saw it, and was all strange and unfamiliar; Queen Street, which used to be the one respectable street, was now only one of six principal ones. Was the Bazaar still there where I used to hire horses when going picnicing? I don't know, I could not find it. Old friends—they were all dead, or married, and done for. Over the town beyond the Observatory it used to be dense forest, with nothing to be seen but tree-tops—now it was a grassy valley with a clear view of mountains beyond. I wandered discontentedly over it all, along Gregory Terrace, down Wharf Street, out by Breakfast Creek, and over the Botanical Gardens. It was all vastly improved, increasing like a wholesome mushroom, but it wasn't my Brisbane, and so I wearied to be out of it.

The first horse which I got from the Bazaar had a fatal habit of shying at all sorts of imaginary objects and at unexpected moments. He was one of those uncertain beasts which would go along as sedately as a policeman on his beat until your confidence was restored, and your thoughts inclined to wander, then all of a sudden he would take a side waltz the width of the road and land his unwary rider in the dust. During one day's ride I kissed the earth a dozen times.

One day I went in to hire a horse, and as I was going with a company of ladies and gentlemen, good riders—for they all ride well in Queensland—I asked for a very quiet safe horse, as I did not wish to distinguish myself before my accomplished friends.

'Here is just what you want—a lady's horse,' observed the owner, leading out a long, glossy, small-headed, sleek beast after the greyhound order. 'You'll find yourself as easy on his back as if you were on a cushioned chair at home.'

He was certainly one of the loveliest horses I had ever seen out of a racecourse, and went as his master had described, with long easy gliding strides, so that I hardly felt any motion.

How proudly I cantered past the window of a young lady whom at the time I adored. I fancy she approved also of my get-up and general appearance, for she smiled sweetly and waved her handkerchief after me, as we all started from Brisbane for a pleasant day at Sandgate, 12½ miles distant.

After going for a mile on our way, and seeing some paddocks before us, by crossing which took something from the road, some of the boys proposed a little steeplechase, so we all set our horses at the fences, and went over them. My horse seemed to enjoy the fun, and took them so easily that it seemed more like flying than riding.

It was a very hot, airless day at the start, but as we crossed these paddocks it seemed as if the wind was rising, while, as I looked behind, I found I had distanced my companions completely; but this I rather enjoyed until I reached the Sandgate road and tried to rein up, when with a pretty toss of his small head, while his ears were laid almost flat on his neck, my steed rather increased his pace than otherwise, and then a horror came upon me—he had taken the bit between his teeth, and was off, past all control.

I looked back—the party were out of sight and the forest before me, with only eight or nine miles between me and the cliffs. How the wind rose and whistled past my ears like a

hurricane as we flew along, for I found out afterwards that
my horse had been a racer; yet but for the thought of that
abrupt termination and other obstacles which might lie between I had no cause for discomforting thoughts, for he was
going along as easily as if I had been sitting on a cushioned
chair at home with a couple of punkah boys fanning me
with all their might.

On, like John Gilpin, for my hat had gone by the board
long before. I passed one or two pedestrians, whose shouts
sounded something like advice to 'get inside and pull the
blinds down,' but taunts like these were lost upon me at
the time, perched as I was like a monkey on the back of
this 'bolting' racehorse.

Then a good stretch of forest road opened up, and by
lowering my head we passed safely under the spreading
branches. Perhaps he will get tired after a bit, and before
we come to the bay, I thought, and tried to glean some comfort from this as we rushed along.

Round a corner we spun like lightning, and then to my
horror I saw directly in front a fallen gigantic gum tree,
which a late storm had thrown down, barring the entire
roadway. It was about half a mile distant, so that I had
hardly time to loosen my feet from the stirrups before we
were upon it. My horse gave one terrific leap upwards and
cleared through between two great forks. I dropped the
reins, and throwing up my arms caught hold of the upper
fork, so saving my head and neck, and next instant was
dangling, like Absalom, in the air about ten feet from the
earth, while my horse, after running a few more paces with
empty saddle, coolly stopped, and turning aside began to
graze without the least appearance of excitement.

It was a narrow squeak. After I had dangled to and fro
for a few moments, I let myself drop, and then went after
my animal; and now the tantalisation of the affair began.

He did not run away again, but calmly went on eating and allowed me almost to touch him, then, with a side look and a mocking curl of his lip, he cantered a few paces away and so on; I coaxed him and tried strong expressions, but all in vain—he had come out for a day's fun, and this was his idea of horse-play.

At last, after wearing myself out completely, I sat down on a log and waited for my companions, while he hung about, and glanced at me inquiringly as much as to say, 'Why don't you catch me?' By-and-by they came in sight, and after laughing at my disordered appearance they caught him and brought him to his senses.

One of the party, a clergyman, changed horses with me for the rest of the journey, for, as he truly remarked, 'this horse was too much for me to manage.'

It was a disastrous change for him as a clergyman, for this ex-racer was one of the most disreputable beasts in the Colony—he could not pass a public-house door. Being a fine-looking animal he had been patronised chiefly by the demi-monde of Brisbane, who at this time were in the habit of showing themselves in the streets on horseback; therefore he had got into their ways, and so scandalised the minister utterly. But on the return journey, and as we got near Brisbane, his evil habits became more pronounced.

Whenever we reached a public-house bar that graceless steed would stop short, and all the spurring or whipping up was so much exertion thrown away.

'It's no good, sir,' observed the bar-keepers as they came each to their doors. 'I know the animal, and you must jist get off his back and come inside for a few moments, then after you mounts again he will carry you right along to the next pub.'

So the clergyman found out, to his humiliation, that he had to enter every bar-shop right through the city. But the grand climax was reached when the infamous horse brought his respectable rider right up to the verandah of one of the most notorious houses in Brisbane, and refused to move on to the bazaar until he got his accustomed lump of sugar and tender caress from the lily hands of his usual mistress. The position was public and awful in its completeness of degradation—a pillar of the Church sitting in front of this palace of pleasure, with one of the most celebrated priestesses hanging lovingly round his horse's neck, and the other giddy nymphs all laughing and chaffing his Reverence from the verandah, at five o'clock in the afternoon!

I had another try at this same bazaar, and fixed upon what looked like a solid bit of horseflesh. His peculiarity was to subside into an awkward, shambling trot at the wrong moment, or stop dead with an Oriental salaam, as if to an unseen angel on the way. The day I took him out of the stable he broke into an easy canter right off, and carried me until within fifty yards of the window of my charmer in that gallant style. There the body-racking canter began, which made my teeth meet and rattle like castanets, my hat dance wildly, and the legs of my trousers work up to my knees. Thus she sighted me coming along, with a vision of bare calf (none too well developed in those days), and a pair of rumpled white socks tumbling over my elastic-sided boots. It was maddening, but mild compared to what followed; for as she looked out, startled at the shivering apparition, my horse saw his unseen angel friend, and made his profound salaam, landing me over his neck upon the gutter. As I rose and led him away, I heard a silvery laugh, which completed my ruin, from that open window. I never looked upon my love again.

With vengeance in my heart I mounted this demon

blighter of hearts, and galloped off to the forest. Wildly I made him go, for I resolved to take it out of him. And now he developed another faculty, which was to take all sorts of sharp corners without considering his rider's head or legs, round tree-trunks and past hut-ends, just allowing the eighth of an inch between his flanks and the object he was passing.

While daylight lasted I managed to evade death a dozen times by lifting my legs or ducking my head at the right moment. Once, when we were flying past a low hut-roof made of sheet-iron I made the duck, and emerged with two inches of my felt-hat. The top had been shaven off as neatly as if with a razor; one half-inch lower and I would have been scalped.

Night came on dark as pitch, and I turned to ride back home, giving my horse the reins as he knew the way best. We were just getting round a corner when I felt a sharp pain in the right knee, and heard a wild shout behind me. I had rushed past a bullock dray, the broad wheel of which had struck me in the knee, knocking the knee-cap right up. With my left leg I dug the spur savagely into the selfish ribs, and rushed on through the blackness, my right leg hanging helplessly out of the stirrup, until I reached Brisbane and the first doctor's shop, where got my knee-cap set at once, afterwards getting home and to bed, where I lay for three weeks. When I think of those merry times I mourn that I cannot fix upon the locality of that bazaar.

The river at Brisbane twists and winds in a serpentine course through the city, with ferry-boats plying from shore to shore at stated streets, and a magnificent iron bridge called the Victoria, which connects Queen and Melbourne Streets at the North Quay. A very fine view of the city and river in its broad sheet, with all the many wharves and shipping, is to be had from Bowen Terrace. Altogether, if it is not quite the homely Brisbane that I knew in my young days, still it has advanced in beauty and stature as well as respectability, and has become a very imposing, prosperous, and charming southern capital of this as yet undivided colony.

CHAPTER XXXIV

MARYBOROUGH

Sugar Plantations and Kanakas—Black-birding—The *Young Dick*—An Idea for the Planters—The Kanaka Melodies of the Future.

BETWEEN Brisbane and Rockhampton lies a very fertile and interesting tract of country and coast.

A well-watered country. If at times the rivers run dry, there are always waterholes left behind, and when the people can come to understand how to keep the water by damming, &c., before it is all run away or absorbed (for during the rainy season the country is plentifully flooded), they need never run short of a constant supply for all their wants or luxuries.

A fertile soil, this Queensland, and more so as we advance towards the tropics. There is not a single acre throughout Australia but can be turned to good account in the way of cultivation, as the land about Sydney, which was originally, without exception, the barrenest and sandiest portion of the continent, north or south, has proved. Therefore, if I point out spots, as yet unoccupied, on the route up to Cape York, I trust that I am addressing men who will understand me, and not foolish sentimentalists who expect to take possession of a land flowing with milk and honey, where no 'sweat of the brow' is required. Australia is in no portion a land where men may sit down and take their ease, any more than England is. All soils, even the richest, require working before they will produce, and virgin soil requires generally even greater patience and perseverance; but I will say to the man who comes out here to work and wait, his reward will be tenfold to anything he could get in England.

The Mary River is a splendid sheet of water which flows past the town of Maryborough, twenty-five miles up from its mouth, and 180 miles north of Brisbane, with at the entrance long sandbanks, and further in woody cliffs; then, as it narrows, flat banks of sugar-cane plantations, for this is the great plantation district of Australia, where black labour is required—a source of deep consideration to humanitarians, and a social problem difficult to solve.

Personally, from what I have seen of the black, or South Sea Island trade, I cannot discern much difference between it, as it is, and the negro-catching and slave-dealing of America long ago. The ways of trapping them are very little different; the transporting them to Queensland is similar; and the retaining of them as nearly alike as it could possibly be in reality, although, to read the laws concerning it, it is altogether a different and benevolent system. Let us look at it from the three points: the natives' view, the planters,' and the legal.

When I was a boy I once went for a trip through the Pacific Islands with a black trader. In those days the law did not interfere very much, so that the traders did not require to resort to any subterfuges or tricks to evade it. All that they had to do was to lure or force the natives aboard, down with the hatches, up with the sails, and hurry back with their cargo to the market, without much query as to how they procured it. Now there are forms and ceremonies to be gone through which cripple their industry a good deal, and render the trade a trifle risky excepting to ''cute' old hands.

In the days I speak about they had not much bother. The trader made friends with the chiefs, who, in exchange for some presents, gave him all their unwounded prisoners of war, and what young men of the tribe they could spare.

The captives went willingly, because if they dared to disobey orders their islands would have been too hot for them. As for the prisoners of war, it was Hobson's choice, slavery or torture; they nearly always preferred slavery, as I fancy most of us would also under the circumstances.

The laws of Queensland demanded that a native should come, first, freely, of his own knowledge and will; secondly, that he was only hired for a space of three years, and sent home again when his time was up. Officers were appointed to see these laws enforced.

These officers, as a rule, did not understand the languages of the natives; therefore interpreters had to be chosen. The traders generally acted as interpreters.

This is how the ceremony was conducted and the articles signed:—

Officer. 'Those who have come of their free will hold up their hands.'

Interpreter. 'Hold up all your hands.'

All hands went up promptly. They had endured a voyage with the interpreter, and knew, from experience, better than to resist.

Down went the report, 'all right.'

Officer. 'You are willing to serve your time of three years? If so, up with your hands.'

Interpreter. 'Hold up your hands.'

Again the report was satisfactory, and the officer went his own way, leaving the planters to come forward and pick out their men, paying their 20*l.* a-piece for them to the trader-interpreter.

The Government officials visited the plantations once a year, in order to see that none of the natives were kept longer than their three years. As a rule, few were kept, because before the end of their three years of servitude, what with the unaccustomed life, the cane swamps, and the home-sickness, few of the South Sea Islanders were worth anything any longer in the shape of work. Rheumatics and consumption had finished them up, so that the planters were glad to get rid of them, and send them home to die. (From this I am inclined to lean towards the side of the Carolina planters, who at least kept their slaves to the last and buried them; but that is a matter of private opinion entirely.)

Still, if some hardy islander managed to rub through without much damage, in his case there was no release.

Before the arrival of the officer the comedy was all prepared, and the sickly ones coached up as to what they were to do.

Officer. 'Hold up hands those who have served their time.'

Interpreter (the planter's overseer this time). 'You fellows to the left hold up your hands.' And the row of diseased skeleton-hands went up, while the cough-racked shadows prepared to see their native land.

As for the healthy slaves, how were they to know that this Government man represented a friend? They were not permitted to learn the English language.

Now each trader must carry a supercargo, appointed by Government, who goes with them through the islands to see that no force is used, and no bloodshed or violence takes place. Some of these men act conscientiously, yet the temptation to act otherwise is very strong. During a long voyage the captain and mates are apt to become chums of the supercargo. It is a miserable life for him if they are enemies on board. It is also to their interest to keep him well primed with drink, and lay little traps for him, so that if he is not very careful and has not great self-control, long before they begin 'black-birding' he is completely in their power, and must shut his eyes whether he feels inclined or not.

There are war-sloops always trading about the Pacific Ocean to look after the natives and the traders, but there is little or no trouble with them. Any novice at the game can hoodwink these gentry and get their assistance.

Perhaps in an island fight a white sailor has been wounded or killed, no one need know how many of the natives fell first. The trader makes his report to the naval captain, and points out the island *where he has been murderously attacked*. Away sails the war-sloop to that island, bombards it straight off, demolishes the villages and gardens with shells, and leaves the horror-stricken survivors on a desolate island to starve to death, their cocoanut trees being their only means of living. Oh, it is a noble occupation for the brave British tars!

There is no use going into details of the foul atrocities which sometimes take place on those fair, sunny islands: the cold-blooded murders and shooting down, the ravishments and violence. Sufficient to say that the women of many of these tribes are perfect in face and figure and dazzlingly beautiful; that the men who hunt them have been months at sea, lawless, most of them, by their occupation, and made up from all nationalities. The reader does not require much fancy in his composition to imagine the rest. Enough that I have been a voyage in a black trader, and could not forget it in a lifetime.

In the hotel where I put up at Maryborough the captain, supercargo, and officers of the *Young Dick* were staying. The sloop itself was lying at anchor in the river, and I sketched it from the verandah—a clean-built, swift-sailing vessel, the ideal of what in my schoolboy days I used to read about as pirate craft. They were *washing* it down, and getting it ready for another voyage.

It had come in a short time before, deluged with blood, and filled with wounded men. There had been a rising of the *cargo* on board, much blood spilt, and many lives lost (this was in 1886), and they were now filling it up with the consumptive exiles whose 'time was up.'

. The captain, supercargo, and mates were all young, gentlemanly, genial fellows ashore. They gave me the information I wanted during the days we spent together, before I left for Rockhampton, and urged me very strongly to come along with them, offering me a free trip round the Solomon Islands, so that I might be able to see the great difference between 'black-birding' now and what it had been on my last trip over the islands. I did for a moment feel tempted to accompany them, but that New Guinea voyage to which I had pledged myself prevented me; I could not undertake both, so, like Mary, I chose the wiser way.

I spent with them my last night, for I was interested in the young men in spite of their trade—they were all so mild, generous, and lovable with each other and me; so after a farewell toast to our different successes, we parted, I for New Guinea and they for the Solomons.

That was the last voyage of the *Young Dick*; nothing has been heard of her or her crew since.

The Government has benevolently put up a hospital for consumptive natives a little way out of Maryborough. While I was there it was filled up, so they had to use outhouses for their crouching patients; so much for the healthiness of the sugar-growing business. I also went among the natives in the fields, watching them cutting down the cane marvellously dexterous they were at it), and afterwards crushing it; I don't think that I saw one contented face amongst them, although South Sea Islanders have always a rather sad expression, but these Kanaka savages seemed to have added a lowering air to the usual melancholy, as if they were brooding on real or imaginary wrongs. Therefore I came to the conclusion that they were not enamoured of plantation life. One cause might have been that very few of them are permitted to bring wives with them. The traders and planters will not be bothered with encumbrances in the form of wives or children for the three years' spell, therefore, unless the natives learn to drink, they have no means of enjoying themselves, but go sullenly to work, and lie fretting for the absent ones at night. I never heard a sound of music or song in any of the huts; silence reigned over the whole of them.

As for the planters' side of this question, they grumble dreadfully about all the hard stipulations of the law with regard to their Kanaka workers; they must feed them too well, the work hours are ridiculously short, they dare not whip them if they are contumacious (as they mostly are); in fact, according to the planters the natives are the masters and they are the slaves. Perhaps so.

With respect to the Law;—well, I think that the Government are doing all that they can under this awful three years' single system; it is the system which is wrong both to masters and men.

I have thought over the matter carefully, for I like to take all sides of a problem and worry over it till I have got it right, and I come to these conclusions:—

Firstly, that for sugar-growing black labour must be employed, for no white man could stand the swamps for six months far less three years; *ergo* we must have Kanaka labour.

Secondly, that the South Sea Islander, under the

despotic control of his chief or king, cannot be very much worse off even if he enters slavery; but according to the glorious British constitution we must not make slaves.

Then the only thing to be done is to treat the South Sea Islander as the Government treat the poor of England: make emigrants of them, send agents to invite them over with their wives and children, give them assisted passages, so treating them like men instead of cattle, and let them settle down, say at Maryborough or Cairns, with their families, and form townships for themselves. Thus they will become acclimatised, work contentedly for their wages, and send over for their relations, while the sugar plantations will flourish all over the tropical colonies, with the maize, rice, and coffee fields; and instead of silent huts where heaving groans and sighs are sent up nightly, there will be dancing and singing and courting on the moonlight nights, with the nursing and squealing of Kanaka children in the huts; there will be melodies composed to the plantations of Maryborough—Kanaka, instead of nigger songs and breakdowns—and the Colony will begin to thrive. Give him his women and his children, with an interest in the country, and the South Sea savage will become one of the main supporters of Upper Queensland.

Maryborough is a well planned out town, and the centre of such rich outlying places as the Gympie gold fields, the Mount Perry copper mines, and Burrum coal field, besides its own agricultural produce, so that it is bound to be great, once these black traders are transformed into emigrant vessels and agents.

CHAPTER XXXV

ROCKHAMPTON

Some Shady Passengers—The Lion Comique and Lionesses—Burnett Heads—Keppel Bay and the Fitzroy River—A Night at Rockhampton—The Fasting Insect—Rockhampton as It Is and as It Ought to Be.

We had rather a rough lot of fellow-passengers going up from Maryborough to Burnett River Heads—sharpers and turfmen principally, with a fair sprinkling of thieves. They were going to the races at Bundaburg. I was amused at the scant courtesy of the captain towards these gentry, and the meekness with which, as a rule, they received his open scorn and broad sarcastic remarks.

'You had better leave your purses and watches with the steward, gentlemen,' he observed openly in the saloon to the respectable portion of his company, while he looked with wrathful eyes over the shady lot. 'Until we get past Burnett Heads at all events.'

'Ain't ye going to take us up the river, capting?' asked one of the scorned ones, mildly.

'No, sir. I'll pitch ye ashore as soon as I can do it,' answered the captain, sternly.

'But, capting, we've paid our fare up to Bundaburg,' remonstrated the others in a plaintive chorus.

'You may have paid your passage as far as H——l for all I care! You pad the hoof at Burnett Heads.'

' How, then, are we to get up ? '

' You can walk it, or swim it if you like, it's only ten miles.'

' But our ladies ? '

'Oh, they're used to roughing it, or ought to be by this time if they ain't ? '

The captain is a king on his own deck and absolute, so that last scoff finished the discussion.

We had a lion comique also going up to Bundaburg—a fat, large, gloomy, heavy-jowled, moustached individual, who growled and thundered hoarsely (but in a low tone) about the injustice of having to ' pad the hoof ' to Bundaburg; but when the captain looked full towards him and requested him to speak out like a man, if he made any pretensions to being of that persuasion, he became very quiet, and buried his triple chin in his flashy waistcoat. On the boards of a music-hall he might have been a great lion and ' comique '; on board this steamer he was a veritable lamb, and moody in the extreme.

He and his lady companions—for he had three with him, all fair-complexioned and golden-tressed—seemed, however, to be on good and familiar terms with the turfites, and condoled with each other on the blank injustice of the whole affair (when the captain was out of hearing), and what they intended to do, with the aid of the law, when they got ashore.

I used to lounge about the deck at night, and listen to their chaste conversation and mutual confidences regarding business, which I discovered from their complaints had been very dull—with the turfites, owing to those darned police getting to know them so well and nipping trade in the bud; with the lion and lionesses, through an infernal travelling opera company getting one stage ahead, and taking all the spare cash out of the townsmen's pockets before they came.

'I tell ye what it is. These cussed foreign hoperas is playing the devil with legitimate business,' growled the lion from his corner, savagely. 'We'll starve, that's what it'll come to if we can't get ahead on them.'

'Why don't you hurry up and make the spring, then?' observed one of the flash fraternity. And the moody lord of beasts muttered, 'I am thinking about it.'

I have often wondered where the legitimate began and the illegitimate ended in the theatrical profession. It seems all so curiously blended and mixed up.

One of the tawny-haired lionesses attempted to make up to the remorseless skipper, but without any marked success. He was too well-salted a bird already to be caught by powder and hair-dye. She tried a mild attack of sea-sickness on him the first hour or two, with drooping head and tottering feet, but he coolly let her droop and totter, unmanly ruffian that he was. Then she appealed to him for protection and justice. She had been robbed of her purse she told him; but even that failed to interest him, for he told her coarsely that crows didn't pick out crows' eyes, or if they did no one had any right to interfere. Then she gave him up, used an unladylike expression about his habits, and returned to her moody mate, the lion comique.

So we progressed past Bingham and Wiangan, and saw our friends go off like a cargo of sheep—or rather blaspheming castaways—in two of the small boats, towards Burnett Head lighthouse, with the sun setting beyond them, making them look like black blots upon a golden shield. Welshers and lion comiques are not held in very great favour amongst the simple-minded Queenslanders.

So we come on to Keppel Bay, outside of which the great barrier reef of coral begins, which stretches right up to Cape York, and makes the rest of the voyage pass as if through a lake.

In front of us lies the Golden shore—a beautiful sandy beach—and over to the side the mainland, with the distant ranges, the chief mountain of which is Larcom (2,060 feet high), with a curious formation of rock on its summit, looking at this distance like the ruins of a great castle, with Cape Capricorn, Herbert Point, and Peak Island rising from the azure ocean.

It is a lovely sight as we look round. I find a note here in my book about the habits of seals, but whether it was some sealer on board who told me the facts at this point, or it had any connection with Keppel Bay, I cannot now remember. My note merely says: 'Habits of seals— Old bulls come on shore to fight over their cows, while the curlews fly about and keep watch, warning them of danger when it approaches.'

Rockhampton lies on the Fitzroy River, 35 miles from its mouth and 420 miles north-west of Brisbane. To me it has in it the makings of the most perfect city throughout Australia, for its surroundings are perfect as far as Nature can make her work when she wishes to adapt it to the wants and comforts of man. It now only rests with the owners to complete the task.

As we enter the wide mouth of the river I notice its muddy colour as the fertilising soil is washed down to the blue sea; then, as we steam up, the rich banks with picturesque backgrounds of ranges.

I learn from my handbook that it is in the county of Livingstone, and owes its origin to the Port Curtis gold rush in 1858, so that it is in its thirty-second year. I remember years ago some friends of mine joining an after-rush and returning to Brisbane in about a couple of months starving, penniless, and in outrageous tatters. When the first shipload of emigrants was landed on these shores, the captain had to sail away, as from an enemy, under the fire of his late passengers, who went nearly mad with horror at being left behind in such a desolate place. My Rockhampton landlord was one of these early pioneers, and was at the time as frantic as any of them, for the shores were all covered with unwholesome mangrove swamps, but he has lived to rejoice that the captain did not listen to their curses and violence. 'We had hard lines at first,' he told me, 'but we got over all that, and here we are, and now I wouldn't change for any other country on earth.'

There is a saying about Rockhampton that the climate is so hot that the bad people who die there and go below are compelled to send up to earth for their blankets to keep them warm. While I was there this last time, I felt it so chilly that I had to order a fire in the sitting-room before I could work, but I believe this was quite exceptional weather for Rockhampton.

The first night I spent there was a night of sleepless anguish of body and spirit. In spite of the cold, the mosquitoes came out in their thousands and contested the field with other enemies of sleep. I have read of those plagues of London—bugs, but never did I imagine that they could be so prolific and daring. They crowded upon me from all quarters, and sucked my veins almost dry, while outside the net curtains the winged fiends dashed themselves madly and sang their song of battle, as I, the victim, writhed and moaned beneath the torture.

Next morning I rose at daybreak, languid and covered with wounds, and wandered along the banks of the Fitzroy, looking on the ships which lay at anchor softly veiled in silver mist, with wearied and hopeless eyes. Yes, I had to admit that the scene was beautiful; but what of that to a victim of the vampires and insomnia? I had, alas! ten days before me to endure this living death and nightly torture. Had I been only thin or delicate, perhaps happy release would come before the ten days were up; but I was robust and sound as a bell the night before, therefore I supposed I would last the time.

I determined to make an effort for life, so as soon as the other hotels were open I went over them one by one, to see if I could better my condition ; but there the traces of my deadly enemies were flaunting on every seam of the weatherboard, darker and more ostentatious than in the lodgings I had left. I gave up the struggle, and meekly returned to my breakfast.

'Take me where you best like,' I muttered, as I lay down that night and recklessly opened up the curtains, for I was resolved that the airy rivals should have a fair chance— if I was to be drained, at least I would make it a competitive game with the usurpers ; then I went to sleep, and wonderful to relate next morning felt a little stronger. I am of opinion that the mosquitoes had waged war on the bugs and sucked them instead of me ; after that partial triumph I felt no more, and managed to enjoy Rockhampton life.

Every place has its own afflictions, so I do not tell this experience to disparage this city, because no one could have been more hospitably treated than I was here. They could no more keep down the breed than Victoria can exterminate the rabbits, or Melbourne its plague of rats since they had underground drainage. I passed one night in a haunted room here, when I thought that an enemy was bombarding the city, the shrieking, thumping, and rushing about was so unceasing and awful.

It was the night before one of the champion fights, and the waiters were all full of it next morning when I got up. The battle had come off at daybreak, so it was all over when I turned out.

'Have you heard the result, sir ? ' said the waiter, as he opened the door for me to go out.

'The result of what?'

'The great fight.'

'No. So there has been a fight after all, has there?' I inquired, thinking of the experience of the night I had gone through.

'Of course, sir. Slavin's won, as we all said he would.'

'I am glad of that, but it was a devil of a row they made over it.'

'How do you know, sir?'

'Because I couldn't get a wink of sleep all night through them; heard them at it banging about and cursing like wild cats!'

The waiter looked me over solemnly for a moment, and then said gravely, 'No, sir, I bet you what you like you couldn't hear that fight, for it took place four miles from here.'

'Then what did I hear in that room?'

'Must have been the rats, they're awful in that No. 46.'

I had slept in the haunted 46.

No, I will never blame my kind host and hostess, or their amiable daughter, for my affliction, for no mortal man or woman could keep them down; but I join with them and the squatters of Victoria in anathematising the two foolish Noahs who introduced the first pair of rabbits into Camperdown district and the first male and lady 'bird' to Rockhampton. The genial climate did all the rest.

I preserved a few of these natural specimens, and posted them home to England to some friends. One of them was sent to a newspaper, and reproduced under the title of a Rockhampton 'soldier ant,' which when I read it afterwards I didn't correct, for it didn't seem a bad title for these bold warriors.

But what was stranger than all, amongst the specimens that I sent home was a strange insect which I put into my letter alive; it had no food, yet went safely through the six weeks' journey inside the mail-bags, and when the letter was opened this insect hopped out on to the table all alive and active, and spreading a pair of new-fledged wings, prepared to use them, when his doom came upon him in the form of a tame starling who chanced to be moulting at the time. Dicky, the starling, made a pounce on the strange foreigner before he could quite recover his presence of mind and gobbled him up.

I never could tell what family that Queensland insect belonged to, but it must have been not only a good-living family but also very good as a medicine, for the tame starling who had been very sickly before this and moping, straightway brightened up and mended every hour afterwards.

In my lodgings I found some of the members of the 'cussed hopera company' who had defrauded the lion comique, and was greatly struck with the homely simplicity of these heroes and heroines; in fact, they gave themselves no airs at all, which astonished me very much. The soprano singer I found very fond of painting; she occupied her spare time painting on velvet, and her art-work was good and true. I enjoyed one night listening to their public performance, and I do not think I have heard better singing anywhere. Poor lion comique, the natives of Queensland were too close to Nature to appreciate your humour! It is only the Old-World masters who can understand such fine flashes of wit as the ' waggle of a bustle' or the genius of a music-hall beast's wild roaring. I am afraid that true music will starve out your *legitimate* line of business before you can get back to the refinements of civilisation.

' 'Ria's *not* on the job' much in Queensland, but good music and honest manliness are.

Rockhampton is the port of Central Queensland, and ought to be the capital of that colony when the country is properly divided off, as it is the outlet of the Dawson, Peak Downs, and Springton districts, all those rich lands watered by the Barcoo, Diamentina, Herbert, Thompson, Alice, and the numerous other rivers flowing from the interior. The streets are splendidly planned out for a semi-tropical city. They have a width of 132 feet, and are lined on both sides with young trees. The town is supplied with water drawn from the Crescent Lagoon, two miles distant, and pumped into an artificial reservoir at the top of Athelstane Range, 150 feet high.

As the original settlers have planned out their city nothing could be better; but as they have built it so far, I fancy that I can add a word or two by way of suggestion.

I wrote a letter to the papers while I was there, describing how I thought it should be built; many of the local readers may have fancied that I was indulging in an ideal picture which could not be realised, or perhaps perpetrating a gentle joke. I was not. Indeed, I never have been more in earnest in my life, and I am always in dead earnest in all my artistic schemes. I don't now remember what I then wrote, but I perfectly recollect the ideal and designs which moved me at the time.

I had gone up to sketch the town from the top of the hill-road leading to the Murray Lagoon and Botanical Gardens. Before me spread the city, like the site of a great city in the plains, with the broad streets and squares only as yet partly filled in with houses, yet all pegged off as it will be in the 'sweet by-and-by.' Beyond the farther line of houses down by the wharves rolled the wide river, with its white-pillared suspension bridge, and with the masts and tracery of the ships lying moored; and behind these again the bold outlines of the rugged Berserker Ranges lying only a few miles distant from the town, with the gorges and cliffs and wooded prominences showing out in most picturesque relief.

The sun was setting behind me, and flung its warm radiance upon the house-ends and the outstanding portions of those perfectly formed mountains (almost a facsimile of the Ochils at Alva in Scotland), while purple shadows trailed along the plains and buried those valleys behind in velvet folds of deepness.

It was all very beautiful, and I gave a big sigh that I must leave it so soon.

People have often asked me which portion of Australia I liked the best, and I can hardly say. When I was in Victoria I think I would have fixed on Birregurra as a home, but that was before I visited Gippsland and the Alps; when I was in New South Wales I thought upon Orange, with a hankering after the harbour of Sydney; again I come up to Queensland and fall desperately in love with Rockhampton, and after what I have written about the nights in bed there you will admit that it must have been very exquisite to make me wish to stay on and endure all this and more, if more could have been endured, for the sake of my artistic sense.

I think, however, now that I have seen most of Australia, I would desire no greater boon from Fortune than to be permitted to pass the rest of my life wandering over it with my camp-stool, sketch-book, and plenty of foolscap, so that I might take it in detail bit by bit, and let the world and posterity know how passionately I love it: the heat, the light, its infinite variety, and those magnificent trees, the rugged gum. I feel like a lonely exile away from it, for it embodies all that is pleasant and free and youthful about me. Those nine letters, 'Australia,' must have eaten themselves in bold Roman type deep into my heart.

But to come back to Rockhampton. As I looked over

that scantily-filled valley, I saw a future city rise over these mean-looking buildings, a city built to suit the climate and the locality, high stone walls, and solid square towers with open roofs, like the Moorish buildings of Spain —those massive houses which are built in a square, with the garden and fountains in the centre, and other gardens around, where the sensible Moors sought to make as much shadow as possible, and planned their principal lounging places on the roofs. Yes, that is how Rockhampton ought to be planned out to suit its surroundings—gardens, streets, with lofty walls on either side of the trees, where people could always walk in the cool shade, and which gather all the breezes there may be about, and drift them down the alleys.

I saw it all in that sunset glow, as I hope the owners of the land will yet see it, when it has become the capital of the Colony, Central Queensland, with its white-walled Parliament House filling out the centre and raising on high its rounded domes, with its squares and boulevards and glinting fountains, backed by those bold Berserker Ranges —saw it so plainly that I have made a sketch of it, to help in the future building of it.

CHAPTER XXXVI

MOUNT MORGAN

The Queensland Throne of Greasy Mammon the Great.

WE are now in the portion of Queensland where the earth is filled with treasures for those who may not be content with its bounteous surface—gold, silver, copper, and other metals. I have a box filled with precious stones with which a prospector presented me before I left the land, all from Central Queensland, and all in the rough: diamonds, rubies, opals, sapphires and other precious ware. They are dull pebbles of uncertain shape and varied low tones, for they require cutting to bring out their beauty; yet I prefer them as they are, because there may be flaws in them, which I cannot discern now, and I don't want to know their faults. Sufficient for me that experts have decided that they are what they were represented to be, real gems from Queensland.

All round Rockhampton the soil is good and productive; that we are getting into the tropics I know, because a man wanted to sell me a living young crocodile which he had caught a day or two before in the river above the Suspension Bridge.

But one of the most wonderful sights about this part is Mount Morgan, which is a mountain of gold.

In all other parts of the world men have to dig down for the precious metal, whether it is in alluvial or quartz form, but here they have only to shift the loose earth, or quarry out the ore in large quartz-block 'gold which is of unusual fineness and unprecedented purity.'

It is not often that a Scotsman misses his chance in life, if he gets one, people are apt to say: but this is what happened about this mountain of gold. A young Scotsman called Donald Gordon had it all to himself, and let it all slip from him at the rate of 1*l.* per acre. It is reckoned to contain gold enough to yield a profit, after working expenses are paid, of nine millions sterling.

About twenty-six years ago Donald took up a squatting station here, and did very well for some years, until the Land Bill for selection was passed, and he was forced to give up the best portion of his run and purchase a selection, about the only one left on his station, being that where Mount Morgan stands—a selection composed chiefly of rubble, ferns, rocks, and tufts of coarse grass. After this the fortunes of Donald declined.

Then the prospectors came along, searching for traces of copper, and went over his land tapping at those loose dark metallic-looking boulders, without ever having a thought of what they contained, it being against all precedent for gold to be found like this. Then Donald took the mining fever, and thought he might find a copper mine, but not knowing anything of geology, he did what he considered the best thing to do under the circumstances, sent for a learned college-bred geological professor, paying all his expenses up, to get his infallible advice on the chances his selection had.

The professor came up with his instruments and scientific 'catchwords,' looked about him, and used regular jaw-breakers over the commonest objects lying about, but could not see any trace of copper or sign of anything else of value to poor Donald. He took him over the mountain, which the learned one on the anatomy of this little planet declared to be merely 'a mountain of ironstone,' and of no value.

That verdict finished poor Donald, who went off to work for his daily bread at Galawa Mine, Mount Wheeler, belonging to the three Brothers Morgan, all keen-headed men and experienced miners.

One day Gordon spoke about his ironstone mountain, and offered to show it to his employers, who, after going over it carefully, offered him 640*l*. for his selection of 640 acres. This he accepted gladly.

For a time the Brothers Morgan kept their find as dark as possible, shipping all the gold to Brisbane for export so as to avoid suspicion; but such a Golconda could not be long hidden, so the brothers formed a limited company to work it, taking for themselves one-half of the mine, and disposing of the rest at the rate of 24,000*l*. for one-tenth interest. It is still kept as quiet as the shareholders can keep it, and as few men employed as possible upon it, which causes great dissatisfaction amongst the miners of Rockhampton, so that they are always trying to 'jump' claims upon it, and getting up all sorts of law quibbles about it.

To jump a claim means, according to mining laws, that if a man can only manage to peg round a claim before he is driven off the ground, it becomes his to work as long as he pays his miner's fee for the use of the ground, so that it is a game of surprise and rebuff. Mount Morgan has to be watched and guarded day and night by the owners, in order that no outsider may succeed in 'jumping' it.

In the Rockhampton weekly *Capricornian* of March 22, 1884, there is an interesting account of this wonderful 'mine,' if we can call it by such a name. I quote from this and other sources in my present description.

Mount Morgan lies 23 miles from Rockhampton in a south-westerly direction, and rises 1,225 feet above the level of the sea, and 521 feet above the batteries at its base. The prevailing colour of the rocks is the rusty red tint of ironstone, so that the poor college-bred professor had some grounds to fix his convictions upon, and therefore did not blunder nearly so much as most of his kind usually do when asked to put their scientific education into practice.

'For the first twelve miles after leaving Rockhampton a low, alluvial country is passed. Out of the clay rise isolated mounds and ridges of graywackes and shales hardened in portions into Lydian-stone and ribbon jasper. When the twelve miles are passed on the heads of Gracemere Creek, granite is seen in a gully—soft, decomposing, and covered with boulders of a coarse, ferruginous, siliceous grit.

'Five miles farther on is the Razor Back Range—a sharp "pinch" on the road, leading up to a table-land, which stands 900 feet above sea level. The rocks here are metamorphosed strata, and this prevails until, five miles further on, Mount Morgan is reached.

'In the immediate neighbourhood of this mountain the rocks are mainly of bluish-grey quartzite—a fine-grained siliceous sandstone, now more or less vitrified, full of minute crystals of iron pyrites and specks of magnetic iron ore, graywackes of the ordinary type; hard, fine-grained sandstone, or mingled siliceous and felspathic materials, now somewhat indurated; and, lastly, occasional masses of shale hardened to a flinty consistency, and a few belts of serpentine.

'The central portion of the upper cutting (of the mountain itself) is a large mass of brown hæmatite ironstone, generally in great blocks of several tons weight, with a stalactite structure, as if the iron oxide had gradually filled up cavities left in the original deposit. The ironstone contains gold of extraordinary fineness, which can be detected in almost every fresh fracture. This ironstone is more or less mixed with fine siliceous granules. Gradually to right and left of the central mass the silica more or less replaces the ironstone. It is a frothy, spongy or cellular sinter, sometimes so light from the enlargement of air in its pores that it floats on water like pumice stone. Fine gold is disseminated throughout this deposit as well as in the ironstone.'

I quote from Robert L. Jack's, the Government Geologist's report here. He considers that nothing but a thermal spring in the open air, similar to the Iceland and New Zealand geysers, could have deposited the material above described; and that the deposits of the mountain are newer than the stratified rocks through which it has burst, as all across the surrounding Dee Valley are horizontally-bedded sandstone cliffs stretching north and south; so that it is conclusive that the valley has been carved out of a once continuous cake of horizontal sandstone, while the hot spring of Mount Morgan was newer than the desert sandstone.

'In active geysers that are accessible to observation, we find a narrow pipe or fissure terminating upwards in a crater-like cup or basin. It may be taken for granted that Mount Morgan geyser was no exception to the rule, and that the upper portion of the mount, where ironstone predominates, represents a basin occasionally filled with a fluid of silica, iron, alumina, manganese, and gold held in solution, to be deposited when the bulk of the water from time to time withdrew into the subterranean reservoirs with which the pipe communicates.

'This Mount Morgan discovery of gold is one of the most important events in the history of mining industry. It is not merely that the quantity is large, but the possibility that this discovery may lead to others of equal importance in a direction where gold has never been looked for, lends it a wider significance. A vast area in our Western interior is covered with cretaceous rocks, and has been covered with the desert sandstone, of which isolated table-lands remain to attest its former extension. Beneath the cretaceous rocks, palæozoic rocks undoubtedly extend, and these doubtless contain many reefs as rich in gold as those which lie exposed to view in the ranges near the coast. Given a hot spring rising from depths in which auriferous reefs lie hidden, we may look for a repetition of the phenomena of Mount Morgan. My own acquaintance with the West has been limited, but I have long suspected that the opals and ironstones met with in certain Western localities have something to do with hot springs. I have heard tales of craters among the desert sandstone and cretaceous regions of the West, and in some instances I suspect that my informants may have been describing geyser-deposits. A few hot springs exist in Queensland, and several cases of " mud-puffs " have been noted ; but there is every reason to believe that the remains of extinct springs —dating, like Mount Morgan, from tertiary times—may be widely distributed. I do not mean that the search for hot springs should be confined to the Western Down. My object is to point out that gold may yet be found over that enormous area where it has, hitherto, been regarded as hopelessly buried beneath mesozoic and tertiary accumulations.'

Dr. Lerbins, in a lecture, says : ' As the mine (or quarry) is being developed caves are opened out, from the roofs of which oxide of iron and silica hang like stalactites the size of a finger, in which gold is readily seen disseminated. The whole hill-top seems to be of richly auriferous stone It is merely cut away to suit the convenience of the miners, so that a quarry or broad terrace has been formed. The cutting is 20 feet high by about 100 feet long, and t stone is of the same character the whole distance, and extends to the summit of the mountain several chains higher. The facility with which the gold-bearing quartz can be obtained may be judged from the fact that a charge of blasting-powder, put in anywhere along the works, will displace tons of it at a time. It is carted after this about a quarter of a mile along a good,

A QUEENSLAND ABORIGINAL.

metalled road down the mountain side, and is then thrown into a wooden shoot, wide and deep, and about 200 feet long, at the bottom of which a cutting has been made for its reception, and barriers raised to prevent it rolling farther down the hill. It is then again carted to battery No. 1, of ten stampers, and next to No. 2, of fifteen stampers, where about 250 tons are crushed per week. The return is said to be never less than 5 ozs. to the ton, and is valued at the rate of 4*l*. 4*s*. 8*d*. per ounce, while the "tailings" left over are said to contain as much as is saved.'

From some samples of the quartz sent by Mr. Hall, one of the proprietors of the quarry, to the Sydney Mint, for testing purposes, by their special Chilian mill, it was found that Lot 1 gave gold at the rate of 39·32–100 ounces standard per ton of quartz, while gold at the rate of 46 ozs. 2 dwts. 12 grs. per ton was left in the tailings; and in Lot 2 the tailings assayed 44 ozs. 5 dwts. 18 grs. of gold per ton. The gold found here is not in the original matrix of gold generally found, Nature having already mined it, chemically treated it, sublimated, and redeposited it.

Gold has been found all round Rockhampton; to the south at Caliope and Raglan; south-west, Crocodile and Morgan; west, Native Bee, Stanwell, and Clermont; north-west, Morinish, Ridgeland, and Rosewood; north-north-west, Bonnie Doon and Marlborough; north, Canoona; east, Mount Wheeler, Cawarral, and New Zealand Gully; south-east, Stony Creek—all highly gold-bearing reefs and rich alluvial deposits.

The *Sydney Morning Herald* gives a fine bit of word-painting of the scenery round this golden mount. I cannot resist taking some extracts from it before I leave the spot.

'The crest' (of Razor Back) 'reached, I look back and see teams of horses and the drays far below, the track beyond winding in and out among the trees till an abrupt turn shuts it out. On every side are round-topped hills covered with blue gums. They are like waves in a broken sea; those nearest dark and gloomy-looking, those beyond flecked with lines of light and spaces of shadow, those in the far distance tinted to the daintiest blue, and wrapped in a tissue of silver gauze, the shimmer of the air quivering in the mid-day sun.

'Passing through a little canvas town with its store, a couple of miles' ride brings me to the mine. The thud,

Queensland 'Gin'

thud of the stampers crushing the quartz, the tents, the great stacks of dark red stone, and the pits filled, and stream flowing, and dyed into the same hue, tell us of the work of the miner. The track dips into the dry bed of the river, which in the rainy season becomes a swift torrent, bearing along branches and trunks of fallen trees.'

He goes on to describe the dams, sluice-pits, into which the washed material is poured (want of water is the great drawback at present in Mount Morgan), the stampers, and the batteries, with the refining shed, where the 'tailings' are treated chemically, in order to extract the gold, which is so fine that much of it escapes the 'ripples' and 'blankets.'

The process of chlorination is kept secret, the works being managed by a professional metallurgist and chemist, employed by the shareholders, and paid according to results.

'In the galvanised-iron shed, one of the first objects noticed is a range of furnaces upon which are placed, one to each furnace, glazed earthenware jars containing chemicals necessary in generating chlorine gas. Next, a number of vats, where the tailings are poured, and the gas injected, which sets free the gold from the tailings. The liquid gold is then filtered through the finest Mediterranean sponges, and so passes from the bottom of the vats into a number of tanks at a lower level. The tanks being filled, sulphate of iron is then poured in, and the gold is precipitated to the bottom, and the chlorine set free. The precipitate is then treated in the crucible, and the gold secured.

'For some distance' (up the mountain) 'a road has been cut, where we meet a number of horses with drays filled with quartz. The prevailing colour is the dusky red of ironstone. The road is a great red scar, the drays are red, the horses red, and the men, as they guide the animals down the steep roadway, loom through a great cloud of red dust.

'The mine is unlike any other I ever saw. It is simply an immense quarry. With the hills of blue gums around it, this great scar, glowing with red, yellow, white, black, and a whole pallet of colours, stands out like a jewel or a many-hued mosaic, in a dead, lustreless setting. It is difficult to convey even the faintest impression of what it resembles—it is so unlike all other geological formations. It is not a reef with defined walls, nor can any trace of distant strata be seen. There are great masses of what look like fused iron, or slag from a furnace. One has to look closely to see the gold, but, looking closely, one sees minute specks powdered over the rock. Sometimes these gold specks cluster together, and form tiny tree or fern-like figures.

'About 250 feet below the first mine is No. 2, the southern claim, where a face of about 700 feet has been opened out, and here the stone differs from that of No. 1. There are great seams and patches of white stone that look like calcined quartz. This stuff is very light, like pumice stone. Standing at the face I put out one hand and filled it with a substance as fine as flour, and perfectly white, while with the other hand I broke off a piece of black, heavy rock.

'In opening up this face small cavities are met with, from the roof of which depend stalactites. In some cases, on the floors of these cavities stalagmites are also found formed beneath the stalactites. At some places they meet; at others an open space is left between.

'But what is very strange, in some of these cavities where there are none of these stalactites and the roof is smooth, the floor is covered with pinnacles exactly similar to the stalagmites, but bedded in as though they had been forced upwards and from it. In one cavity I saw a wondrously brilliant bit of colour. The lower half had been torn away, and only the upper left, and this was crusted with nodules, coloured with the richest metallic tints—crimson, violet, green, and other half-tones.

'Returning from the mountain I stopped at a wayside inn, where a tall, weather-beaten, grizzled-looking man took my horse to a well to drink. This was the original holder of the freehold (Donald Gordon), who parted with it to the Morgans. He said that he had always believed the mountain to be of ironstone, and never dreamt of the fortune which had been so long within his grasp, and which he had sold for 640*l.* In olden days he used to sell this pumice-stone-looking gold quartz in Rockhampton to clean the hearths and doorsteps of the houses.'

CHAPTER XXXVII

COAST SCENERY

Suburbs of Rockhampton—Olsen's Caves—Towards Townsville—Whitsunday Passage—Bowen—Two Nice Young Passengers—A Breakdown at Bowling Green—Cleveland Bay and Townsville.

BEFORE leaving Rockhampton I went for a drive, with two friends, to Olsen's Caves, along a fine bush road, with the warm tropical mists overlying the country (the mornings are mostly misty on the Fitzroy River, and bad for ague before people get acclimatised). What a fairylike picture the bush looked, with the great spider meshes, heavy with the moisture, trailing over all the branches and leaves!

We crossed the bridge and looked down the river, all pearly and soft, with the ships at anchor repeating themselves, and the wooden posts of the wharves with the terrace above, ships and lines drifting into tender spectres of objects, and delicate washes. One of my companions on this trip was the editor of a local paper, and the other a lover of, and exceptionally good painter of, pictures for a non-professional, so that we had tastes in common and enjoyed ourselves.

Up towards the weir the river was lined with trees and wooden huts all blanched with that soft atmospheric effect.

Past woodmen's shanties and Chinamen's huts, picturesque in the extreme as they stood glowing in all the tints of different-coloured preserved meat and salmon and sardine tins which John had lined them with—gay structures, if a trifle uncertain in their upright lines and shaky on their pins.

I liked that bush drive in spite of the clusters of ferocious tiger mosquitoes which went with us, hanging hungrily on to us, and perhaps if I had not dropped my favourite pipe down one of the holes, and broken the amber stem, or passed over without seeing the Fish River Caves, I would have been delighted with the glowing wonders of Olsen. As it was, my admiration became a little qualified. Still, they are something to be proud about in the way of caves, vast and lofty in some places, with a delightful soft carpet of bat droppings underfoot, and long roots of trees dropping like snakes from roof to floor ; narrow passages where one has to squeeze hard to get through, and countless families of bats hanging head downwards from the ledges. We spent two or three hours boring mole-like through the earth, with unexplored caves on every side of us, and hollow chambers underfoot. Outside it is very rugged, with dense bush about it and charming, extensive views all round, with blue and scented gums making the foreground sweet, and clusters of the zamia, that half-way plant between the fern and the tropical palm, the pith of which is good for food on the tramp, and the outside for making eider-down couches.

Next day I went to Gracemere, a pretty suburb along the Crocodile Road. Next to Breakfast Creek, and round the Berserkers, getting some quaint sketches.

I did not get to Jericho as it was too far distant, but I heard all about it and its expectations, and the pretty bathing-places along the coast, and after seeing the meat-preserving works at Lakes Creek and the scalping-huts, I was ready to depart and say farewell to my friends the *ladybirds*. By the way, I completely disgusted them before

I left by anointing myself nightly with oil of lavender, which is a very potent charm against midnight marauders.

That evening I went down the river, under a heavy shower, in the little ' Dolphin,' and joined the ' Alexandra ' at Keppel Bay.

It was all summer weather after this, for we were now within the protection of the Barrier Reef, so that there was no longer danger of sea-sickness. We might look at the storm raging outside in the ocean, inside we were protected and safe. All I had to do was fix myself comfortably on deck and sketch the passing landscape, while the captain lounged beside me, when off duty, giving me the names of places from his chart, and telling me incidents about each landmark as we passed. A very fine fellow was the captain of the ' Alexandra,' and his chief steward was also one of the most obliging and gentlemanly of waiters. If it had not been for the easy and elegant manner in which he waited at table, I should have quite felt to see such a man standing while I sat; as it was, he gave a dignity to the post, and stood like a genteel protest against the vulgarity of those he seemed to patronise by attending upon. I admired him prodigiously, not only for his kindness and affability, but also for his aristocratic appearance. He had a refined, pale face and classic features, with expressive eyes, a slender figure, and languid air, while his carefully-cultivated moustache might well have graced an *habitué* of the Army and Navy Club. From what I have heard, lady passengers liked to travel on board the ' Alexandra,' and I don't wonder at it—I should have doated on my soup if handed to me by such a drooping cavalier, had I been a susceptible young lady. May he live long to adorn that neat little saloon, and his shadow never grow less as it glides gracefully along the snow-white deck.

The sea is of that delicious cobalt-green tint, with

violet streaks caused by the snow-white beds of coral over which we are sailing day after day, with softly clouded skies and warm breezes fanning our faces from the distant ocean. Every hour it is becoming warmer and more beautiful, with constant changes of coast, and islands dotting all round, some rugged and bare, some clustering with trees.

We pass the Clara Group and Steep Island on the one side, cliffs 409 feet high, covered with herbage, while on the other lies the mainland, soft greys, greens and purples, with snow-white clouds half veiling the distant ranges. It is still the black-fellow's country this mainland, for we see the smoke of their fires curling upwards on Edwards Islands, the Beverley group, Cape Townsend, &c. Then to Flat Top, near the entrance of the Pioneer River, and Port Mackay, a rising town and great sugar centre. Over twenty-five sugar mills are working here, the River Estate mill being lighted by electric lamps; and although barely twenty years old, Port Mackay has over forty miles of streets, and a public library of nearly 2,000 volumes. We are once more in the land of free libraries.

Talking about libraries reminds me of the State schools of Australia, of which I have as yet said nothing. The whole country is fairly studded with schools, and must be one of the finest places in the world for teachers, and, as the education is free, also for pupils. All the schools are supported by Government, and where trains run past them the journey to and fro is free to scholars. I have seen the slow train stop every few yards, like a tramway car, to pick up or let down the children as they come from or go to school—a pleasant sight, even though it made slow travelling.

Captain Cook has given names to a great number of the islands and points along this coast, and fortunately they have not been altered, for they are all most expressive and descriptive.

We pass Temple Island, Cape Palmerston, Fresh Water Point and Round Top, Flat Top Island and Port Mackay, Slade Point and Shoal Point, and with Anchor Island, enter Whitsunday Passage, reckoned to be one of the most beautiful straits throughout Australia. A lovely place it is, with thickly-wooded and rounded hillsides and green banks, with cliffs starting boldly up at parts, and high ranges behind—Cape Conway, Dent Island, Pine Head, Cid and Molle Islands to right and left, as we steam close to them both, with the High Peak, 1,900 feet high, all wooded, and Mount Jeffreys on the mainland, Grassy Island, Double Cone, Armit, Gumbril, and George Point.

Cape Gloucester is one of the most diversified and rugged promontories we have come to yet, standing boldly, with its boulder terraces and grassy slopes, high amongst the sunlit clouds, and the smooth waters lapping its rocky strands.

We now approach Bowen, and a pretty picture it makes from the sea, as it lies behind Gloucester Island and lighthouse, brightly sparkling with its purple background of hills.

The people of Bowen do not hurry or excite themselves over trifles; there is no need, in this quiet, undisturbed cove. It is pastoral and sleepy in its character, for there has not yet come any great rush to disturb their repose. The situation is delightful, land-locked and safe from tempests; all they have to do is to live and let live, which they try to do.

Two young men come aboard at Bowen. One has been sheep-farming and become tired of Australia, and having got a little cheque from home, is returning to England, like a bad shilling, to loaf upon his relations. He has not a happy look about his weak face, and is an unpleasant object to look upon, so that I expect he will be one of those returned exiles who abuse the country when they get back.

The other is a pudding-faced boy who is being sent to England by his fond parents to be educated, under the stupid impression that he will come back more accomplished than the colonial schools could make him. It is his first parting from his mammy, and he is blubbering at the awful thought of the long voyage. Unfortunately for my peace of mind he fancies, as he mopes his fishy eyes, that he sees a gleam of sympathy in mine, and straightway becomes one of the most awful afflictions any one could have thrust upon him, for he feels lonely and wants company, is chock-full of senseless questions, and never leaves me for a moment or ceases in his everlasting prattling, until I get away from him at Thursday Island. I vainly attempt to sit upon him. All rebuffs are thrown away, for he is too conscious of his own niceness to take the broadest hint to leave me alone for a moment. A great lubberly boy he is, who hangs over me while I am working; like a half-grown Newfoundland pup, only less interesting. When I think of him now, I wonder how I kept from knocking him on the head and tumbling him amongst the sharks during some of the many nights when I was trying to enjoy the lovely starlight, and he would maul about me, tempting me to murder. Sometimes, when desperate, I turned on him and curdled his marrow with stories of what they would do to him when he got to college; but that was a trivial revenge for all I had to suffer.

I think that either he or his shipmate must have been our Jonah on board, for after we had got clear of Mother Buddock's Stone, Abbott's Point, and Cape Upstart, and were approaching Cape Cleveland, having behind us Bowling Green Lighthouse, the engines stopped suddenly, while a quick thud from below startled us on deck; our

THE BARRON FALLS

propeller had snapped through the middle, and the rest of our journey into Townsville had to be done by sailing at about the rate of two knots per hour.

I would not have minded this had I not been in a hurry to catch the 'Victory,' the only boat possible for a month to New Guinea. Knowing the day it was to sail, I reckoned upon just having one day to spare at Thursday Island. Now, unless some unforeseen accident favoured me, I would have to waste a month or six weeks, perhaps forego my Papuan trip altogether.

However, the captain kindly came to my rescue, and as a boat was to be sent into Townsville for a tug to help him in, he permitted me to go with the boat and gave me a letter to the captain of the British India mail steamer 'Duke of Westminster,' to take me on with him, and charge my fare to his company.

A splendid moonlight night that was, as we progressed towards Cleveland Bay, and a delightful experience going over these tropical waters, with the men straining at the oars.

Cleveland Bay, land-locked on three sides, with Magnetic Island at the entrance, is one of the finest roadsteads I have seen, and capable of sheltering all the ships at present afloat.

Townsville had, at the last census (1881), seventy-five miles of streets and roads, 1,450 buildings, and a population of 9,000. It is picturesquely laid out on the north bank of the Ross Creek and partly climbing up Castle Hill, which rises to a height of 1,000 feet from the sea. There is a large shipping trade done here, Townsville being the main outlet of an immense territory, several gold fields, and vast pastoral districts, including such flourishing places as Charters Towns, Hughenden, Norwood, Ravenswood, and the stations lying between it and the Diamentina River.

As a port of call, however, it has its disadvantages, for large vessels have to lie over two miles from the shores, the water gradually shallowing up to the beautiful sandy beach. But for this drawback I would be inclined to fix upon this place as the future capital and the *third* colony of Queensland; as it is, however, we must look for the locality about 200 miles farther north.

Townsville is plentifully supplied with water, as the supply is drawn from two great wells sunk three and four miles distant, where they believe that they have tapped a great subterranean stream. The water from these wells is pumped up to a reservoir of 650,000 gallons capacity on Castle Hill, at about 180 feet above sea level, and from there distributed through the city.

The approach to Townsville is very fine, and almost resembles the Bay of Naples, with, instead of Vesuvius, that abrupt Castle Hill towering over it, and the other ranges behind.

Barges and small ships lie scattered over the waters, with the houses glistening at the base of the mountain and along the yellow beach. On Magnetic Island they have built a quarantine station, and on a little rocky island in the entrance to the bay is placed a lighthouse to guide vessels in.

I was in time for the mail steamer; indeed, the other passengers were also, for as morning dawned over the bay the 'Alexandra' came dragging along behind a disreputable little tug, and my beautiful boy-bear smiled genially at me over the side, preparatory to coming aboard. I groaned in spirit as I saw those prominent teeth glisten in the morning sun.

As I was going along the saloon passage where the baths were, I heard my name shouted out, and, next moment, was seized upon by a party in a towel-wrapper. It was one of our old passengers from the 'Parramatta' going to China. This world is very small now, and I don't know the place where a man may safely hide his identity if he has been once on board a P. and O. or an Orient steamship. We were soon busy, recounting our adventures since we had parted company at Melbourne, until the breakfast bell rung.

After breakfast there was a little disturbance about the young man from Bowen who was going home to loaf on his friends, and his slobbery friend the future collegian came up to tell me all about it and ask my advice.

It appeared that the young man's friends had sent him out a second-class ticket, but on board the 'Westminster' they had no second class, so the captain had told him either to go ashore or accept the accommodation which they had. However, this did not suit the dignity of the youth, and he had sent his boy friend to see if he could not take the hat round and collect the difference for a saloon passage for him.

As the boy explained the charitable project, and ended up by coolly asking me if I'd take round the hat, my disgust broke out in rather strong expressions.

'So this young gentleman would sooner be an object of charity amongst the passengers than rough it a bit in the steerage, would he? Tell him from me to go ashore. He hasn't given Australia half a trial; he hasn't got a quarter of the "Lion and the Unicorn" kicked out of him yet.'

The boy delivered my message, and as the captain would not be any more charitable than I or the other passengers felt inclined to be, this poor young man was shunted ashore, weeping very pathetically over his own injuries and misfortunes, to finish his education of colonial life, as the Bowen boy was going home to commence his.

CHAPTER XXXVIII

HIGHER THAN NIAGARA

The Future Capital of Northern Queensland—Why the Town of Cairns should be Chosen—The Barron River and Falls—Mr. Monk's Idea, and Description by Mr. A. Meston.

CAIRNS is the place which I have been forced, by many advantages which it seems to possess over other northern townships, to think about as the most suitable site for a future capital of Upper Queensland.

It lies 900 miles north-west of Brisbane, 480 miles from Rockhampton, and so is about an equal distance between this city and Cape York, the topmost cape of Australia—just where it should be when an equal division takes place.

It is situated at the mouth of Trinity Inlet, on the western shores of Trinity Bay, with a very fine harbour, where vessels of all sizes can go alongside the wharves, once they get over the bar. This bar is the one, and only drawback, as at low tide there is only seven feet of water over it. It is of a width of about a mile from the fairway buoy, and an inlet would require to be cut this length for the convenience of vessels drawing over ten feet. But this is merely a trifle in the way of future expense.

Cairns lies on level ground, and is surrounded by miles of the finest sugar-lands in the entire Colony. Indeed, it has space enough about it for a city as large as London to be built in comfort upon the plains before the ranges can stop the extension, which is advantage No. 2 in its future aspirations.

The climate is most salubrious and healthy (if hot), and will be made more so when the ground is drained and cleared of its virgin scrub and mangrove fringes, a fine long sea beach extending in front of the present town. It is surrounded by gold-fields, tin and other mines. Herberton, with its tin mines, fifty-five miles distant, to which a good road has been made as well as a fairly good railway line, is one of the richest of mineral districts, not only for tin, but copper and silver lead, the lode and alluvial covering over a space of forty miles. I am understating the extent and wealth of this district, as I want to be well within the mark, but fresh lode discoveries are of constant occurrence. Indeed, it is so exceedingly rich in minerals that it can be compared only with Cornwall, and it will be able to give employment to 20,000 miners when the capital to work it is forthcoming.

Cardwell, the Tate River, and Port Douglas are all within easy distance of Cairns, both Cardwell and Port Douglas being centres of a great cedar and future wood trade, as behind these towns extend vast primeval forests of the finest wood in the world. So much is there hereabouts inland that the world may be supplied for the next century or two without danger of this magnificent timber land being cleared off. Hope No. 3.

Innumerable large and small rivers and creeks water this fertile land—rivers plentifully supplied from the Bellenden Ker Range, the highest peak of which towers 5,400 feet above the level of the sea, and which lies south of the town—while to the north rise the, as yet, unexplored highlands of Cape Tribulation and Peter Botte Ranges, the lofty peaks of which are nearly always covered with rain-clouds, and which make the most sublime scenery that can be imagined. So we find, first, space enough; second, splendid harbourage; third, mineral wealth which cannot be surpassed; fourth, fertility of soil; fifth, immense timber-land of the rarest quality of the valuable cedar; sixth, inexhaustible supplies of water; and lastly, healthiness of locality. What more can be desired by mortal man for a future capital to a splendid tropical country, where everything may be grown, dug out, or supplied for his wants and comforts!

About nine miles from Cairns, and in the Bellenden Ker Range, is one of the largest, if not *the* largest, waterfall in the world. It is some hundreds of feet higher than Niagara, and pours over the rocks a most tremendous and unceasing force of water, cold as ice, and pure as crystal, into the Barron River, which flows past Cairns into the sea.

Some miles above the Barron Falls the river flows in a broad, smooth sheet, widening out at this point like a great pond, and very deep, while beyond this again it runs along unobstructed, right into the heart of the cedar country for many miles, being fed by countless mountain streams, and rushing along, a full flood, through forests and deep gullies.

One of my fellow-passengers from Thursday Island to Cooktown was a Mr. Monk, a Government surveyor and resident of Cairns, who gave me a great deal of information about the Barron River and surrounding country. He also explained to me what I considered a very reasonable and practical mode of utilising this fine flow of water, now running, like Niagara, to waste.

Upon the banks of this smooth bend of the river above the falls he would plan a township, and wharves for woodrafts and vessels to transport the cedar logs from the forest as they were felled, and tin, copper, silver, and other produce from Herberton, close to which town the Barron

River passes, and beyond which it is deep and wide enough to float vessels.

This pond or basin he would partially dam, so that logs, rafts, and vessels could get no farther down. He would direct a portion of the water into canals, for the purpose of lifting trains up the face of the rocks at the fall by water power and cables on a zig-zag line, similar to the Blue Mountain railway, and from there along the remaining few miles to Cairns, whereby the cargoes could be first floated down the river, afterwards taken by train to Cairns, and thence shipped to all quarters of the world direct. Cairns would be the seaport city, and this upland city a midsummer resort and commercial river-port and highway to the interior.

I cannot resist bringing in here a description of these stupendous falls, written by Mr. A. Meston to one of the Queensland papers, and which, I trust, the author will permit me to use as the text to my illustration. It will give the reader a fair idea how the grandeur of the Falls affects some spectators.

The Barron Falls in Flood Time.

' My first description of these famous falls was written when the river was down to its lowest level. The present article describes the falls during the highest flood in the Barron for seven years. Byron says that no picture can give us an idea of the ocean; and no word-painting can give a clear outline of the unimaginable scene at the Barron Falls on the first three days of the present year. I find the blacks have two names for this tremendous cataract—"Biboohra" and "Kamerunga." They appear to avoid the locality, as during visits extending over four years I have not seen a myall near the falls, nor the tracks of any on the gravel beds of the river. I am not yet on terms of intimacy that would enable me to learn any legends they may have regarding the falls, but shall acquire that interesting information when my relations with the dark sons of the forest are less "strained" than they have been in the past. The actual height of the falls is now ascertained to be about 600 feet, or 436 feet higher than Niagara. From the edge of the precipice the river falls 900 feet in half a mile. The Herberton railway will pass right along the top, and the finest view of the whole falls will be seen from the carriage windows. That view, in flood time, will have no rival in the known world.

'" Stand back," said the dying Raphael, as the first glories of the world of spirits appeared to the parting soul—"stand back until I sketch that heavenly scene!" And standing by the Barron Falls on the second day of the new year, I, too, felt disposed to say, Stand back until I sketch that mighty picture, hung there on the Primal rocks among the everlasting mountains, like an immortal replica by Raphaelistic Nature, from some divine original in the picture-gallery of God! Before me was a torrent of water 300 yards wide, and about sixty feet deep, rushing resistlessly along at the rate of twenty miles an hour, tumbling in a solid wall suddenly over the edge of the enormous precipice, launched clear out into space, and descending for over 600 feet into the "waste wide anarchy of chaos, dark and deep," yawning abysmal in the depths below. I look up the river, and see it come sweeping round the bend, divided into three streams that rush together like wild horses as they enter the straight in the dread finish of their last race. They come with the sound of a tempestuous ocean dashing its surges through dark passages in the caverned rocks. Weird fancy pictures them as the rivers that roll through the gloomy realms of Pluto. Imagination

hears the sorrowful wail of Achero, the lamentation of sad Cocytus, and the hoarse roaring of infernal Phlegetho, "whose waves of torrent fire inflame with rage." They roll over the cliff, strike the first ledge of rock, and the water is dashed into foam and mist; rolling billows of vapour are projected with terrific force, in vast fantastic forms, down the entrance of the Titanic avenue of the river beneath, and clouds of spray float away upwards for 1,000 feet, and condense, and drip in showers of emerald dewdrops from the trees on the slopes of the mountains. The currents of air, created by the cataract, waved the branches of trees hundreds of feet overhead as if they were swaying in the contending winds of a storm.

'The thunder of the waters was awful. The rocks shook beneath you, like a mighty steamer trembling with the vibrations of the screw. The very soul within you recoils appalled before the inconceivable grandeur of that tremendous scene. These falls stand alone among cataracts, like Chimborazo among the mountains. Eternity itself is throned there on those dark rocks among the wild whirlwind of waters, and speaks to you in solemn tones of the Past, the Present, and the Evermore. You stand voiceless, "mute, motionless, aghast," in that immortal Presence.

'The human tongue has no utterance for the thoughts within you. They are not dead, those black rocks, those vast columns of descending waters! They tell you of

> Vastness and age and memories of Eld,
> Darkness and desolation and dim Night.

'Once only in each year do the flood waters of the tropic rains sweep the total surface of the bed rock. The wear of that brief period on the adamantine formation is imperceptible. How long, therefore, has the river occupied in cutting down 1,000 feet into the solid rock? You must look back through the shadowy vista of hundreds of thousands of years that bridge the period of time intervening between us and the dim morning of the world! The Night of Time hides for ever the birthday of that cataract. Empires have risen and fallen, barbarisms become civilisations, races of men flourished and died, religions triumphed and disappeared into eternal oblivion, thousands of plants and animals vanished for ever, the face of Nature changed its aspect in the long wear and waste of centuries, and still those waters roll down that precipice with a wail of lamentation over a dead Past, like the voice of a lone spirit in the agony of unspeakable despair!

'The gulf has a weird and fearful fascination. You feel a mad impulse to leap out into vacancy—to launch out, as Lucifer did, into the wide womb of uncreated night, and disappear for ever into that yawning chasm, from the vast depths of which rise the sheeted columns of vapour—

> White and sulphury,
> Like foam from the roused ocean of deep hell,
> Whose every wave breaks on a living shore.

'At intervals there are deafening explosions, like the discharge of enormous cannon, and the waves of spray roll out like cannon-smoke, and recoil upon themselves with the force of the impetus, to be swallowed up in the downward-driven current, and finally swept into the abyss. Imagine some Titanic race battling with the demons! There is a rock fortress 600 feet high, with huge cannon projecting from a hundred embrasures, discharging a continuous shower of projectiles, "winged with red lightning and impetuous rage," into the ranks of the advancing foe! Terrible beyond conception is the diapason of that cannonade!

'On the left of the main falls is the circular pool, 200

feet in depth, whose sides slope inward from the top, with a narrow outlet, not twenty feet wide, at the bottom. Into this frightful cauldron poured a vast body of water from the main river. It fell clear down, struck the surface of the pool as if it were solid rock, dashed itself into vapour, and threw a dense shower of spray far up the face of the opposite rock, whence it descended in a thousand little rivulets of silver that sparkled like a flood of moonlight on the dark surges of the midnight main. On the left came down a torrent that poured itself out from the dense scrub overhead. That, too, fell clear down on to the pool below in a sheet of glorious spray. Around the face of the rocks grew beautiful and tiny orchids, and ferns, and innumerable little plants looking serenely down, with their green faces, into the awful Maelstrom underneath, indescribably beautiful, amid the war of winds and waters—

> Resembling, 'mid the torture of the scene,
> Hope watching Madness with unalterable mien.

And gorgeous, blue-winged butterflies emerged from the crevices of the rocks, fluttered slowly down until the spray caught them, and vanished, like a flash of light, into the vortex of remorseless waters, like lost spirits drawn in where the firmament of the Miltonian Hell spouted its cataracts of fire, until caught in the descending flames and swept down into the infinite abyss, nameless in dark oblivion there to dwell. From the still pools up the river came magnificent blue and pink and scarlet lilies, with superb, fan-like green leaves attached. On one of them was a splendid butterfly, floating along like the Indian Cupid in the Nelumbium flower, down the swift current of the sacred river.

'Swift and painless death for all life once closed in the

pitiless embrace of that deadly surge, cleaving the azure with the rapidity of light! One step from where you now stand and you have passed the confluence of the two infinitudes—eternity is before you, and this world, with all its madness, is behind you; your body is dashed to atoms among those jagged and savage rocks; the spectral winds play your death-march on their Æolian harp of pines; the giant cannons fire, in volleying thunder, their last salute; the cataract wraps its white foam-shroud around you; and the mighty mountains, throned on the Primary rocks, stand there aloft in the majesty of eternal silence and immensity as your everlasting monuments! What was the pyramid-piled grave of the Egyptian kings compared to this? A tomb here more worthy of divine Cleora than the old Leucadian steep! This is the home of Poesy, first-born of the gods, and Romance, the parent of golden dreams. Alas! that the cold hand of Science has dragged the Naiads from the waters, and hurled the Dryads and Hamadryads from the woods!

'Twilight is descending, and I gaze once more into that awful realm of swimming shadows and enormous shapes, with fearful chasms, rolling billows of foam, vast cloud-like vapours, descending columns of yellow, water-like liquid fire, opalescent and iridescent, fantastic rocks scarred and rent by Æons of ages, towering mountains crowned by mournful pines, showers of spray and wandering mist, mingled with the roar and rush and howl of immeasurable waters plunging in their death agonies into the "fathomless and thundering abyss," in unutterable sublimity of unfettered chaos and illimitable madness. Alas! after all I have only proved how impotent is language to give more than a vague and shadowy outline of that mighty picture, hung there, on the sullen rocks among the grand old mountains, as a presentation picture to Australia from the Art Gallery of the Eternal!'

CHAPTER XXXIX

TO CAPE YORK

Mr. McNaulty of Thursday Island, and the Everlasting Ego. The Alexandrine Ranges—Cook Town—Albany Pass, and the Land's End.

ALL the road up to Cape York after this is a series of beautiful, fantastic or sublime scenery, a constantly-unfolding panorama of change, which keeps me very hard at work, so that I have little time to observe my fellow-passengers. Yet they are all nice, for most of them are Queenslanders, and they are pleased with my enthusiasm over their land, and delighted to help me with anything I require, from a field-glass to the shade of their umbrellas.

I think an artist is about the most selfish individual in the world when he is engrossed in his work. One day I kept an Australian knight, who was going to England with his daughter, standing behind me, holding his daughter's parasol over my head, without intermission, from breakfast time to tiffin, only flinging a word at him when I wanted to get the name of a promontory or island, and forgetting to thank him or apologise for the martyrdom he must have suffered for all those hours, standing as he did full in the blaze of the sun while he covered my sketch-book with shadow. His daughter, also, a charming young lady, who relieved her papa in the afternoon, I spoke to like a Nero, ordering her to stand on one side and hold it properly, as if she had been a born slave of Imperial Rome. And still they were pleasant and admired my work, playing in the evenings for me, the knight on the violin and the daughter on the ship piano, to soothe my excited brain.

Although I did not show much gratitude at the time, I shall ever be grateful to that kindly Australian knight, and even more so to his amiable daughter, because she drew, with the unconscious magnetism of her charms, a great deal of the attentions of my cub friend from me, and so permitted me to enjoy the landscape and changes going on. He was no sooner on board than he fell a victim to a violent fit of calf love, and followed her about like that innocent suckling roarer is apt to do its mother, only coming to me for encouragement after she had retired for the night.

I was glad also to find amongst the passengers the genial old man who had told us that narrative of how he was saved by Pears' soap at New Guinea. He was going up to his pearl station at Thursday Island.

When he heard that my destination was also there for the present, he gave me some friendly advice, which I afterwards acted upon with benefit to myself.

'You will likely put up at McNaulty's Hotel when you get there, as it is the only one' (I found out that there was another, but he wanted me to go to the best place). 'Well, take my advice and don't put on any airs with McNaulty, for he can't stand it.'

'You surely don't think I'd be such a cad?' I remonstrated a little indignantly.

'Well, no! I don't, but as a warning in case you might be inclined to try on the high falutin', I'll tell you how he served a man in the same line as you are—one of the special correspondent kind, you know.

'This cad was a Yankee, and had gone on bouncing all

up the coast, as he had done all over the Colonies, in a high and mighty way about the almighty Ego. Well, you must know that passengers are landed in small boats at Thursday Island, and are expected to look after their own traps; the ladies are carried in the boatmen's arms over the wet sands, but the men are expected to wade ashore.

'Well, this everlasting Mr. Ego, who had patronised our Colonies in the newspapers and got kicked out of one or two clubs for his infernal brassy impudence, comes up to Thursday Island, and mighty indignant he was when the boatmen chucked his traps ashore just above low-water mark and made him wade up to the hotel. I suppose he expected a convoy of Government officials to be ready to welcome him ashore, only that's not our system of doing things up here about.

'He strode up to the hotel in a flaming rage, with his wet trouser-ends dangling about his sopping socks, and shouted out when he got to the verandah:

'"I say, landlord, have you such a thing as a —— Chinaman, Malay, black or white fellow about who could cart my luggage up here and be —— to him?"

'McNaulty, who, as you will see when you get there, is a big made and independent fellow, came out and looked over the object who was raising the echoes in this way for a while, then he lifted his eyes with a languid air and gazed down to the sea sands where Ego's traps were lying, and answered with a drawl:

'"No, stranger, I hain't got a —— Chinaman, Malay, nor yet a —— black or white fellow to cart your luggage up and be —— to them, but I'll tell you something you don't seem aware of. The tide is coming in, and if you don't look —— sharp after your luggage it 'll be washed out to sea before you can get it, and be —— to you."

'With which McNaulty disappeared within his bar,

leaving Mr. Ego to hop down to the water's edge and save his traps from wreckage the best way he could.'

I laughed over this yarn, for I had heard all about Ego as I had gone along; it seemed very characteristic of this gentleman. When I afterwards got to the island and interviewed Mr. McNaulty, I saw one of the finest-looking Irishmen I had ever looked upon, with a head like the statue of Achilles, and over six feet of graceful proportions. I left what I could not carry on the shore out of reach of the tide, and went into the bar with my hands full.

'Can you give me a shake-down here, Mr. McNaulty?' I asked as I laid down my bundles.

'Yes, I think we can put you up with a rope across at any rate,' answered the landlord graciously, as he served me with a drink, putting the bottle before me to help myself according to the fashion of Queensland. 'But have you any more luggage?'

'Yes,' I replied. 'They are on the sands, but I'll be able to fetch up the rest next turn.'

'Oh no, you don't. Here boy,' shouted out McNaulty to a Malay passing: 'Go down and fetch up this gentleman's luggage.'

The Malay disappeared, and then I said to my host: 'I thought you didn't encourage laziness up here, Mr. McNaulty?'

'Ah, sure you've heard that story about poor Ego, have you?' said he, laughing, as he helped himself to a glass. 'Well, he was a skunk of a fellow, but we treat decent boys differently.'

McNaulty was a fine man, and shrewd, yet most particular in his rules. I lured him once to break through his habits, and have a drink with me, and the islanders told me that it was the first time they had known him do such a thing; so I suppose I must reckon myself a favourite of

ALEXANDRINE RANGE

his. He said that a landlord had no right to accept drinks from his customers, as he thought it low and mean; so when a man invited him to drink he always stood the drink round. Brave old pioneer McNaulty! He has passed away since 1886.

We pass Great Palm Island with White Rock—we are in the latitude of the palm now—the Frankland Islands, Cape Grafton and Port Douglas, with the main road to Herberton and the interior, passing over in a serpentine line the Ranges. Port Douglas is hidden by the Island or Heads as we come up to it.

Over vast stretches where Captain Cook groaned as he crawled along with slow pace and flapping sails, Cape Kimberley, Schnapper Island and Cape Tribulation, with Peter Botte pinnacle towering above the clouds. Cook was a-weary when he got the length of Peter Botte, and so called the place Tribulation.

What splendid ranges those Alexandrine Mountains are, full of colour and mystery! We look up with wonder and awe as we sail along at the base of these marvellous highlands of purple green, dun colour, and softest of dove-grey, as the straight lines of cloudland stand before the suggestions of deep valleys and waterfalls over mighty precipices.

Now we pass a grassy land, all untenanted except by the kangaroo and the wandering black natives, at this part all cannibals, and savage in the extreme to unwary rovers. Then we see what appear like towns of clay huts, the townships of the termites, who are good architects, and can lay out vast cities on the plains when they like; or it may be a mound of rocks on the seashore, standing isolated like a great castle with grass all about, and those tent or cornstack-like termite buildings dotting the country beyond, for all the world like a ruined baronial keep beside a city of serfs' huts.

Weird and lonely is this brilliantly-lighted land, as we sail along it, day after day, with the slumbering seas around, and the dark blue ocean outside miles away over the Barrier Reef. Now we pass a lightship, moored to the reef, from the deck of which the lonely keepers, man and woman —no, it was only a woman—wave a dish-towel to us as we pass; I tried to realise their feelings, in the day, in the night, in the sunshine, and the storm, from which they were also isolated as they were from humanity. I can somewhat remember that lonely, yardless barque as she lay baking in the sun, so I give a sketch of it.

Past Cape Melville we glide, and my friend who shades me for the time, tells me his theory for those great boulders and detached stones lying about—a submarine earthquake. Past Castle Rock and Cape Flinders and on to the Pass of Albany, with the coral islands in process of formation all about us, and pelicans standing stupidly upon the glistening strips of sand.

We have passed Cook Town and the 'Endeavour' River, where Captain Cook beached his ship for repairs in 1770, and which is one of the most thriving northern seaport towns, having a large mixed population of Europeans, Chinese, Malays, and Kanakas. This is the port most of the *bêche-de-mer* and other traders make from the south end of New Guinea, as it lies nearly in a straight line from it, although Thursday Island is nearer. It is a clean, well-built city, and the centre of a good country, although not to be compared for productiveness to Cairns.

We see ant-hills all along the coast, ranging from four to ten feet high, like beehives in shape and carefully finished. They look, in the distance, like golden sheaves of gathered corn, and those nearer like clay huts, with streets between each line.

Through Albany Pass and Somerset, once the most

northerly settlement, and 1,500 miles from Brisbane, but now sadly neglected since Thursday Island came to the fore as a place of call; it is now used only as a pearl-fishing station, and a pretty station it is. After this we come to Cape York and the islands lying about it. We have reached the extreme limit of the land, and will shortly pass beyond the limits of civilisation.

CHAPTER XL

AT THURSDAY ISLAND

Mr. Kerry's Account of a New-Guinea Massacre.

It was at Thursday Island that I met Mr., or, as he is called amongst his friends, Captain Kerry, the young man who discovered gold in New Guinea.

I was sitting writing the night I first met him, going over my notes, with a dense cloud of mosquitoes humming about me, and trying to singe their tiny wings in the oil lamps in McNaulty's public sitting apartment, when a shy, little, fresh-coloured, fair-haired and blue-eyed youth (as I thought) sat down beside me, and observed in a gentle voice:

'Mr. Hume Nisbet, I presume?'

'Yes,' I replied, laying down my pen and looking at him, and thinking of that historic meeting of Stanley and Livingstone in Africa.

'You have just got back from New Guinea, I am just going over again. My name is Kerry. Hope you enjoyed the trip.'

'What! Kerry the gold-finder?'

'Yes, I did find gold, but they would not believe it, so the less said on that subject the better. I know where to find more, and intend to find enough for myself before I attempt to communicate the fact to my fellows.'

So we struck up a friendship. I told him some of my

adventures, and he told me a few of his, during the few days we spent together, before the steamer arrived which was to carry me south.

'It was on December 20, 1885, that I arrived at Kattau, a village to the west of the Fly River.

'Going ashore here I found some native teachers, with their wives and children, who had been sent by the Rev. Mr. McFarlane from Murray Island to found a new mission for the civilisation of the natives—a very mixed race about these parts. One of the teachers I had met before, and owed a debt of gratitude to, as he had saved my life when with the *Melbourne Age* Expedition, at the time we were forced to abandon our captured vessel, May 24, 1884.

'Here I met with a hearty welcome, and after spending the night beside them, sailed up the Kattau River next morning, accompanied by about forty natives as guides and carriers. However, as this river is a very small one, and in parts so shallow that I got fast and grounded several times, I had to return without proceeding very far.

'Next day being Sunday, I went to the little hut beside the native teachers' house, under which service was usually held, to listen to the native service and watch the effect which it had upon these untamed savages. This little house was built of bamboo posts, covered with the dried fronds of the palm, and raised about six feet from the earth. To gather the natives at the hour appointed for service, a boy went round the village beating two pieces of wood against one another, which did duty for a bell.

'The natives came in great numbers, and squatted on he ground, while the black teacher tried to explain to them, in his own quaint symbolic manner, his message of grace; but I observed an air of insolent mockery pervading the assembly; the natives nudged one another, laughed scornfully, and although they listened to the words uttered in their own language, paid but small respect to his earnestness.

'As I stood watching these ominous signs of disaffection around me, with my back against a pile next to the teacher (two of my own "boys" beside me[1]), and keeping a keen lookout for danger from the outside, I saw a man rush double-quick from the village, shouting all the way along the beach as he ran.

'In an instant the church was deserted, men, women and children decamping in a regular stampede, *sans cérémonie*, which seemed to astonish the poor teacher very greatly.

'The women and children passed into the huts, while the men ran to the large "tapu-house" where their meetings are held, and where they keep their war-implements. Here, quickly arming themselves with bows, arrows and clubs, they marched in battle order and with great haste into the forest.

'The teacher, fearing that they meant some mischief to the house and my schooner, got out his gun to protect his family, while I looked to the state of my revolvers and rifle, and warned my boys to be ready for action. However, hours passed away without any signs either from the bush or the village, the women and children keeping indoors, so that we could get no information of their movements or intentions.

'It was about sundown that we heard the distant sounds of the war-drums beating, so, taking my two black "boys" with me, I went out in the direction of the noise, and getting on to a ridge where I could command a good stretch of country, saw them returning in a most excited state of exultation.

---

[1] 'Boys.' Malay or Kanaka seamen are so called by the traders in the Straits.—H. N.

'They had been fighting with some rival tribe, and evidently had gained a great victory, for they were all yelling at the highest pitch of their voices, dancing with most jubilant antics, and beating upon their iguana-drums furiously, while two of them bore on their shoulders a long bamboo cane, from which were suspended a number of bloody, human heads, rove through each mouth, as we sometimes see fish gilled.

'On they came with their ghastly trophies; thirty-three heads I counted, as they rushed past the ridge on which I stood watching them, on their way to the tapu-house, which is the house of the village set solely apart as a place of meeting (a kind of temple or club-house, where men only are allowed to enter).

'I watched them lay the heads down in front of the tapu-house. Then they held a great talk for some time, after which one of the men and a boy, who had joined from the huts (at the doors of which the women had now appeared), lifting up three of the heads, bore them towards the house of the teachers, who had barricaded their door, and now waited inside with fear and trembling.

'Following the head-bearers to the mission-house, I heard them shout to the teachers to come out and see what they had brought home, but receiving no reply they carried them back again to where the rest were lying, and taking them all up, they put them into the pots, which meanwhile the women had brought forth, after lighting large fires in the open spaces.

'It had now grown quite dark, being about eight o'clock, and the large wood fires flared out luridly to the night, with the dark forms around them, dancing their war-dance and beating upon their drums, while the thirty-three heads were cooking in the pots. A weird picture it made, and the more horrible to us knowing the contents of those pots.

'After looking for a time I went down to the shore, where I had left my dinghy, and rowed aboard the schooner, which lay at anchor very close.

'About nine o'clock, and while I was trying to swallow some tea (not an easy task, with the thought of the supper the natives were having in the village), I was interrupted by hearing a loud shouting from the shore, and my name being called; so hastily leaping into the boat, and going over to the bank, I saw the teachers with their wives and children, standing all in a group, greatly excited, and crying: "Very good! You go, get all gun; man going to kill."

'On hearing this, I went again on board, and getting together all my guns, dynamite, and ammunition, I hurried with my boys up to the whare,[1] where the teachers and their wives had now returned, after which we fastened the apertures, and putting out the fire inside, waited for the attack.

'We had not very long to wait before the natives came on, shouting again for the teachers to come out and join in their feast, surrounding the hut and making a terrible din, to all of which we paid no attention. The wives of the teachers were in a state of mortal fear, as they could see through the crevices, besides the savage crowd near at hand, others walking and rushing about the beach, carrying fire-sticks, and the skulls of the slaughtered bushmen.

'I made sure that we would have a hard fight for it that night, as they were maddened by their victory, exasperated by the teachers' refusal to join in their revels, and afraid, if they allowed any of us to escape, that we would tell the "bom-bom," or war-ship (of which they have a wholesome dread) of these evil actions, so that we could see that they

---

[1] Kerry is a native of New Zealand, and uses the Maori name 'Whari' for native hut.—H. N.

CAPE MELVILLE.

had resolved to go on the principle of dead men telling no tales, and meant to kill the whole party.

'After a time, finding that they could not force us out by threats, and afraid to break in upon us, knowing that we had firearms, they retired once more to their fires, leaving us comparatively free to decide what was next to be done.

'When we were thus left in peace, I proposed to the teachers that they should bring their wives and children, and come on board as soon as the tide turned, and that if they did so I would take them over to Murray Island, it no longer being safe for them to stay with the tribe after this hostile manifestation. With this proposal they all seemed delighted, and agreed to it at once.

'So till midnight we were engaged packing up the things they wished to take with them, rice, &c., and then, looking out and seeing the coast clear, I prepared to go aboard, so that I might quietly get the schooner ready for sailing, telling them before I left to be sure to come to me as soon as the moon rose, as it was then that the tide turned, also agreeing as to a signal between us, so that I might not mistake them in the dark for a war-canoe.

. . . .

'It was at two o'clock A.M. that the moon showed a faint yellow section above the clouds and inky palm-tops. We were ready to sail, and only waited upon the coming of the refugees.

'On shore the fires were dying down, and now shone with dull red sparks in the direction of the village. Above the moon, in the darkly clear space, the stars flashed brightly, and repeated their lustre in broken reflections, which danced about and mingled with the dull crimson of the dying embers ashore, and the amber-yellow, lustreless light of that duskily-rising morning moon.

'We had been on the *qui vive* all night, and while I was watching and listening for the signal, I heard the soft splash of paddles, and suddenly caught sight of what appeared to be a canoe crossing the faint moon-track towards our bows, from the shore. As it slid into obscurity again I could make out another in its wake. It was in too dangerous proximity for me to feel satisfied, as I could not see enough to make out whether it contained friends or foes, so I hailed them before they could have time to come near enough to surprise me, giving at the same time the signal agreed upon between myself and my friends. No reply; but I could hear that they were advancing rapidly.

' "Who goes there?" I called out again, without getting any response except the quicker splash of the paddles.

' Six times I hailed them without any reply, and just as I was about to give my boys the command to shoot, the teachers' friend sang out " Siby!" which caused my heart to leap almost into my mouth. Another second, through their careless inattention to my hailing, and we would have had the blood of them and their families upon our souls. I suppose the intense excitement under which they were labouring at the moment made them forget all about our agreement.

' I had got them all safely aboard, and was just ready to start, when, after taking one or two uneasy turns along the deck, and some regretful looks ashore, the teachers stopped in front of me, and asked me to take their wives and children out of harm's way, but as for themselves, they had decided to go ashore again and see it out.

' "We came here to be killed, if God wished it, and so we cannot run away."

' I sought to reason with them, talking all through that moonlit morning, until the day broke over the distant banks, but it was of no avail. They only shook their heads sadly, turning their big melancholy eyes towards the bent heads of their crouching wives, from whom they were probably parting for ever, this side of the grave, in that fatalistic and blind adherence to what they considered their duty, and replied to all my reasons with the words, "If God wishes us to be killed, we ought not to run away."

'Just before day dawned the natives in the village awoke, and we could hear them all talking at once, making a great noise with their tongues and the clashing together of their weapons, at which the poor fellows who seemed resolved to win crowns of martyrdom shivered and grew leaden-hued, but still they asked me not to delay setting them ashore; so at last, very unwillingly, I got down my boat from the deck, while they were bidding their wives and children farewell.

'Natives of the South Seas do not make so much of partings as we white people do. I suppose they feel as keenly as we could possibly do, only they don't show it. They were ready as soon as I was, the leave-taking being got over without a sound, and indeed had scrambled over the side and into the boat before I was quite prepared, leaving the bereaved women and children a shapeless mingling of shadows on the deck in the faint light of that breaking morning.

'When we reached the beach the fighting-men of the tribe gathered around us, making a big talk, but with a vast amount of yesterday's courage slept away. They were evidently very uneasy in their minds about this victory of theirs, and wanted to make me promise not to tell upon them to the Government or big ships—"Bom-boms" as they called them. I had told them, when threatening us the day before, that I would send the man-of-war to blow them up, and break down their cocoa-nut trees, and to-day they were remembering these words with gloomy forebodings.

'They did not attempt to injure us as we passed through them, but followed us all up to the mission-house, howling like bad schoolboys caught in the act, and imploring me not to tell upon them, a promise, however, which I would not commit myself to.

'After I had settled the teachers into their old quarters, I resolved to spend that day with them, partly to see if they would not alter their minds, and partly to see if the natives would settle down, but was a little astonished to hear my friend propose to go and burn down the great tapu-house. He had taken a notion that the devil dwelt in that tapu-house, as all the evil was concocted there, and that Kattau would always be a bad place while the house was permitted to stand.

'I tried my hardest to point out to him the danger and folly of such a step, but he was as obstinate in this conviction as he was firm in his desire to become a martyr, so that, being only his guest, I was fain to yield and permit him to act as he felt inclined.

'He then took a fire-stick and went to the upper village, I going with him and the other teachers, to see that he came to no harm, and a crowd of the natives following after us to watch what we were about to do.

'This tapu-house was about two hundred feet long, of one floor, as these buildings are west of Motu-Motu; as you go eastward of Moresby you see spires and double floors, but about the Fly they are all in the form of a flat shed or barn raised on piles, with palm-thatched roofs and sides, and one aperture at each end for ingress and exit; the roofs are fashioned like inverted boats, with a decided lean to one side.

'Of course, being composed of dry bamboo posts, split

cane, and brittle palm-fronds, it needed very little to set it in a blaze, and soon it was reduced to ashes.

'The natives, although armed at the time with spears and bows, &c., did not offer any active resistance to the movements of the teacher, doubtless being afraid of our revolvers and Winchesters, and knowing from experience the effects of dynamite. Daylight also is apt to take the pluck out of most people in the fighting way, and particularly natives, who have had a little experience of, without too great an intimacy with, the magical powers of gunpowder and shot. They are apt to imagine the slender tube to be a living object which can blast them at any moment, as surely as lightning does the forest trees.

'While the house was catching fire they only howled and made frantic motions of despair, but hung back from it, even although at the time it contained most of the wealth of the tribe; and when a few charred stumps alone remained in the midst of a little mound of white ashes surrounded by a blackened circle of burnt grass, they only flocked together, crying and moaning all day long, till sundown, after which they got up and shouted that they would murder the incendiary when I was away.

'All through that second night we could hear them lamenting the loss of their tapu-house, and shouting vengeance at intervals, so that, tired out as we were with our previous nights of anxiety, we dared not think of taking a rest, and I spent the hours of darkness striving my very hardest to turn my friend and his companions from their reckless resolves, and to induce them to come with me to Kawai on the Fly, where I intended, for the present, to leave their families; but nothing I could say seemed to move them in the slightest degree.

'"Take our women and children to Kawai, we'll stay and be killed."

'I had to go next morning, and as I could not kidnap them I was forced to leave these three noble and devoted, but most rash men, to their self-imposed fate. However, I left them what I could spare in the way of weapons and ammunition, showing them how to use the dynamite if required, and then I sailed away for the Fly River, but with a very foreboding heart.

. . . .

'Upon my return from my journey up the Fly I again called at Kattau. On shore all was quiet, and the huts seemed deserted. It is no uncommon sight in New Guinea to pass a thriving community one voyage, and return to find only deserted huts fast going to decay. The burning of the tapu-house may have broken up Kattau, I thought. Besides, as I was suffering at the time from a wound in my leg and could, only with difficulty, limp about, I sent one of my "boys" ashore to find out about the teachers. Very soon the "boy" came back and told me that they had been killed, on which I at once went over to the house, to find it empty. I shouted at the top of my voice, but no one replied, until at last one small boy crept out of one of the huts (thereby showing me that the natives were only hiding).

'On questioning the little fellow he informed me that "teacher-man ran away into bush, and that all *man* want head belong of me," so that if I wanted to keep that article safely between my shoulders I had better go aboard, and inquire no further about the matter.

'We stayed at Kattau two or three days, firing dynamite by day to let them know that we were there, if they were alive, also beating about the bush as far as we dare venture, besides keeping large fires burning each night on the beach, but without any success; so at last I was forced to the conclusion that the little boy was telling lies when he said they had escaped, and that there were three more victims added to the long and bloody list of New-Guinea massacres.'

CHAPTER XLI

SAVAGES

At Thursday Island—Kanakas—Superstitions of Savages—Will-Power—Cannibalism.

THURSDAY ISLAND lies about 1,500 miles from Brisbane, in lat. 10° 33′ south and long. 142° 10′ east, just off the northern coast of Australia, and between the other Cook-christened islands, Prince of Wales, Howe, Hammond, Friday, Wednesday and Good. They all range at about a distance of between one and five miles from one another.

The port is called Kennedy, and is the regular place of call for steamers coming by way of China and other northern ports; a nice little settlement of about fifty or so houses, two hotels, one store (Burns, Philp & Co.'s), one Roman Catholic chapel, and the Government residence. The population is very mixed, Chinese, Malays, and Kanaka pearl-divers being the majority, with a small sprinkling of Government officials, and migratory pilots waiting on vessels to take down through the reefs.

The ladies are very scarce at Thursday Island. A short time before I got there, two lady passengers, seeing the scarcity of their sex, had landed between mail steamers. The genial but morality-loving Governor, Hon. John Douglas, promptly packed the nymphs off the island by the next ship, but not before they had done a vast amount of damage amongst the young men under his charge. The ladies went off to other fields, laden with unset pearls, while the young men remained to mourn their advent.

The Kanakas are the divers here, and are much prized by the pearl-station owners. They get 60*l.* per month for their wages, besides all the pearls which they can find in the shells, as it is only the shells that their masters prize. A pair of good shells sell to the traders for 15*s.*; therefore, as these divers can make besides their wages in pearls sometimes 80*l.* or 100*l.* per month, they are very lavish and extravagant with their money; indeed, all the time I was at Thursday Island I felt like a very poor white man.

They go about carrying great rolls of bank-notes in their outside coat pockets, and when they enter a bar, order their gin by the case, pitching down their bank-notes carelessly on the counter for the landlord to pay himself out of them, and hardly ever looking at the change as they shovel it up and stuff it into their pockets again, drinking from the tumbler and by the tumblerful without diluting the gin with water.

They are mostly all Roman Catholics, yet are exceedingly kind to their poor brethren who are working amongst the savages as Protestant teachers at the rate of 20*l.* per year, and finding themselves out of that small yearly stipend. These reckless divers are constantly sending over money from their plenty to help the poor martyrs in their wretched poverty, otherwise I fear there would be even greater mortality amongst the South Sea Islanders than there is, through dire starvation as well as fever.

These Kanaka divers are very shrewd in worldly wisdom, in spite of their superstitions. I went to the morning mass at the little Roman church at Thursday Island, and felt much amused by the French priest there and his dusky congregation.

He was lecturing them on the virtue of giving to the

THE LIGHTSHIP

poor and the Church. 'You see, children, de poor Virgin dere, all bare and unadorned—is it not a shame?'

He paused, and looked at the stolid rows of faces fronting him, but no one seemed to take the hint. Then he went on afresh:

'Not for mine self would I ask of your plenty, which you waste on gin, but for de Church, de Blessed Virgin, and de poor.'

No apparent comprehension was expressed on the part of the hearers. They were attentive but irresponsive.

'Ah ha! Now I know you have pearls—many good pearls—in your breasts, under your shirts, hiding.' Every black paw made a clutch through the open shirt-fronts, while the men looked as if a dark secret had been discovered.

'Ah, do not be afraid, I would not take one little pearl from one of you. But yet see, de poor Virgin has not yet one single string of de pure beautiful pearls to hang round her neck for de good of de poor, and yet you melt them down your own necks every day!'

Poor foreign father! He was deeply in earnest I could hear, but as I went out I did not see any of the pearls forthcoming. I have often wondered since if the Virgin has been provided yet with a little chaplet.

The superstition of savages has long been a careful study of mine—their wonderful will-power, cannibal customs, laws of tapu, &c.; and as I am shortly going to take you amongst the savages of New Guinea, perhaps it would not be amiss to say a little about them before I go on.

Will-power amongst Savages.

If it is a hard matter for the civilised races to comprehend the calm endurance of the savage under moments of torture and agony which would break down the most heroic resolutions of a European, the peculiar will-power which makes him able to give up life at an allotted hour, and pass from robust health to a painless death, without any of those artifices being resorted to by which the wearied of existence try to get surcease in our barbarous western climes, is utterly beyond solution.

Another wonderful point about this is that the savage is never tired of his life. He can endure torture stoically when there is no other escape (but no one dies harder when in the hands of his enemy), as he can die quietly and consistently at the time appointed by his medicine-man or omen.

That savages cannot feel pain is the common verdict given by those who have watched them suffer; but this is not the case, their nerve-tissues being exactly the same as ours, and their feelings as acute as our own. But I am of opinion that they have qualities which we, the more favoured races, have lost; a will or soul power which, at emergency, can sujubgate the physical, and make them as insensible to pain as chloroform or ether can make us; a brain-force which can either act as an opiate or deadly poison as the possessor wills at the time, and which it is as utterly impossible for a European to acquire as it is for him to master the magical secrets and gifts of the astral brotherhood.

These are all gifts of race, and the slow development of centuries of peculiar training, and are as impossible for us to comprehend as it is for the refined Buddhist or high-caste Brahmin to comprehend the coarse brutality of our daily habits of life. We, with a characteristic method all our own, cry 'Bosh,' and laugh at, as imposture, what they accept from constant experiences, completely and naturally beyond our efforts to disprove.

All the Eastern experiences of the present day the religious or credulous amongst us accept with faith as having occurred in the past, but as utterly impossible now.

There are no ghosts or re-appearances at the present day in England.

All our supernatural phenomena came from the East; but the last of those manifestations, according to even the most credulous of our thinkers, closed with St. John at Patmos, nineteen hundred years ago, when he wound up his Revelations with the words, 'He which testifieth these things saith, Surely I come quickly,' &c.

In the East they still have revelations and powers which we allow them to have experienced or possessed long ago, but scoffingly deny to them now.

However, it is not the gifts of second-sight, soul-reading, or spirit separation, and materialisation, which are solely confined to the century-prepared and uncontaminated Eastern, but this life-yielding quality, which is shared alike by the lowest-caste Pariah, the least intellectual of the Africans, and the most primitive savage of the South Seas.

They can, by will alone, stretch out their limbs and pass from existence, when inclined, as completely and as easily as we can turn down and extinguish a lamp-wick.

At Kandy, when I tossed coins with an ordinary Indian and a Buddhist, I tossed and they guessed. With the Hindoo, who stood apart, it was an ordinary game of chance, such as might be played between Englishmen, but with the Buddhist, who stood near, and always touched lightly with his finger-tips the back of my hand which covered the coin, it was not guessing, but telling, for he won each time.

I have seen two Scedy men, and several Maoris, and one aboriginal of Australia, die because they had a warning or omen that they were to die.

Where the warning came from, or how they received it, I cannot tell, and they either could not or would not explain. One day they would come up in perfect health and calmly announce to their friends or tribe that they were going to die at a certain time next day, or two days or ten days after date of announcement, and the friends never doubted the statement or tried to combat it, but straightway began their preparations for the funeral, and the *corpse* never disappointed them.

On the voyage to Australia on board the P. and O. steamship 'Parramatta,' I have mentioned how one of the Seedy boys struck work. 'What is the matter with him?' inquired the officer of the rest of the stokers, for he would not speak.

' He got big dibbles in him inside and going to die.'

' When ? ' again inquired the officer.

' To-morrow, at tiffin-time.'

The officer shrugged his shoulders and walked away.

'Will he really die?' I asked of him.

' Up to the moment,' replied he, ' and all the medicine and talking in the world won't alter his determination '; and, in spite of the doctor trying his utmost to rouse the negro, he was dead at tiffin-hour, and buried at sundown.

I was once going through the bush of New Zealand with a Maori, when, as we were resting, a lizard ran over him; he caught the lizard, and after quietly counting some marks upon it, said to me, as if it was an ordinary event, 'This fellow tell me I die in eight days more,' and calmly continued the interrupted conversation.

' But he ran over me also, and I don't feel like dying.'

' P'raps! Pakihi not Maori.'

No more was said at that time, and we went on and joined the tribe. When in my friend's, Wharé's, the lamenting began while the doomed one made his preparations.

On the eighth day his prediction had come to pass, and his wife was a widow. I watched him go about day after day, apparently in usual health, and eat as usual, only by himself. On the seventh day he took his last meal, and, drawing his mat about him within his circumscribed tapued space, waited motionlessly until the end came. When the sun rose on the eighth morning he was still sitting on his haunches, with his knees drawn up, and his head drooping upon his breast; but the sun-shaft, which darted over the hill-top and lake-surface to the tapued cliff whereon he perched, smote dully upon the glazed eyeballs of a staring corpse.

Amongst the aboriginals of Australia, if a man points a bone at another it bewitches him, and draws him to death, and he will perish as surely as if that pointed bone had pierced his heart.

With the savages of the South Seas it is the same. Although each island and tribe has its different omens and bodes, the fact remains the same, when the fiat has gone forth, and the native knows that he is doomed, he never attempts to struggle against his fate. He sits down, or stretches himself out, and when the appointed time arrives his heart stops beating, or that subtile fluid which he bears within him passes through his brain by the force of his will, and liberates his spirit without a gasp or a groan. He is alive one minute and quietly waiting, and the next he is annihilated.

Cannibal Customs.

Cannibalism is the most atrocious habit of primitive man; that is, to us, the more favoured, who have only been addicted to the devouring of the flesh of the lower animal world—pigs, oxen, sheep, &c.

It is only to be compared to those atrocities which have lately convulsed the East End of the world's Metropolis with appalling horror—that is, to the stranger unaccustomed to savage manners and traditions; but cannibalism, to the

European accustomed to the savage and his daily life, can no more be compared to the doings of 'Jack the Ripper than an East End coke fireplace can be compared to a smelting-furnace. No, this modern monster must carry off the palm, in the grades of atrocity, from the savages; he is unique in these later centuries.

To kill and eat the flesh of a man is bad, very bad; even the savages themselves in some cases shiver at the thought of the 'long pork'; but this nineteenth century outcome of the decline of civilisation is what I would term the dilettantism of decay. We find a precedent for it in the later days of the Roman Empire, when empresses and patrician ladies went into the shambles, and vied with the courtesans, tearing the hearts out of their living victims, and returning, as this modern fiend has done, by a natural rebound, from the hypercritical stage to the primitive.

In all this we may read the constantly-recurring history of man, and a proper interpretation of the Flood, the burning of Sodom, and confusion of tongues: the young nation, savage and robust, becoming civilised, loving song and poesy, growing into correct sound, independent of meaning, sinking into the critical *or used-up stage*, wallowing in the mire of disgust, lacking enthusiasm, and incapable of enjoying life, rushing by the natural sequence of over-refinement and inanity into ' Lustmordt ' some grades below the rude savage, to be finally merged into, or lost before a coming race of sturdy barbarians.

We, as a nation, have now reached the farthest stretch of the elastic band of civilisation : a little further, and the band snaps or becomes released, and it rebounds, and we are as we were when Julius Cæsar first discovered the utility of our land.

Our best writers cannot get subjects ghastly or morbid enough to serve up to the jaded tastes of their super-refined readers. Our best actors must go to the most grotesque of weirdness and unnaturalism before they can find a place in the world of fame. 'Jack the Ripper' is the natural outcome of this age of *blasé* education; he barely takes the one step beyond the writers of the age which is required to complete the age's dissolution.

The original savage is a man who has been born and bred up to the belief that the flesh of *an enemy* is good to eat, as *we* have been born and bred up to the belief that the flesh of an unoffending animal is good to use.

When the savage becomes more advanced he gets ceremonies, institutions, superstitions, and laws of *tapu*, which I shall hereafter describe; thus the sacrifice of *his enemy* becomes a religious rite, and added to the pleasure of the flesh-lust, is the more intense delight of revenge.

To eat an enemy, with the most primitive man, is to enjoy an exquisite pleasure.

To eat an enemy, with the semi-educated savage is to disgrace and degrade that victim for ever afterwards, added to the animal pleasure before mentioned.

The last and worst savage is he who has received the teachings of centuries: he has gone on from stage to stage, from the warlike, the romantic, the scientific, the *dilettante*, to the ferociousness which only torture and warm blood can rouse up *just a little*.

In New Guinea we find the most primitive savage. The Papuan native of this island has no religion, very little superstition, and no reverence for Tapu, that widespread law of sacredness which governs other natives of the islands of the South Seas and New Zealand. He kills his enemy, but only his enemy, wherever he can catch him, and naturally cuts him up and eats him, as we might do a fish we had caught, or a deer we had stalked.

There is no more feeling in the matter with him than

the most inoffensive alderman may have towards mankind while he is enjoying his first plate of turtle soup. He has no blood-guiltiness about him, but may be as gentle in his demeanour, while enjoying his *grill*, as any benevolent philanthropist who has ordered a beefsteak at Gatti's or the Criterion; and this is just what I want my readers to understand as I go on to describe this uninviting habit of the savage in his native state.

I want him, at once and for ever, to banish from his mind all preconceived notions, and be able to place himself exactly on the same platform upon which the cannibal stands, and regard the subject as the human-flesh eater himself does —*i.e.*, merely as an everyday occurrence, or rather as a choice bit which does not come every day, and which, therefore, ought to be enjoyed all the more when it does come.

Not at all to be compared with the feelings which, I naturally suppose, must animate this East End midnight solitary reveller in the blood of his victims! The debasement and horrible fascination of cruelty and danger are wanting, the haunting dread of discovery, the weirdness of that lonely hour when he is beside his victim, the after-effects of suspense and unsated longing for more excitement—these are removed altogether from the placidity and utter unconsciousness of evil with which the true-born cannibal will tell you that 'it is good, very much nicely good, much more better than pork.'

There are, of course, even amongst the Papuans and South Sea Islanders, tribes which view this habit with great abhorrence; natural in their case, as they are closer to it, and occupy the same position to their man-eating neighbours as our sheep and cattle do with us. Having had dealings with both cannibal and non-cannibal tribes, I must say that I would much sooner trust my life with the cannibals than I would risk it amongst the non-cannibals, and I think in

A NEW GUINEA DANDY

this opinion most travellers who have had intercourse with the savage tribes will agree with me without demur.

The true cannibal is an open-hearted, easily-satisfied, and confiding friend when he gives his friendship. No man, in the natural state, ever forgives an enemy, that being an artificial abnegation utterly at variance with the laws of Nature and of man. He wears no stamp of ferocity upon his features, no assassin-scowl or evil, sidelong glances, but, holding his head erect with all the consciousness of rectitude, he will meet you with a smiling, candid look, and give you an honest embrace.

He will also invite you to his feast, if he loves you—an hour will win his affection towards those who know how to gain it; he will offer his friend a share of his allotted piece of the broiled flesh, and look with pity upon him for refusing to partake of such a treat; he will be tender and affectionate while he picks the bones, which are afterwards to be carefully polished and worn, as ornaments and trophies of war, about his person. Such a genial, good-natured, honest fellow is the true unbiassed cannibal.

The non-cannibals—*i.e.*, the hunted ones—are timid, cowardly, suspicious, and treacherous, as they ought to be under the circumstances. They give no friendship, place no faith in anything or any one, and, wherever they can with safety, lure and murder the stranger.

So much for the effects of cannibalism. Now I will give a few descriptions of the modes of using the victims after they are caught.

Throughout all the tribes the body is always divided either before or after being cooked, and carefully apportioned off according to the social position or grade of the natives. Amongst the Maoris the chief gets the eyes and brains, in New Guinea he takes the breast, as the most honourable portion, to himself; so that a visitor who has learnt their habits may know the chief or nobleman from the plebeian by the bones decorating his person or house.

Mr. Andrew Goldie, naturalist, of Port Moresby, informed me that he once arrived at a cannibal feast in the eastern peninsula of New Guinea just in time to rescue a little maiden of about ten years old, whom the cannibals were about to roast alive. He succeeded in buying her from them, by exchanging for her a pig and several pounds of tobacco, with the alternative of shooting them all down if they refused his offer.

The custom of this tribe was to prepare the victims by giving them a cathartic, after which they forced them to eat bananas and yams until they were replete almost to bursting, and next they placed them fronting a fire, and slowly roasted them alive for the sake of the *vegetables* within them; this was a tribe of epicures who would not cook killed victims, and their tit-bits were the stuffed entrails, which they prepared as I have stated.

Some travellers are in the habit of telling wild stories which must be received with great caution. I once met a gentleman who had lived in the Northern Island, New Zealand, and who not only ought to have known the natives better than to tell the story he did, but from his social position ought to have been most guarded how he deviated from strict facts.

He said that he once lived in an out-of-the-way part of the bush, where he was near some friendly natives, a family of whom, comprising the husband, wife, and a young child, attended to his wants at odd times. They lived some distance from his house, but used to come backwards and forwards as the whim took them.

When they were there—the father breaking wood, and the mother cleaning the house--they generally brought the baby, a fine little boy of about five years old, who used to play about in the sun.

One day they came without the baby. When the master asked where he was, the mother made some excuse, and went on with her work. Again and again they came, but never brought the boy, until at last, growing suspicious, he asked the mother for a straight reply, upon which she answered, laconically and carelessly, ' In the pot and eaten.'

This white man said that the Maori mother told him that they had been hungry, and having no other meat, they had killed, cooked, and devoured their only son.

Another of this veracious gentleman's tales was of a Maori husband, who had gone out hunting the wild pig, and on starting left instructions with his wife to prepare the oven against his home-coming with the spoil. After some hours, during which his Waheni got ready the pit or oven (an operation which takes some time, and which I will describe hereafter), he returned empty-handed, with the exception of his meré, or club, and hunting-spear.

' Have you got the pit ready for the pig ? ' he asked.

' Yes, but where is the pig ? ' inquired the wife.

' You are the pig for this day,' he replied, with grim jocularity, knocking her on the head, and tumbling her into the heated pit amongst the potatoes and other vegetables; and then, like the respectable widower he was, sat down to enjoy a pipe while his dinner was being cooked.

That both these were clumsy lies, even although told for the purpose of exposing the awful state of the benighted heathen, any one with the slightest knowledge of the laws of Tapu would at once know, but still they imposed upon some portion of this gentleman's audience, and because they did so I expose them now.

It is impossible for a Maori, above all men, to kill, mutilate, or eat his own blood relations, because that would disgrace himself and all his family, making them lose caste and become slaves for generations according to the laws of his own faith or religion, a degradation which they fear more than a thousand deaths by starvation.

Kill and eat an enemy if you like—the more the better for your prestige as a Toa—but never a friend.

This same lecturer, I found out afterwards, had been compelled to vacate New Zealand for some nefarious dealings with baked Maori heads. He had traded for them with the natives for museum purposes, without inquiring how they were prepared, or how obtained.

If the wife of a Maori offended him mortally, and he wished to disgrace her utterly and all her relations, he might, as the keenest revenge he could perpetrate, kill and eat her, but in such an extreme case he would prepare himself for a life-long vendetta, worse than any Corsican feud.

The story of the first cannibal in New Zealand was a case of the same sort. A chief caught a faithless wife with her paramour, and, after due deliberation, killed and ate them both as the worst form of hatred, contempt, and disgrace he could think of inflicting upon the guilty pair; and from this rose the custom of cannibalism with them, purely a scheme of revenge.

The feast of slaughter is a very sacred ceremony amongst nations where Tapu or Dabu holds sway. The partakers must be careful not to touch the flesh with their fingers or their lips, therefore they use special forks or prongs for the purpose, and are very cautious how they insert the pieces into their mouths; the flesh is chewed slightly, and bolted as quickly as possible.

The body is divided and cooked by the priests, who are always sacred, and therefore may touch what they like as far as they are concerned themselves. The priesthood is an isolated, accursed, but feared class, as were the embalmers of Egypt.

Amongst nations where Tapu is a dead letter, or unknown, no forks are used; the women cook the victim, and each man gets his own share according to the grade he holds.

In New Guinea the tit-bit is the breast-piece; in New Zealand it is the eyes; in other parts it is the brains, or tongue, as the fashion may run.

A story is told of two rival chiefs who were brought to London by different Missionary Societies as specimen converts. They both behaved themselves very well in the drawing-rooms and on the platforms, but it was thought advisable to send them back in different ships.

By bad luck it chanced that the two ships touched the Cape of Good Hope, and the two converts landed and met one another on neutral ground for the first time; religion was forgotten in the heat of the moment; they rushed at one another and fought desperately, one of them going down under the club of the other, who, before he could be interfered with, had swooped down upon his prostrate enemy, gouged his eyes out, and swallowed them, thus disgracing his rival for ever.

Then he suddenly remembered that he was a Christian, and looked round appalled.

I cannot vouch for the truth of this anecdote any more than the other two; indeed, I doubt it much from all I have seen, amongst native races, of the sincerity and child-like earnestness with which they embrace the benign tenets of Christianity; but it goes to show the portion most relished by the Maori.

The Maori and the South Sea Islander make the most sincere converts I have ever seen; their faith is perfect, and their endurance, under no ordinary trials, for the cause to which they give themselves, is beyond all praise, and reflects the highest credit upon their noble teachers. I am only sorry that, as yet, I cannot say the same for the Papuan; but then he has no religious belief of his own to start from, which makes the task the harder for the missionaries. They have, as it were, to *create* a faith where there is none. It is much easier to prove the fallacy of a time-worn belief than to build up a spiritism in a born materialistic mind.

The Rev. James Chalmers relates, as the origin of cannibalism in New Guinea, something like a new version of the original temptation and fall of man. As Eve tempted Adam to eat of the forbidden fruit, so the wives of the natives gave them the idea to eat man.

The legend gives it that once, after a successful hunting expedition, when they returned shouting, with their canoes laden with boars, cassowaries and wallabies, their women met them with mockery, crying, ' Is that the dirty stuff you are singing about; who is going to eat that?' Then, when the men wondered what they meant, one of them suddenly became inspired with an idea, started up, saying, ' I know what they want: it is man.' Then, casting away their spoil, they all started to a neighbouring village and brought back ten bodies, but without any shouting as they returned. However, when the wives saw what they had with them this time, they all shouted, ' Yes, yes, that is it; dance and sing now, for you have something worth singing for.'

It is a cruel legend of the gentler sex, and must have been invented by some disappointed native woman-hater; but one thing about it is verified, and that is, the verdict then pronounced—that it was good, and vastly superior to any other flesh, which is the opinion of every New Guinea cannibal of the present day.

The story of the missionary, who tried to convert the cannibal, may be quoted here as evidence. Seeing the native almost convinced by his arguments, and inclined to relinquish the evil habit, he concluded his remarks by saying, 'It is not only very wicked to kill and eat your fellow man, but I am sure it must be very nasty also.'

'Oh, no!' replied the native, pathetically, 'it may be very wicked, but oh! do not say it is nasty.'

The cannibals of New Guinea eat from choice, as do some of the tribes of Central Africa, preferring it to the flesh of any other animal; but the aborigines of North Australia become cannibals only from necessity, and in times of scarcity and dire distress. They are the lowest order of cannibals, and eat their own children to prevent themselves being burdened with a large family—a misfortune to tribes constantly on the move as they are; but they much prefer a dish of white ants, an iguana, or a snake, if they can get it, to this revolting alternative. They are a simple and harmless race, and totally unlike the more ferocious, but wiser and more industrious islanders of the South Seas.

CHAPTER XLII

CAUSES OF MASSACRES

Savage Customs and Superstitions—Laws of Tapu.

In reading about deeds of native atrocities, such as the murder of Captain James Cook at Hawaii, in the South Seas, or of Captain Marion du Fresne in the Bay of Islands, New Zealand, or the more recent records of bloodshed which come from the New Hebrides and New Guinea coasts, it should be borne in mind, as some palliation of those native massacres, that there may be some intricate, yet unaccountable reasons and foregoing causes, which we, from our very imperfect knowledge of the habits of the people, cannot in reason be expected to penetrate.

A few of the causes which do lead up to the punishment of death (for I will not here call it murder when the victim is to be regarded in the aspect of a condemned criminal), I shall endeavour to set forth from my own personal experience of the South Sea Islanders and the Maoris.

The European wanders amongst the savages, unacquainted with their languages, totally ignorant of their customs, and from the moment he puts his foot ashore until he leaves it commits blunder after blunder, as unwittingly as the man not initiated into the mysteries of society may be outraging very important codes, even while he is inwardly congratulating himself that he is doing extremely well, and acting in exactly the same fashion as

A PAPUAN QUEEN

those around him. If you look in this light upon the intercourse between the stranger and natives, who are more conservative and strict in matters of ceremony than we are, you will get the solution of many a disaster which is put down to the inconsistency of treacherous savages.

Happy the stranger who trusts himself to the care of a friendly guide, who will prevent him from committing any capital offence! The man is blest who has a true gentleman for his friend and host, when he ventures into unknown depths in the society to which he has not been used.

When the offender, wittingly or unwittingly, offends society's laws, *if he has not money enough* to carry him through the breach, he is put into 'Coventry'; but with the more direct sons of Nature, who have no alternative or power to make a loophole, if the offence is capital, there can be no chance of *buying off*; the offender is condemned by his own action, as a brother would be condemned, and executed upon the first occasion.

The grand law of Tapu looms up for ever before the stranger, and against this he must not transgress, if he would retain his life, as no influence can save him from the punishment.

This Tapu is a protective law, and to be Tapu is to be sacred; *i.e.*, to touch anything Tapu makes you at once Tapu and deadly to all about you.

To explain my meaning fully :—When Death steps over the threshold he lays the spell of Tapu on the entire house and all within it, the mat on which the body lies, the implements and dishes, &c., which in life he used; whoever ventures past the proscribed limits becomes, as it were, infected with this spell at once sacred and evil.

Those who have become Tapu have the immediate and terrible power of making everything Tapu which they touch or pass over, if left to themselves; and so a person under the ban of Tapu, if ignorant of the evil he carries unconsciously about him, may infect a whole district and lay it waste by simply taking a walk abroad; natives will fly with horror at his approach, and dare not, under peril of being Tapu themselves, pass over the earth which his sacred but devastating feet have trodden. If he takes up a dish, or a stick, it is Tapu, and as virulent as he is himself, so that he becomes a living curse, and something to be removed, as speedily as possible, from the face of the earth.

He must either at once isolate himself, and so remain until the time has elapsed needful to remove the ban, with the ceremonies which require to be gone through, or else be slain.

A native of course knows exactly what to do under the circumstances; he will at once remove himself to the place set apart for this purpose, and place himself under the protection of the priests, who alone have the power to take away the evil spirit.

All priests in office are Tapu; chiefs may act as priests, but are Tapu all the time they are so acting.

To prevent the influence from spreading, and enable the priests to move about, a certain mixture or pigment is prepared and painted over the parts which are in communication with the outer world; dishes are set apart for the use of the infected party and their attendants, and all the food is cooked inside the sacred circle; those who have to move about and wait upon the victim are painted from the feet to the waist, while the outer attendants, who have to bring provisions, are coated all over, so that they have no virtue to remove Tapu; also, although so protected from being made Tapu, they only go to the verge of the limit line, and place their provisions, &c., inside for the more active performers to lift up.

It is a long and tedious quarantine for those who have been imprudent or unfortunate enough to become infected; if they wish to take the air they are carried on the shoulders of the gaily-painted priests, and never permitted to touch anything while out. A chief, when first elected, is for a time Tapu, and has to be secluded until it can be removed, while those who are engaged in removing the spell have to go through a similar ordeal before they can enter into free intercourse with their fellows, wives, or children. It is only removed by degrees, so that in every tribe there are old men and women devoted to perpetual Tapu, who do no other work, cursed with a fearful isolation, as the disembowellers of ancient Egypt were, gifted with an awful power. The tribe contribute to their support, and they always have work on hand—either a death or a birth, for both events will create Tapu.

Graves are sacred until the corpse is entirely decomposed, after which they must be exorcised, like all land trodden by a Tapu person, before they can be utilised for ordinary purposes.

If, therefore, a priest was at hand and properly painted, and a stranger to their laws were to transgress and become Tapu, he would first of all try to arrest the dangerous object and persuade him to go at once into quarantine. He would rather do this than kill him; but if an ordinary native were to become aware of it, he would either fly from him to save his own person, or at once, for the sake of his tribe and possessions, make himself also Tapu by killing the transgressor, after which he would place himself under the hands of the working priests; he could have no alternative once the evil was done, no matter how well he liked the victim, unless the victim could understand his explanation of the magnitude of his offence, and obey his directions at once. With a native guide, a stranger would be able to avoid the evil in most cases, only to do so he would find his personal liberty and progress very greatly circumscribed.

If he wanted to take a short cut over the country, his friendly guide would say, 'Not that way.'

'Why?'

'Tapu.'

At every turn the fatal prohibition would start up, until his patience was completely exhausted; then, perhaps, he would daringly push past his guide, and before the other could interfere the deed would be done, and he himself at once doomed to isolation or death.

The guide would make no further objections; probably he would himself be infected by a casual touch, in which case he would follow the other, to watch exactly his route, and note the amount of ruin he was causing. If he could get away he might do so, but, as a rule, he would prefer to incur the infection so that he might report properly the amount of evil done in that fatal walk. If the spot was suitable for a murder, he would unhesitatingly club the offender to limit the mischief; if it was not suitable, he would wait his chance, suffering agonies of consternation at the delay. Love or gratitude could not stay his hand from slaughter; with grief at his heart, he would brain his dearest friend, and weep for him afterwards. This is the exact significance of the word Tapu as nearly as I can explain it in the short space at my present disposal—a ban more paralysing than excommunication was in the olden times, a curse to be avoided as we avoid the dangers of hydrophobia.

Amongst the Maoris and the natives of the South Sea Islands it was the greatest curse and bar to civilisation, until the mightier influence of Christianity taught them the folly of a superstition so utterly demoralising to social progress or intercourse, and banished the power of an evil witchcraft.

Throughout the islands of the Torres Straits and New Guinea I did not find any trace of this abominable superstition; they had no Tapu, so I had to look out for another cause for the murder of strangers, for, knowing the habits of savages as I do, I could not discover a single act of violence to cause this cruelty on the part of the natives; it must be caused by the instinct of self-preservation or superstition—the direct result of fear, or revenge for a wrong committed.

In New Zealand Captain Cook was badly received on his first visit, before the natives learnt that his purpose was good-will and peace towards them; and they afterwards confessed they were terribly afraid of this strange appearance, and it was the desperation of fear which roused their resentment; they all expected to be killed and devoured by this monster flying-fish, as they thought the ship 'Endeavour' to be, and tried, by combining their forces, to kill it first.

Brave to utter recklessness, the Maoris have always shown themselves to be shrewd and not easily deceived, yet I have always found them generous and noble towards those who can understand their nature. Their first greeting of Captain Cook and his party certainly displayed their pluck, if not the amicable side of their nature. Four men, with lances only, rushed out of the woods to attack the pinnace and yawl, both filled with armed men; two volleys fired over their startled heads did not daunt them. Yet that gunpowder-report must have sounded awful when heard for the first time by these four plucky savages who dared to tackle two boatloads of fire-eaters, and their first fears were fully realised by the third volley, which shot one of the four through the heart.

So death preceded Captain Cook on the New Zealand coast, and the great discoverer made himself Tapu the moment he first put his foot ashore, when he handled the body which his coxswain had slain.

'Upon *examining* the body we found that he had been shot through the heart,' &c.

Knowing what we do now about their laws, we do not wonder that he was badly received all round the coast, and warned from it after this, on that first visit. We only marvel that he was not slaughtered long before.

No one who has read the records left by this truly wonderful navigator, can think of him otherwise than as a most sagacious, far-seeing, and kind-hearted man, the *beau ideal* of a brave and generous sailor, just commander and powerful leader; nor can we blame him in any way for the unfortunate disaster which occurred on his first visit to the Maoris. His experiences amongst those softer natives, the Otaheiteans, ill-prepared him to deal with the sterner cannibals of this more stormy land; he had been greeted at Otaheite by plantains, the natives there having already had some experience of white men from the former visit of Captain Wallis, who must have treated them kindly when they were so ready to make friends of Captain Cook and his party; the after-visitors always reap the benefit, or pay the penalty of their predecessors, but with the Maoris it was altogether different—their natures were as totally different from the Otaheiteans as was their climate.

Over Taheta the ocean breeze wafts balmily, and the coral-protected waters are seldom ruffled. The natives are gentle and trusting as children, and make splendid, long-suffering missionaries; their diet is mostly fruit, and they have little necessity for war.

But the Maori is a different specimen of manhood, having a stern education in warfare, trained by necessity to pluck his food from his enemy, as were the hardy and needy Bordermen of Scotland in the Gothic times, with greater reasoning powers and more suspicion, as well as hardier in their natures and not so impulsive as natives of the colder climates are liable to be. The South Sea Islanders could be enraged at a moment's notice and conciliated the next, forgetting the offence as they forgot the benefit; but the Maori required to be roused up by his war-song before he could fight, and once roused was not easily appeased; slow and deadly in his wrath, and as unforgiving toward the enemy as a Scotchman, the effect of that fatal shot would not be forgotten in a hurry.

Afterwards Captain Cook made friends of these suspicious savages; possibly when they came to understand his purpose and appreciate the benefits to be derived from the intercourse, they consented to condone the offence of killing, seeing that he abstained from disgracing the friends of the victims, for with the Maoris the killing of a man is not so serious a fault as the utter disgrace which eating him would be, cannibalism in the first instance being originated in the desire to degrade the enemy, for it was an insult not to be forgiven for a Maori to say, 'Ha! ha!! my father baked your father's head.' In that case the descendants were reduced to the level of slaves, to the fifth and sixth generations, a stain which could only be wiped out by returning the ghastly compliment.

Possibly, in view of the future benefits to be derived, the priests during Captain Cook's absence purified him by ceremonies and a substitute from the effect of Tapu, probably killing and eating an enemy in his name, and so were open to receive his friendly advances upon his return. I can think of no other reason to explain why he and his men were even permitted to land again upon the coast. Be that as it may, he came and left New Zealand, and the natives had cause to bless his memory in their droves of pigs and fields of kimira—*i.e.*, potatoes.

Before taking up the close of this useful life at Hawaii, I would glance at the other great murder which occurred on this coast—that of Captain Marion—and attempt to explain it on the premises which I have taken up.

Between Captain Cook's first and second visits the 'Mascarin' put in at the Bay of Islands, along with the 'Castries,' May 11, 1772.

Two years before the landing of Captains Marion and Crozet a relation of the chief Takowii had been carried away against his free will by Surville, an injury which the Maori was bound to revenge on the first European arrival, for death would have been a less injury than this disgrace brought upon the tribe. Good cause No. 1 why the unfortunate successor to the wrong-doer Surville should be slain and his body outraged.

Thirty-five days they lived in friendly intercourse with the natives, who, shy at first, vied with each other at last in showing kindness to the strangers.

Many attribute their conduct to cold-blooded calculation and treachery during those thirty-five days of kindly attention, but from many little incidents, I incline to the belief that the intelligent Takowii had given up all thoughts of revenge. He had plenty of opportunities of snaring the sailors during that interval.

On May 23 Captain Marion examined the interior, and discovered a forest of splendid cedars; it was not in this tour that he transgressed, for the natives still lived in close intimacy with the seamen.

On June 8 he was made a chief, on the 12th he organised a fishing party, and went off to Takowii's pah, and was seen no more alive.

'Takowii killed Marion.' Why? Out of revenge for the

COAST SCENERY, NEW GUINEA

loss of his relative and to wipe out the disgrace from his tribe? A fair enough reason from a Maori standpoint, yet he did not require to wait thirty-five days to encompass this act of retribution; indeed, from a Maori standpoint the sooner he took his revenge the greater the *éclat*; but from the story of Turner, who witnessed the affair, I draw my conclusions thus.

Takowii had a wrong to avenge on the white man, but Marion had become his friend, so he reserved his retribution for the next arrival, in whom he might feel less personal interest. His fishing invitation was given in all good faith, but between the shore and the pah was Tapued ground, which the impetuous Frenchman stepped upon before he could be warned or prevented by his Maori friends; then Takowii had his duty and his revenge to perform in one act, and the thirty-five days' friendship had to be obliterated. Marion was doomed.

The savages rushed forward and lifted the Frenchmen upon their shoulders (they would have permitted them to walk if they had not become Tapu), and in a moment they clubbed and speared them. They bore them into Tapued ground and slaughtered them before they could devastate the untapued lands.

It was an act of duty done upon the instant of the offence, with a dormant old grudge paid off at the same time, and not the premeditated atrocity which some writers lay upon the shoulders of this grand race of now almost extinct savages.

To return to the final act in the life of Captain Cook at Hawaii in Honolulu, in which there can be traced no wicked motive, as he had inspired the natives with only respect and affection, and after the execution they all united, even the executioners, in a universal wail of sorrowful regret, as Abraham might have done had he sacrificed his well-beloved son.

Cook wrote on his last pages: 'I never met with a behaviour so free from reserve and suspicion, in my intercourse with any tribe of savages, as we experienced in the people of this island. It is also to be observed to their honour that they never once attempted to cheat us in exchanges or to commit a theft.'

For two months and a half they continued in the best possible relations with each other; indeed Captain Cook, or 'Lord' as the natives called him, had been venerated as a deity, as has been described by Captain King.

He says: 'The ships being in great want of fuel, Captain Cook desired me on February 2 to treat with the *priests* for the purchase of the rail that surrounded the top of the *morai* (*i.e.*, sacred or Tapu house). I must confess I had at first some doubt about the decency of this proposal, and was apprehensive that even the bare mention of it might be considered by them as a piece of shocking impiety.'

Captain King, from his knowledge of the strictness of Tapu, felt the impropriety of this order of Captain Cook, who appears at this stage to have lost his usual keen sense of justice and gift of adaptation; possibly he was blinded by the excessive freedom and friendliness of his dusky friends, and felt that he could take this liberty on the strength of his new position as a deity; and from the priests not exhibiting any surprise or indignation at the request, it is just possible that they were also, for the moment, dazzled by their veneration, but the reaction was soon to come. They gave the wood readily, without ever stipulating for anything in return; they also assisted the sailors in the sacrilege, being resigned even to the taking away for firewood of one of their carved images.

Kavo, the priest, on being spoken to by King, stipulated for the restoration of the image, which, when obtained, he carried into one of the priests' houses.

So far had Cook, in his taking, only acted up to his new character as a God; but the unexpected restoration of the image was the first false step. To the native idea, a god might be rapacious and cruel, but he must not be inconsistent; by giving back the idol, he proved that he had been offending a deity whose power he owned superior, since he feared it enough to pause at destroying the centre image, although he had not paused at the spoliation of the temple.

They would naturally reason in this fashion:—' This god intends going away before the other god has learnt what he has done, leaving us to suffer from his vengeance.'

Then they became very inquisitive about the time of the departure, and Captain King took some pains to satisfy them and himself as to their motive for asking, but as yet they were evidently in too great a state of awe to explain their fears and growing suspicions.

At the night talks hints would be thrown out as to why ' Lord ' Cook feared this other god so much, and if after all they had not been imposed upon, and might have to suffer in consequence.

I must blame Captain Cook that he, in the first place, permitted himself to be deified, and that he did not imitate St. Paul at Corinth, and try to enlighten them as to the true God when he had the opportunity. It gave him for a short time a fictitious power, which, when he lost the prestige, placed him at the mercy of an imposed-upon and outraged enemy; their hatred was intensified by the former kindness which had been misplaced and trifled with.

It took some days to awaken them, during which their kindness continued seemingly unabated; still, that they were watching the strangers and testing them, is proved by the invitation which Terreeoboo gave them on the 3rd of February, when the people brought their presents to their own king instead of to the newly-found god. ' If he is really a god, he will be angry that our king is placed before him.' Captain Cook did not express any anger at the preference, and appeared satisfied with what the chief gave him out of his own leavings; if a god, he was a very paltry god, of less account than their chief—so from veneration they had progressed to suspicion and silent contempt; the rest became easy and natural.

The same day the charm of Tapu was removed from their lodgings and themselves, and they were delivered into the hands of the natives.

On the 5th, the weather becoming rough, the natives left them, but left on board their women, who became seasick and much dissatisfied.

Then the weather became worse, and we can fancy the natives attributing the disasters which this storm caused amongst their canoes to a foretaste of the vengeance of the god whom this impostor had outraged.

'Towards the evening of the 13th the officer who commanded the watering-party of the " Discovery " came to inform me that several chiefs had assembled at the well near the beach, drawing away the natives, whom he had hired to assist the sailors in rolling down the casks to the shore. He told me that he thought their behaviour extremely suspicious, and that they meant to cause a disturbance.'

A marine is sent ashore, and things become worse, the natives grow tumultuous and arm themselves with stones, but upon King, who appeared to be a favourite, speaking to the chiefs, they are permitted to get the casks filled; and, having quieted matters so far, he goes to meet Captain Cook, who is coming ashore, and who on hearing the disturbance, orders ball to be used by the sentinels, instead of small shot, if any repetition of the trouble takes place.

It is now open warfare between the natives and the seamen; a state of matters to be expected after the reaction from the former hero-worship.

Shortly after this they were alarmed by the firing of muskets from the 'Discovery,' directed at a canoe; and supposing it to be a case of theft, gave pursuit into the woods after the fugitive without success. The natives now began to amuse themselves by fooling the pursuers with false information; the goods had either already been restored, or, what was more likely, never taken. During the absence of Captains Cook and King a more serious difference had happened. One of the officers had taken upon himself to seize the canoe of Pareea, while this chief was on board the 'Discovery,' and instead of giving it up when Parlla asked for it, he knocked the chief down with a violent blow on the head with an oar, upon which the Islanders, hitherto peaceable spectators, attacked the crew of the pinnace, and but for the timely interposition of the injured chief, would have demolished them. So far as we read, the Europeans, by a most deplorable series of mistakes, were the aggressive party, and the Islanders had displayed great forbearance under their injuries. Captain Cook certainly had not acted with his ordinary prudence or humanity, for when he heard this last incident, which certainly redounded more to the credit of Parlla than of the officer who assaulted him, he said, 'I am afraid these people will oblige me to use some violent measures, for they must not be left to imagine that they have gained an advantage over us.'

During the night the cutter of the 'Discovery' was found missing, and Captain Cook prepared to go ashore and capture the chief man, taking with him his double-barrelled gun loaded with ball—his usual system for recovering stolen property. Reaching Kowrowa, with his lieutenant and nine marines, he invited the king to come on board the 'Resolution,' to which the king readily assented, and got up to accompany him. He was not permitted to go, however, for some of the lesser chiefs, with his favourite wife, used force to keep the king back when he was inclined to accompany Captain Cook, until, what between the urging of the one party and the insisting of the other, the poor king was left in a most dejected state of fear. At the moment when he would have given in, the climax was reached, for the tidings came that the seamen had killed a chief of the first rank.

What followed was rapid, decisive, and blood-curdling; the women and children hurried from the scene, while the men rushed for their war-mats and spears, and, arming themselves with stones, closed round the doomed men.

Captain Cook fired his first barrel at the leader as he came on flourishing his *pahooah* with savage yells. The first shot did no more harm than to irritate the enemy; then he fired his second barrel and killed his man, drawing the first blood in the fray, and leaving himself defenceless in the midst of a maddened crowd.

Four of the marines were slaughtered while retreating to the rocks, three more dangerously wounded, and the lieutenant stabbed between the shoulders.

Captain Cook was last seen by those in the boats, standing on the shore shouting for his crew to come to his rescue, while he faced the natives. They, the natives, hung back, as if still half-afraid of the sham divinity which he had weakly allowed them to hedge him with; but, as he turned from them to give his orders to the boats, the rush was made, a quick stab in the back, and he fell face downwards in the water.

Then, like the assassins of Cæsar, they plunged upon the poor body, dragging it ashore, and snatching at the weapons which made the first wound and showed how mortal he was, and each one vied with the other in their savage eagerness to share in his destruction.

So perished one of England's greatest commanders, and most excellent of men, who was so far fortunate in that he lived to finish the work entrusted to him. He was regretted and lamented by all the sailors who had good cause to love him, and by the Islanders, who had cut him off, after their just rancour had passed away, and they could think upon the man whom they had received with generous friendship, and not the impostor who had permitted them to think that he was a god, and who, by profaning their temple and their Tapu, had condemned himself to death.

CHAPTER XLIII

NEW GUINEA

A General Survey of New Guinea—Its Possibilities, &c.

NEW GUINEA, the largest island in the world, is being forced upon our notice more and more every day by the conflicts between natives and Europeans. The noble abnegation of the missionaries, who so frequently fall victims in their efforts to make peace between the offended Papuan and the acquisitive adventurer, the appalling stories of outrage and cannibalism, and the vague rumours which float towards England of vast possibilities and wealth in future to be gleaned from these coral-bound shores, tempt me to tell you what I know about it.

During this present tour throughout Australasia I went over the British portion of New Guinea, and besides, had the good fortune of being fellow-passenger from Cook Town to Brisbane with Dr. Knappe, who had just returned from his country's portion of this land of wonders; so that while I had the advantage of seeing from Motu Motu to East Cape on the southern side of the island, I likewise had the benefit of his experience of the northern side.

I did not go to New Guinea as a geological, botanical or geographical explorer, but rather in my capacity of artist and author, to observe the people and their ordinary habits, to learn how they built their houses, and cut their canoes, ornaments and general utensils, what they occupied themselves with on working-days, and the amusements which filled up their leisure hours; how they looked and talked amongst themselves, what ideas they had of this life and the future state, their myths and legends, if any, and whatever else I could find out personally about them and their comparatively unknown land.

As I had the honour to be the first, and I believe, as yet, the only *painter* who has travelled in New Guinea, I was particular to see and sketch as much as I possibly could in the limited time at my disposal, every moment of daylight being utilised. Favoured as I was by fair weather and happy circumstances, I missed very little of the coast-land from the Papuan Gulf to the top of Milne Bay. The Owen Stanley ranges indulged me with exceptionally clear views of their wonderfully lofty and rugged peaks; the owners of the land were universally kind and friendly; the missionaries and traders helped me when they could, and, best of all, I escaped the greatest of dangers to venturesome travellers in these parts—the New Guinea fever—so that I was able to return to England with my sketch and note books literally crammed full of work.

While going round the country I kept my eyes open and my pencil busy. By making a great number of rapid sketches I did not require to write down many observations, beyond the names of places, distances and heights, with a few touches of local colouring, so that I was able to carry away far more vivid impressions of the country than I could have done with pages of word-memoranda; which is, I consider, a decided advantage to a traveller, when going over a hot country where every extra package becomes an incumbrance. A light suit of pyjamas, my pencils, and one or two small note-books sufficed for my purpose, and I think did me better service than a dozen of carriers could have done. I went amongst the natives lightly clad, and feeling hardly any inconvenience from the heat.

Before going, I took great care not to read any works already written about the country, as I did not desire to carry away any preconceived notions or theories of other travellers. I wanted to take away with me only my own ideas of what the people were, and what the country was like, intending to compare, by reading when I got back, my own theories and the notions of those who had gone before me; so that when I saw the first savage, I was utterly ignorant of his peculiarities beyond having a vague notion that he had a taste for eating strangers, but whether raw or roasted I was not in the slightest degree aware.

With the usual egotism of Europeans, I thought that of course he would naturally prefer my flesh, as the representative of dainty refinement; however, like many other insular conceits, I quickly discovered that in this I had been flattering myself, and woke to my mistake with a feeling of humiliation. I found out that the Papuan prefers many kinds of food to a white man; for instance, the pig is much more to his taste, while a Chinaman is a real delicacy. As for the white man, he is only to be endured when there is nothing else to be had; so I suppose to the contempt of the natives I may attribute my indemnity from danger while with them.

Years ago, when sojourning with the Maoris, I had learnt that their human feasts were not so much the outcome of flesh-lust as the desire for revenge, and in order to degrade, in an effectual manner, the relations of their victims. The descendants of a man who had been devoured could not take rank as Toas or warriors—they were degraded for several generations to the levels of outcasts and slaves; still, I have heard an old tattooed fighting-man revel in the memory of these olden feasts, and say that man-flesh was better than pig; so that one of my earliest investigations amongst the cannibals of New Guinea was to find out if religion or revenge held an equal prominence in their feasts. I found out that revenge made them, in most cases, kill, but relish alone ruled the roast—religion holds a very slight place in their esteem.

They have their superstitions, that is, they believe in bodes and omens, evil eyes and witchcraft, and practise a kind of spiritualism, having mediums and *séances*, when masks are set up like hobgoblins, before which they tremble and appear terribly afraid while the performance is going on ; but I could never believe in the reality of their horror, as they are quite ready to handle the hobgoblins, and sell them for a few sticks of tobacco to the first stranger who comes to them, so that they cannot regard these masks as any other than what they are--painted and carved bits of wood. They believe also in ghosts, but do not appear to trouble themselves in the smallest degree about Ghostland.

When a man dies, he is dead to his friends for ever. If he has a ghost they are very anxious to chase it as far away as possible, and content themselves with utilising his mortal relics as far as they can, making necklaces of his smaller bones, prow-ornaments of his skull, the larger bones being transformed into lime-spoons or daggers. The remains of a relative are used in pretty much the same way as those of an enemy, so that in this they differ totally from the Maori, their descendants incurring no disgrace because some ancestor may have been roasted.

In speaking about New Guinea native customs, it must be strictly remembered that every few miles the natives have a different custom of betrothal, marriage, burial, and even language. A general belief, or rather non-belief in a future world, prevails over all. The missionary, when he preaches to them, has first to create a want before he can fill it up with his glorious promises. They do not aspire beyond this life, and their precautions are all taken for the guarding of the present state of things. Now, with a thorough-going idol-worshipper the work is comparatively easy, for he has his spiritual wants and cravings already generated, to which they administer, substituting a better heaven than the hereafter which he has already been taught by tradition to regard as an object of life; but with the Papuans, who have no soul-aspirations, and who are the most thorough-bred materialists going, he has difficulties innumerable. Therefore the results which have been gained by such men as MacFarlane, Chalmers, Scott and Savage are the more wonderful with such a nation.

Every native of New Guinea goes to bed with his war implements handy, and sleeps warily. These missionaries have taught him that if he shows mercy to his enemy he will make his enemy do likewise, so eventually he flings down his arms, and sleeps soundly without dread, and common sense brings him over in no time.

Teach him also that burying his dead in front of his house, with only palm-leaves as a covering, is the cause of the fevers and mortality amongst his tribe, and that there is no other evil influence at work, and in time he will abandon this most pernicious practice.

At Port Moresby they have not yet succeeded in instilling the importance of sanitary laws, but they have taught them the value of living without war, so that the other will follow in good time; then, when the excitement of war and the troubles of disease have departed, and when the active-minded native is satisfied in all that pertains to this life, will he crave for the something beyond.

As I found the natives of New Guinea, they were industrious, artistic and moral in their habits, regarding their women with affection and respect, sharing the daily labour, ready to adapt themselves to the customs of the stranger, if those customs were in any way an improvement upon their own, and with general tastes simple and natural.

As cannibals they are not ferocious, having about the same taste for a human breast-piece as we have for a rump-steak; they do not gorge as the Maori did, but eat only to satisfy their hunger, whether the food be pig, human flesh, wallaby, fish, or yams; they are great tobacco-smokers and betel-chewers, which latter they use as a preventive for fever; but they have not yet acquired the taste, nor do I think they ever will, for the fire-water of the Europeans. I do not think it possible that a nation such as this, which indulges in no excess of eating, will soon be exterminated by strong drink.

I wish now to take New Guinea as a future field for planters, gold-seekers and agriculturists, and from what I saw in my short visit I consider it not only possible, but as having every feature to recommend it, if so be that we utilise the natives instead of exterminating them. I consider that no other native labour can be of use except that of the Papuan himself, in the same sense that I regard the eucalyptus as the best tree and future source of wealth for Australia.

As I travelled through Western Australia, South Australia, Victoria, New South Wales, and Queensland, to my regret I saw miles of country covered with dead gum trees—miles with the bare white trunks rearing up like gigantic and fantastic tombstones over vast graveyards, trees ringed and rendered useless by selectors and squatters, who thought only of the grass and earth, plucking out and destroying the wealth which Nature had provided to their hands, in order to secure a competence by hard work and uncertain results.

In New Guinea the natives still wait unmolested, on our side of the Astrolabe, but they wait to be educated as helpers who will grow rich while they enrich their teachers, or, like the gum trees of Australia, to be cut down or left to die unutilised.

I had no opportunity of going to the German side of the land, but, as we travelled on that return journey from Thursday Island to Brisbane, Dr. Knappe, who is the German Consul at Samoa, kindly gave me much information regarding the doings of his countrymen there. He had explored the Augusta River, and found splendid land on both sides of it, the river itself being safe for traffic for over 400 miles. Down this they can transmit their timber and produce, and they have begun in earnest to people the country. He did not say how they got on with the natives, but as they have taken possession of the land, I do not suppose that they will trouble greatly about negotiating with the original owners, except by means of their gunpowder. Now my own estimate of the Papuans leads me to conclude that they will not submit to force. Each native has his own private property: there is not a fruit-tree standing which has not an owner, nor an inch of land which can be taken without resentment; therefore I believe that the natives on the German land will be exterminated. Dr. Knappe informed me that he and his party had excellent health while there; that there was less fever, and of a milder form, than on the British side; yet for all that, I do not think that any European can work and live in New Guinea, whether on the German or English lands, any more than a European can work and live in Java or Ceylon.

I am of opinion, however, that a European can live and enjoy health in New Guinea by taking the same precautions that he would in Java or Ceylon; that is, if he directs the native labour and is prepared to pay out and reap the benefit, dealing fairly with the natives, and employing them instead of trying to subdue them, or force them off the ground.

The Germans are sending out emigrants by shiploads, paying them a salary for staying on the ground. From what I have seen of the German emigrant, I do not think that there is a better colonist alive, excepting, perhaps, the Chinaman, yet I doubt if the Germans will make any good of the country. Working wrongly, as I believe they are doing, they will die off wholesale, and so at the present time I regard German New Guinea as only a graveyard, until they learn to buy from the natives their labour, and rest content with this result.

The Papuan already has all the instincts for work :—he has his rest-days and his days for fishing-pot and canoe-making, building, gardening, spinning. He does not wear clothes because he does not feel the want of costume, but he embellishes his house, paddles, canoes, lakatoes and weapons; everyone has his duty to do, and he does it, in New Guinea. I found as much real work going on as I had left in England, not the hurry and bustle perhaps, because there was no necessity, but something rather like an ideal England according to John Ruskin, without steam-engines or coal-smoke.

The Papuan has his house of council where the men meet to discuss the welfare of the tribe, while the women attend to the household wants; he can enjoy a joke, be cynical, or earnest, while as a business man I do not suppose he can be well beaten when he knows the value of things, and he jumps to that discernment with a very rapid bound.

Formerly I used to think that the Maori was of the lost tribes of Israel, from the keenness with which he could drive a bargain, although hospitable as a Jew after the bargain was concluded; but now I think the Papuan has a keener instinct for trade than the Maori, therefore I consider him before even the sons of Judah in that respect, and expect great future possibilities from him in consequence.

He has also a keen sense of honour and probity. At Gilé-Gilé I saw this displayed in a case of theft, by a white man, of hens which were left under the charge of the native chief by the missionaries ; our party tried to prove that the fowl were his from being abandoned, but he could not endorse this logic—he considered that they were his in trust only, and stuck to his idea of right and wrong. This I speak more fully about later on.

The Papuan has also a most apt and quick mind to learn from strangers. At Hula one of the natives learnt the chorus of a song in one singing, air and words, and sung it afterwards correctly, without aid.

Also, at Moresby one of the Brothers Hunter showed me a native drawing of a horse, brought from inland. One of the inland tribes had seen him pass on horseback, and from the hasty glance supposing it to be some new animal, made horse and rider as one beast with five legs ; any one could see, however, what the artist meant. These are both trifles of themselves, yet are full of significance of future results, for the native who can learn four lines of a song with its air at one hearing and remember it afterwards, or reproduce so nearly correctly an object which he has seen only once rushing past, is possessed of an intellect capable of mastering anything in the system of civilisation.

MISSION HOUSES, PORT MORESBY, NEW GUINEA

CHAPTER XLIV

THE LAND QUESTION

A General Survey of New Guinea (*continued*).

THE question now comes to be : How much must these so-called savages be taught by Englishmen before it is worth an Englishman's while to go amongst them in order to gain an easy competence? I would reply to that, no more than it would take to teach a Saxon labourer accustomed only to tilling the ground, if a manufacturer planted a mill in his district, or opened a coal mine, and make him adroit as a mill-worker or a miner. Less effort, I think, would be required to teach the clear-headed Papuan than it takes to drive the simplest idea into the befogged, beer-soaked brains of the majority of Saxon labourers. From what I have experienced as yet, I would rather fix the standard comparison of brain-power and reasoning capabilities as about equal in the Papuan at present and a labouring native of Scotland; in fact, the New Guinea native resembles this latter more than any other in his independence, self-reliance, and quickness at taking offence, but has a much greater love of home and country.

Putting the cannibal propensities aside (which will shortly be shamed out, and which have not the same significance to travellers who have lived with cannibals that the empty sounds have to people who live at home), the Papuan is no more to be regarded as a savage than the native of India or China, much less than the African in his native state, or the American Indian. To me, he is several degrees higher in the social scale than the lower level of British subjects; it is an easier task to make a companion of a New Guineaite than it is to do so with our own home clodhoppers, the first having already in activity the instincts of right and wrong, which I fail to find in the majority of the latter.

At Teste Island, which I will describe presently, I met a trader who is working on the right system with the natives. He has gone amongst them as a friend and employer. I found his station in first-class working order, and the owners of the island working willingly under his direction and producing splendid results. He acts as their physician when sickness overtakes any of them, and as magistrate to settle their disputes, by native choice. It is a model trading station, as he is a model trader. If a few hundred men of his stamp settled out there, what missionaries like Messrs. Macfarlane, Chalmers and Vergus have begun so well might become an accomplished fact.

I would not like to be misunderstood when speaking about the Germans in their connection with New Guinea, or lead you to think that I regard them as one degree more remorseless than the British would be, and have been, in their dealings with natives, for I do not. I consider the German, as a colonist, to be as industrious and kind-hearted a man as any Englishman can be; but as regards New Guinea, I do think that they have no business to be there, and I think that our Government did both a foolish and a selfish stroke of policy when it weakly permitted this nation to take possession of the northern quarter of that land.

I think, in the first place, that it was our duty to protect the other half of the country as the Queensland Government desired at the time, and permit no other Power, either

French or German, to land, except as British subjects under the control of the officials appointed by our Government for the protection of the original owners. But having allowed this prize to slip through their fingers, I hold it to be doubly foolish, under the guise of this protection, to throw all sorts of impediments in the way of adventuring traders who risk their lives in order that they may deal with the natives, while at the same moment the German landowners are being paid instead of being extra-taxed.

To quote an instance of how men are discouraged at present on our side of the Astrolabe Mountains, I met a trader from Melbourne, at Thursday Island, who had gone in search of cedar up one of the rivers in the Papuan Gulf. He had employed native labour and secured his cargo at considerable personal risk, with a vast outlay of time; when he reached Thursday Island he was not allowed to go on until he had paid a new tax about which he knew nothing when outward bound, a heavy tax of so much per foot on the cargo of wood. He had before him the long and uncertain voyage round North-Western and South Australia before reaching his destination, Port Phillip, where he would again be taxed before he would be allowed to land his cargo, by the Victoria Government.

It was his first voyage to New Guinea, and he declared it would be his last, as, before he got his cedar home, taking all the expenses and waste of time into consideration, to compete with the market price he would be a heavy loser. The cedar he said was good, but of an inferior quality to the American cedar, while he could sail quicker over to America, and have less duty to pay, for a superior cargo.

I will now touch upon the country as it affects strangers. While I progressed towards Torres Straits all the people who had not been there constantly warned me about its extreme unhealthiness, and told me to prepare to leave my bones there, and the nearer I approached to my goal the more gloomy became the evil croakings; but the few traders and pearl-fishers whom I met and who had coasted the land, without exception flouted the idea of its being more unhealthy than any other virgin tropical country, so I did not pay much heed to the croakers.

Personally, while there I enjoyed my ordinary health; but then I took small doses of quinine as a tonic before each meal, kept myself always busy and on the move, slept on board whenever I could do so, and always avoided the night damps.

But I must admit that at present the land is unhealthy on the low parts for any one careless in his habits, although not more so than any other new, unworked tropical land would be; and the causes are quite apparent to any one who has been there.

There are swampy and mangrove-covered flats all round the coast, which require to be drained and cleared before any one can expect health. From all virgin soils there exude gases fatal to human life, which escape when the land has been once turned over. The mountains rise abruptly and to a great height, with deep valleys where the waters congregate and rot the vegetation, the decayed *débris* of which has been accumulating for ages in some parts untouched—a wealth of natural manure which only requires to be utilised in order to produce splendid results to the future planter, and which can only be utilised, without risk, by the nations who are already acclimatised, for the poor South Sea Islanders, who are there as teachers, suffer as much as do the Europeans.

By day the sea-breezes blow strongly inland and then there is no danger, but at night the wind veers round and returns from the mountains, bringing down to the valleys and hollows white, vegetable germ-laden, malarial fogs, and these are the hours when strangers, glad of the coolness of the night after the heat of the day, carelessly go to sleep under outside verandahs and get inoculated with New Guinea fever.

On the heights, however, it is always healthy, winter or summer, and also out at sea; therefore the inland tribes build their villages on mountains, ridges, and tree-tops, and the coast tribes in many cases raise theirs on high piles out on the reefs, half a mile or a mile from the shore; their gardens and plantations are on the flats, but they live themselves, when they can, on a level above the mist-line.

At Port Moresby, one of the least picturesque and most unwholesome places along the coast, I saw some of the white men's residences lying on a lower plain than the native huts. Mr. Andrew Goldie has built his house on what I consider to be about the worst part of the bay. He lives where he is surrounded by the night fogs, and has the day breezes poisoned by the constant fumes from native graves, so that he is a victim to repeated attacks of fever, which is not at all to be wondered at.

The Mission Station is better placed, much better than even the Government Bungalow, and Mr. and Mrs. Lawes appear to enjoy good health ; and from what I have seen of the country, if any white man can live at Port Moresby he need have no fear about squatting upon any other part of New Guinea.

In order to comprehend the capabilities of this land, I will now say a few words about its formation.

From Caution Bay to Table Bay the British coast-line is protected by a wide fringe of coral reefs ranging from four to eight miles wide, with good openings very conveniently placed at almost regular distances from each other, within which the largest vessels may, with perfect safety, enter and find good anchorage; these disconnections occur at the mouths of the large freshwater rivers which lead inland to the vast chain of backbone mountains called the Owen Stanley Range. Such are the Basilisk Passage at Port Moresby, Round Head Passage, Beagle Entrance, Hood Lagoon, opposite Kerepuna one of the most important native towns, with rich flat lands behind. Between the Aroma and Ammarupa districts is a stretch of growing district over twenty miles in width, and spreading from Keremu to the Robinson River in Cloudy Bay, over ninety miles in length, well drained, and watered by rivers and streams throughout.

Again, from Cloudy Bay to the North Foreland in China Straits, there is a fine spread of diversified land—forest, swamp and plains, with occasional mountain land—over 150 miles in extent, and ranging from 15 to 30 miles in width.

Westward, from Caution Bay to Bald Head, a distance of over 180 miles, we find the same description of land; after which, from the rivers Fly, Baxter, and so on, to the Dutch boundary, it is flat and swampy, well cut up by rivers, some of great volume and extent, as those lately discovered and named the Douglas and Jubilee, by Mr. Theodore Beven, who was sent out at the private expense of Messrs. Burns, Philp & Co., of Sydney, in the interest of future trade.

The country east of Port Moresby has been fairly gone over by the Rev. James Chalmers and other able explorers, but much of that lying west has yet to be explored. Mr. Beven sends glorious news of what he has explored, and considers the new rivers to be the future gateways to the interior. He penetrated far inland in the same steamer, 'Victory,' which I used while over there, and passed some most stupendous gorge scenery, as well as fine level stretches of rich land; all the party enjoyed, as I did, good health.

After getting past the coast belt of mangrove forests,

the country opens up—in parts grass-covered, and in parts densely wooded—the timber being in some parts of gigantic size—cedar, camphor, nutmeg, mahogany, tamarind and other denizens of the tropical forest. Some of the bush-tracks are very difficult to penetrate owing to the dense undergrowth, but in other places the ground is more open, large spaces of grass-covered country, with, here and there, cotton and gum trees breaking the monotony. In these open spaces the wallaby and bush turkey are to be found plentifully.

The specimens of the eucalyptus which I came across in New Guinea were not to be compared to the gum trees of Australia; but this is owing to the heat, as there are no trees north of Brisbane to be compared to the giants of Gippsland and Tasmania.

On the mountains the natives cultivate the ground right to the top, making terraces and ridges to prevent their gardens from being washed away by the rains. Round by East Cape the appearance of those garden-ringed hills reminds one strongly of the cultivated mountain ranges of Ceylon.

Crotons and orchids are to be found in great variety and beauty all over the island, and there is a very rich harvest to be gleaned by any future botanist who may wish to make a name for himself and find out novelties in the vegetable world.

It is also ridiculous to suppose that a country so closely connected with the gold-bearing continent of Australia, and in many respects so similar in geological formation, will not yet yield a heavy return in minerals and ore, both in alluvial and quartz form; specimens have been picked up by nearly every traveller who has spent any time in the country. That the natives themselves have not discovered gold, or used it in any of their ornaments, is no evidence, as it needs a *certain kind* of civilised taste to be acquired before this metal can be appreciated. I saw myself some specimens in the possession of a trader whose word I had no cause to doubt, particularly as he has discarded all other means of gaining a livelihood, and is devoting himself altogether to New-Guinea gold-seeking. He is working alone and quietly, as he wishes to find enough to remunerate himself sufficiently before divulging his knowledge to the world at large. Personally I have no desire to see a rush of miscellaneous gold-hunters on the field, before the rights of the original owners are fully recognised and themselves protected. I am hoping for better results to be gleaned out of the soil than can be dug from under it, for a gold-field, however prosperous it may be, is a dreary sight to contemplate. I would much rather see New Guinea transformed into a planters' paradise, with contented natives tilling and reaping the ground, than a miserable waste of upturned earth, crushed quartz, and drinking shanties, with the exhibition of unbridled lust of gain which all newly-discovered diggings display, and where the worst passions which can degrade mankind seem to be let loose. Rather than this should come to pass, I would prefer to see the land locked up as it now is, and left in the undisturbed possession of the missionaries and their converts.

I would like now to speak of the natives as I found them during my visit, and show you as briefly as possible their daily life, if only to prove to you how little is required to bring them into close community with strangers who may think about living amongst them. We leave England, with its bustling activity, its trains, steam engines, tramways, factories, and thousand distractions, to rest for about six weeks on board ship, seeing the varieties of foreign scenes, Malta, Egypt, and Ceylon, with the long spells of ocean expanse, where the passengers grow to be one family as it

PORT MORESBY BY MOONLIGHT

were; then we land at Melbourne to find England with its bustle and traffic repeated.

As we progress towards the North we appear to be gradually living back time, and drifting into the period of the old coaching days, when men took time to breathe upon their journeys. Then, as we leave Thursday Island behind, it feels as if we had dropped centuries in an hour, and were approaching the Britain which Julius Cæsar came to subdue. Yorke, Murray, Darnley, all lovely islands, which we stop at, help to acclimatise us and accustom our eyes to the change of scenery before us. We have been gradually getting used to tropical verdure as we sail up the Barrier Reef of North Queensland, while the distant effects of mountains and coast with colouring are pretty similar in all parts of the world—a difference in outline, cloud changes a trifle more vivid, but the same blue-grey and purple haze over all.

We have a summer sea while in the Torres Straits, like to the rippling calmness which we have enjoyed since leaving the golden sands of Keppel Bay, with bright green waves and tawny sea-snakes floating languidly past; then we leave the friendly protection of the coral reefs and get into the rough tumble of the Papuan Gulf, where we have a couple of days of misery, before the table-like outline of Mount Yule rises up on the horizon, and gives us the first glimpse of our promised land.

Half a dozen fine young men welcome us as we drop anchor. They have come in their canoes, and bring to us desperately hard bunches of bananas from Yule Island. They are splendid specimens of manhood, with cassowary head-ornaments and dog-teeth necklets, painted on the cheeks with alternate stripes of black and white, with the brown skin left for the third tint, wearing bone and coral nose-bars, hair-spun armlets, a fine string tightly braced round their middle, and all their other perfections left as Nature designed them.

We are not much afraid of them, and they do not appear to be in the slightest degree afraid of us, until our engineer gives them a sudden blast with the steam whistle, when they all simultaneously plunge overboard, to reappear in another moment laughing somewhat awkwardly at their betrayal of consternation.

I dare say our forefathers, in the olden times, would have bolted also if the noble Romans had startled them with a steam whistle.

We go over Yule Island and investigate the gardens and fields, the plantations of sago, and the groves of cocoanut and betel palms. The natives are a friendly race who are living at peace with the French missionary, and rearing home vegetables and fruits from the seeds which he has brought to them and shown them how to plant.

CHAPTER XLV

THE PAPUAN AT HOME

General Survey of New Guinea (*continued*).

Our next rest is at Port Moresby, where we discharge cargo and take in fresh water before going eastward.

The natives are the workers and take off the cargo in their canoes, bringing fresh water from the springs in iron tanks which we lend them for this purpose. They work well for about four hours at a stretch, when they strike and will not go on until they are paid for what they have done; they will not give trust until the work is finished, but go on cheerfully again, when their demands are satisfied, for another four hours, when the squaring-up has again to be repeated.

Horses have been introduced at Moresby, so that they have become used to them, but they are very much afraid of sheep; we had to land half a dozen, and it was with great difficulty we persuaded three stalwart fellows to come alongside and lend a hand to take them ashore. They told us with loud voices that they were not afraid of sheep, but they laughed nervously when they saw them kicking, and trembled very visibly as we hoisted them overboard. 'Now steady, and catch,' we cried. Six brown, trembling arms were outspread from the canoe to receive the first instalment, which we had tied at the feet, and three most anxious, pallid faces, with wildly staring eyes were upturned towards it.

'Flop!' Their screwed-up courage has failed them, and the poor sheep slips through their nerveless fingers, and splashes into the water.

All the shouting and cursing on the part of the seamen will not move them to stretch out a hand to save that drowning quadruped, so some of us are forced to jump overboard also and fish it out; then, as we get the others over they shrink back from them, and make no disguise of the horror that possesses them; they consent, however, to paddle the canoe ashore while we sit and look after the live stock: and that is as much as any one can expect from them the first day.

That night, when the tribe gathers round the fires to cook their yams and taro, they will give a graphic account of their awful experiences, while the wives will listen with awestruck faces, until some daring female, not particularly interested in the narrative, will throw a doubt on their story and make laughing-stocks of them—for it is always the women who penetrate the mysteries. Then next day these three frightened canoe-owners will swagger up to where the sheep are grazing, and when they see the poor things run away, they will jeer at them and return to tell us that they were only shamming fear the day before.

Pot-making is the principal craft carried on at Moresby. These pots they fashion from clay, blackening them with plumbago while wet, and firing them afterwards until they look like ironware. Some are beautifully elaborated with quaint carvings; these they take about to friendly tribes and barter for provisions and other articles not made by them.

They are also great at canoe-making and sail-spinning, but do not use such an extent of decoration as will be found at East Cape, where the hull is one mass of carving and shell-embellishment. The canoes of Hanuabada and Elevari are made mostly with an eye to use rather than for show, some of them being sixty to a hundred feet in length.

The smaller craft with one sail are used for fishing purposes and short coasting voyages, but when they have to go upon their long western annual voyages in search of sago and rice, &c., they lash three or four of the longest hulls together, raising over them a strong platform, with wicker gunwales and cargo-houses out of water reach; then they hoist their swallow-tailed sails, two, three, or four, and with flying streamers of palm fronds, locks of human hair, skulls and shells dangling about, and cassowary tufts raised above the carved prows, they sail away in grand style.

These united canoes are called lakatoes, and are capable of holding all the fighting-men of the tribe.

In their daily communion with women they are respectful and subservient rather than masterly; they marry mostly from affection, and have to court their brides as well as pay for them. The female has her own choice out of several suitors. If one pleases her during courtship, he is permitted to purchase her from her parents at the appointed time. They observe a strict etiquette in matters relating to courtship and marriage, and, even after marriage, are most careful not to be seen too much together. Their children come at longer intervals than is usual amongst us civilised Europeans, and a married couple would be shunned by the tribe and compared to pigs and beasts if they had a second child before the first could walk.

It is a rare occurrence for a man to beat his wife, and he does not like to be reminded of the fact if hasty temper has led him into this mistake. The other women generally make a song about it, and sing it whenever he appears; and as no one is so sensitive of ridicule as a New Guinea savage, he will endure a great deal, even from a shrew wife, before he attempts to lift his hand.

He will marry more than one wife if he can afford the luxury and the first mate is quite agreeable, as she very often is, in order to have a fellow-houseworker; and at odd times, if they cannot agree, he will repudiate the offending member. But, as a rule, he is content with one wife, and divorces are very rare occurrences.

Therefore, with these facts before you, I trust you will agree with me in saying that our own unwashed savages of England, and even some of the dress-coated ones also, do not compare favourably with the hibiscus-adorned savages of New Guinea. Of course it is not all unadulterated perfection with them any more than it is with other nations on the face of the globe. They are terrible fighters amongst themselves, and, as a rule, fight treacherously; as great fighters and as treacherous in their manœuvres as were our own Celtic feudal tribes when they were in force. They have no sense of chivalry where an enemy is concerned, and never spare the death-blow when they have the opportunity to deliver it.

They have very abominable burial rites—indeed, their corpses are the greatest nuisances to visitors; they come under your notice at every turn of the road, and ruin many a good appetite before the memory of them can pass away.

With their domestic pets also they are more quaint than nice, according to our Western ideas. They are very fond of pigs and dogs, and if very particular not to nurse more than one baby at a time, they do not at all object to take up a young pig or pup and suckle it along with their own offspring.

Pigs, puppies, and babies all cuddle together in the one cradle, and seem to have equal attention from the fond mistress and mother.

Their houses are clean and comfortable, carefully thatched with palm fronds, and raised on high posts with wide platforms from which they can visit one another when inclined. They do their cooking mostly on shore, except in those sea-built towns such as at Tupuselei.

Their gardening implements are of a very primitive order, yet effective enough to serve their present purposes—a pointed stick or two to scrape the earth, Nature being left to finish the job; but it is a lavish Nature in these parts and a generous sun, so that they have not much room to grumble at the results.

The gardens are picturesque if not very orderly, each plot being protected by large palisades to keep the wild boar and other beasts of prey out, with long lanes between the different properties, over which swing the broad leaves of the mammy-apple tree or more pendulous filigree-work of palms.

Their fishing-tackle is simple but effective—nets for trailing along the reefs, net bags fixed on bamboo poles for dipping through the waters, many-pronged fishing spears of black palm. They do not elaborate the implements of peace much, but show some very beautiful designs and specimens of native art on their war implements—their shields, swords, axes, and poisoned arrows.

Their calabashes and bau-baus, or native pipes, are also wonderful in the symmetry and beauty of their designs, no two being exactly alike. These designs they take from passing events or surrounding objects—flowers, passing clouds, animals, fish, and all sorts of incidents, which they transfer to ornamental scroll-work, working freely, yet always telling their story with definite purpose.

The colouring which they use is always quiet and subdued, no glaring reds or blues or greens, but soft tones of brown, yellow, black and white.

The men embellish themselves lavishly about the head, face, neck, and arms with flowers, hair-combs, shell and bone ornaments, leaving from the neck downwards fully exposed, with the exception of the waist-string. The women seldom use necklaces, but cover their breasts and arms with tattoo-work instead, wearing bunchy petticoats of coloured grass, about which, by the way, they are very particular.

The men in general are tall and finely formed, with mild, intelligent faces, good features and expressive eyes; some are of a dark copper colour, while others vary from copper tint to a tawny white. The women are not so good looking, being mostly under sized, although there are some graceful exceptions.

I think I have now said all that is necessary at the present to give you a fair idea of the daily life of the Papuan and his capability for work and pleasure, and how easy a matter it is to get along comfortably with him, for any one desirous of doing so in earnest. He knows keenly what are his dues as man from man; he is open to conviction and of good reasoning powers; he is not unreasonable in his demands, nor unduly suspicious of strangers; he is jealous of his honour, and will not tolerate encroachments upon his rights either as a landowner or as a husband; but if he is met by candour and treated as a white man expects to be treated, there is no man on earth more inclined to open his heart and welcome, with delight, the stranger and the comforts he may bring with him.

I trust also that I have shown that the climate is not too unhealthy, and that the land is only to be dreaded in the same sense which we, in this country, dread a bad drain. Clear the drain and the infection dies, clear the land and the malaria must also pass away.

The present owners have proved themselves willing, when approached properly, to sell the land to Government as it

HEATH ISLAND, EAST CAPE, NEW GUINEA

may be required; so that there need be no bloodshed to be feared, so long as they are not forced to remove from their property; there is plenty of room for both strangers and natives, the one to buy and the other to sell, and after that the one to pay for labour and the other to labour for payment. I have also pointed out how the many and wide, deep, and swift-flowing rivers from the mountain ranges, and in some instances penetrating them, will prove the open roadways from the sea to the interior, which at present appears to be locked up by those steep and rugged lofty ranges lining the coast, and separating us from our German neighbours.

I can tell you that nowhere have I seen more splendid and beautiful scenery than in New Guinea. As you pass along the coast from Round Head to China Straits, it is a perfect feast of ever-changing panorama—range behind range of mountains, from the steep grass-covered sides nearest to the sea, with their deep valleys and watercourses, the forest-clad hills behind, to those far distant inland giants, the Owen Stanleys, tier above tier, growing fainter and more mist-like as they tower above and behind one another, until, when we think we have sighted the loftiest, and look on the rolling banks of snow-white clouds, we are still astonished by the faint but rugged outlines of yet more lofty peaks, staining like a delicate wash that limpid space beyond.

At portions of the passage, as we near China Straits, vast precipices start out as if from the sea, sheer walls from ten to fifteen hundred feet in height, with those purply masses again receding and melting into mid-heaven, then on to Dinner Island and East Cape, with the vegetation dense and overhanging to the water's edge.

Up Milne Bay or Gulf, with the other inland bays opening from it, a glorious play of sunlight on the hillsides, and penetrating into deep fertile gorges without a single yard of monotony anywhere.

To Teste Island with its surrounding cliffs and islands—for the ocean bed is dotted with those isles, all islands of loveliness, such as Boat, Cliffy and Western Islands, Cliffy Island being like an immense iceberg on the point of toppling over; and so on to other islands, and more romantic coast formations, pictures of fertility and pleasure.

This is a rough picture of the only spot on the face of our world which has not yet been thoroughly explored, and which is so well worth the trouble, with no greater natural difficulties in the way than have been already encountered in Africa, and having the advantage of being, with the exception of alligators, free from ferocious beasts of prey; snakes are not plentiful, while there is game enough to be had for the shooting.

Here is a nation interesting from the fact that it is the only and last primitive nation to be found in its pristine vigour and the simplicity of ages, as yet uncontaminated by the contact of the invader; a race quite as ready to adapt themselves to the necessities of civilisation as were the ancient Britons, after the Romans had taught them how to exist according to Rome; new blood which would do the old blood good to blend with; a race of antique men and women ready to be led forward and upwards of their own accord, or dragged backwards and downwards with the same easy facility.

CHAPTER XLVI

UP MILNE GULF

New Guinea—East Cape—From Samarai to Milne Gulf—Natives on the Rampage—An Errand of Peace—Scenery going up.

On August 7, 1886, we left Samarai, or Dinner Island, to try what we could do to conciliate the natives of Gilé-Gilé, who having been wronged, or imagining themselves injured, were up in arms, blowing their conch-shells, and demanding, by way of restitution, the life of a white man.

It was a disagreeable task which we set about, but it was strictly necessary for the safety of any European who might hereafter visit these parts that we should investigate this matter and leave the natives entirely satisfied. This is a duty which travellers must on no account shirk, however dangerous to themselves, as many of the massacres occurring in New Guinea are entirely owing to the carelessness of traders or travellers, who, knowing the cause of discontent, but feeling secure themselves, sail away, leaving the natives unsatisfied, to wreak their vengeance on the next party, who, all unsuspicious of the fate hanging over them, may land. And as the Papuan does not openly express his sense of injury, but cunningly waits his time, the danger is all the greater.

The present cause of complaint was what to Europeans may seem a very trivial one to demand a punishment so heavy, being merely a case of 'hen-lifting'; but to the simple directness of the natives, who do not observe degrees of wrong-doing as we do, with proportionate award of punishment, a wrong is a wrong, and an injury an injury, with only one mode of wiping it out, particularly if the evil-worker is not a relative. He is promptly judged and condemned to death, and straightway hunted after; if captured, he is carefully taken care of, and cooked as tenderly as his age or occupation will permit; but if he escapes, then the vengeance is kept and increased until it may embrace the whole of the next company who chance to land in this evil hour.

In the present instance the case was somewhat complicated, in this way:—A hunter who had gone ashore to shoot the bird of Paradise and other feathered game, after being kindly treated by the natives, had, without asking leave, taken one of a brood of hens.

Now the curious part of the affair was that the hens did not belong to the natives of Gilé-Gilé. In fact, it was rather a difficult point of law to decide whether that particular fowl did not belong quite as much to the poacher as to any one else, it being a young fowl, many generations descended from an original family left, by the Kanaka missionary, when he abandoned the station some fourteen or fifteen months prior to this date, to run wild, breed, and serve as food for the natives or any one else coming after who liked to catch them. But that was no matter from a native point of view; they laid no claim to the fowl themselves, but claimed that they had been placed or left under their special protection until the return of the missionary or his successor, and that therefore their honour had been outraged, to which no salve could be applied except an inward plaister of carefully-roasted European thief, or, failing him, a substitute of the same colour.

So the case stood as we left Dinner Island that misty

early morning to negotiate for the pardon of the poor criminal, who waited for our return in fear and trembling; Such a strange, changeable sort of a chameleon is this porcupine called honour, in all parts of the world for ever setting up its back of bristles where least expected, and of a colour the most difficult to define!

We carried with us a Greek outlaw and beachcoomber, who, having lived a long time in outlandish parts, believed in but one method of settling a dispute of this description, viz., his cutlass, Winchester and revolver, which weapons he carried constantly about him. We had also a gigantic jet black South Sea Island teacher, the successor to the owner of the hens, who, not seemingly thinking that his Testament or hymn book would be required on his present mission, had left them behind, and taken in their place a couple of revolvers and a little half-caste, reddish-haired, lob-eared native boy to carry and load them for him. This little boy was covered with the curious but harmless skin eruption so common to the coast tribes, and which I attribute to their strong distaste for salt, and the unvaried yam and taro food; whoever his progenitor may have been, the mixture of races was not improved in him, for his appearance, when compared with the other little pure-bred native boys, was currish to the last degree—he was undersized, thin and ugly. The black teacher seemed to lament that he had not a spare round of cartridges, but brightened up considerably when he discovered that my size fitted his bore, and eagerly accepted from me three spare rounds for each weapon—a grim hint that the people we were about to visit were not lambs.

The other members of our party were—a trading agent of the enterprising firm of Burns, Philp & Co., whom I accompanied as he went from point to point on the look out for probable future stations, and who kindly humoured me when I wished an hour or a night longer to prosecute my artistic investigations; a young man who had come to spend his well-earned holidays from the heavy duties of a Government Office at Thursday Island, and who had already learned to suck and swallow the smoke from the 'bau-bau,' or native pipe, with nearly as much freedom from choking as the natives themselves; an explorer and his plucky wife, who braved the dangers of New Guinea in company with her husband, and who now honoured our company with her presence, putting us all in a very great flutter as to how we were to accommodate her in our limited and rough quarters.

We always admire enterprise on the part of the ladies, though we beg to doubt the expediency of trying their devotion so far as to bring them to a land like this, where the male portion of the natives promenade with a necklace of dog or human teeth by way of costume, and where adventurers have to make all sorts of shifts for convenience of room, &c. For an hour on our upper deck her presence would have been delightful, but the contemplation of a whole day and possibly a night with us, was a much more serious matter than people at home would be apt to imagine.

'What will we do with her and ourselves?' was the consideration which engrossed us during the entire evening of the 6th. Our little steamer had only one very small compartment, which we used as a saloon by day and a sleeping-cabin at night, while what with cargo and curios, every corner was so completely filled and crammed above and below that we had hardly space ourselves to move about, far less accommodate a female. However, it had to be faced, and we made up our minds to do our best under the circumstances, and trust that our efforts to please would compensate for our lack of ability.

We fixed upon 6 A.M. to weigh anchor, and as our guests were expected about five, we stayed up all night so that we might be dressed in good time, taking our baths by turns while the others watched for signs of movement ashore, and tortured ourselves for the first time inside stiff collars, coats, and shoes. On ordinary occasions we had roughed about in our pyjamas and bare feet, but now we tried to look happy and respectable with a day of utter misery before us.

The morrow would be the anniversary of my birthday. How was it to be spent? Giving a friendly drink round to my companions on board, in which I could participate, or being the means of a feast ashore, during which I would be also present, not as one of the partakers, but as one of the partaken—a solemn thought, which I daresay crossed all our minds at times, like the shadows which fell upon the waters of the gulf and hollows of the mountains, as the clouds flew over the surface of the sun. No matter, we had all our time to run, and a smash from a club or the cut of a sword are not the worst deaths on record, while it does not much matter, beyond the sentiment of the thing, whether afterwards we become incorporate with brother man or brother worm.

My friend the swarthy Greek found his way to beside where I was sketching, and now stood puffing at his pipe, a lurid gleam in his dark eye, and an angry flush on his sunburnt cheek. It appears that one of the gentlemen on board had first asked to be introduced to him, and when his request was granted, deliberately turned his back on him and snubbed him—a singular method of showing superiority and dignity, which I have observed in other parts of the civilised world as a preventive lest the something which God fashioned exactly like ourselves, but which chance has placed in a slightly different sphere of life, should presume upon his similarity to our own ordinary clay. From a standpoint of honesty and honour I could not altogether regard this treatment as undeserved, although it might have been administered before rather than after the solicited introduction.

'Humph! A fine explorer he is, with his gentlemanly airs,' muttered the insulted Greek (Nicholas, like many of his class, was apt to mistake caddish arrogance for gentlemanly refinement, I suppose because under this form the quality was most frequently displayed before him). 'He has got indigestion next, and is going in for smelling-salts and cold-water cloths on his head.' Our visitor certainly had exhibited a few varied ailments since his advent aboard that morning.

'I bet he never reaches the top of Mount Owen Stanley unless he is carried up in a litter.'

Nicholas puffed savagely at his well-used pipe as he muttered this, and after feeling the edge of his cutlass, relapsed into moody silence, with his brawny arms folded across the taffrail, and his eyes fixed upon the rugged coast ranges which we were passing.

'Have you ever landed on that coast?' I asked him, to change the conversation.

'Yes, twice, and had hot quarters of it both times.'

'Then they are savages?'

'Savage ain't the word! They torture you before they cook you over there. I tell you what, I once came upon them just beginning to roast a young maid after they had stuffed her chock-a-block with hard bananas.'

'Why did they do this?'

'Well, you see they have their own ideas of cooking in these parts. They like to eat their bananas done that way, and when they catch the grub they force it to eat as much as they can stuff down of the fruit; then they put it before a slow fire, alive, and when they think the bananas are ready cut them out and eat them. The flesh they don't care much about.'

'Horrible! But did you save the girl?'

'Of course I did. I let them have the contents of my Winchester right off, and when the rest bolted, got her away. She wasn't much the worse except for the fright and the gorging, and as soon as we were safe became quite lively.'

Nicholas did not mention the ultimate fate of this maiden, and at the moment I was too busily engaged with my sketch to ask about her after-history. We were getting well into Milne Bay or Gulf; for although it is marked down on the charts as a bay, from its magnitude it may well be termed a gulf, and also to distinguish it from the numerous bays which lead from it.

On both sides we could see the land rearing up very high: mountains with steep sides and deep indentations and valleys with some portions grass-covered, but more frequently close jungle while, looking down the chasms and valleys constantly opening up as we passed along, we could see vast stretches of immense timber-land—cedar, tamarind, and other tropical trees, while numerous stream-beds and torrent-courses proved the plentiful supply of water.

Overhead, the sky was broken up by sunny and swiftly-sailing rain-clouds, summer showers which fell very frequently and served for a few moments to cool the air, as the thin drops rained upon us like fine spray, to be quickly followed by intervals of fierce glittering sunshine.

A soft grey atmosphere lay over the landscape and smooth surface of the gulf, till it seemed like a lake only, slightly ruffled by the passing breeze. Indeed, the effect was exactly similar to that which I have seen on Lake Derwentwater and the hills of Borrowdale, mellow-grey purple shadows shifting perpetually—now rushing down the mountain sides, as if chasing the sunshine into the deep hollows, now sweeping over the distant waters with the dazzling gleam of quicksilver in front, a constant scene of change and motion, producing the first home-like feeling which I had felt for many months.

So we slowly steamed along and approached our destination, Gilé-Gilé, passing many points of beauty, and delicious stretches of sand with mangrove fringes, while behind this foreground babbled down little streams, and tiny waterfalls leaped over cliffs, and played round boulders, hiding amongst foliage and rippling over golden beds, on their way to annihilate their laughing freshness in this marriage with the briny flood, as the straight shafts of sunlight struck through the cloud-apertures and pierced into many an awful chasm.

We saw no signs of life or smoke as we passed along, but we knew that the natives were there in force, watching from concealed places the strange smoking monster which went puffing and snorting along, and beating the waters into white foam with its wriggling tail.

As we draw near to the native village of Gilé-Gilé we see the land closing in till it stretches away like the banks of a thickly-foliaged river, with ranges of misty blue mountains beyond. On one side of this narrowing neck we observe a stretch of sand in front of a dense thicket of palms and other trees, with a copra station composed of store and drying sheds, where the natives prepare the cocoanuts for the traders who occasionally call here; on a narrow strip or tongue of land dividing the mouth of a fresh-water river from the broader estuary, we see the pile-raised huts of the village, with groups of natives sitting round large fires, while their canoes are drawn up to the beach.

No one amongst those squatting groups makes a movement or seems to betray consciousness of our presence, although the unusual sound of the shrieking of the steam-whistle must have startled them. They sit sullenly with their backs to us, a dangerous sign with savages, so that we are forced to lower our dinghy and row over to the deserted copra station, leaving the engineer, firemen and sailors with rifles and pistols to guard the little steamer in case of an attack, while we take with us our weapons and ammunition.

Nicholas fires off his revolver in the air to attract their attention without producing any effect, after which Tom the native teacher, who knows their language, stands up in the dinghy and shouts out our errand, asking the chief to come over for a consultation.

We wait a little longer and then see a movement taking place. One figure with a conical-shaped cap rises and comes slowly down to the canoes, followed by about fifty men, naked but carrying with them spears and other weapons. They prepare to get into the canoes, when Tom stops them by shouting out that we are determined to shoot them if he brings more than a dozen with him, the half to be women. Tom explains that they mean mischief when they leave their women behind.

At this the chief once more retires, and we can observe a very excited discussion going on in the camp, during which pause we look to our weapons and prepare for action. However, it does not appear that we have this extremity to face, as we can see the chief once more returning, with half a dozen warriors and three women, one of whom carries a baby, but they appear to come much against their inclinations.

'All right,' says Tom; 'they won't begin fighting—I think we can manage them.' So we all sit down on the sands to watch them paddle across, while those who smoke charge their pipes and prepare to light up, so that we may appear quite unconcerned.

I daresay we all looked quite cool and composed as we sat thus, waiting on the approach of the chief of Gilé-Gilé, whether we felt so or not, the more so on account of our lady-visitor, who had insisted on coming ashore with her husband, and who, although the only one unarmed, looked as cool as the others—a little woman she was, with grey eyes, grey hair, and a complexion milky from the quantity of the new arsenic fever preventive which she had been compelled to take since coming to New Guinea, and clad in an æsthetic-cut gown made of a light, soft grey material. As a son of Scotland, I could the more enthusiastically admire the real Caledonian courage of this daughter of Scotland who kept her feelings so well under control in that time of indecision and danger.

One of our company and Tom had come to loggerheads on the passage about the vexing theft question. Tom was prepared to accept the native view as to the ownership of the hens and claim them in the name of the missionaries, so as to leave only the wounded honour to be settled; while this gentleman wished to teach the natives a new point of law whereby they might consider the fowls as their own property when they had been abandoned so long; and so after much wrangling poor Tom had to sulkily acquiesce and act as interpreter only—*i.e.*, to state the case as the othe chose to represent it, the white man being dominant. Poor Tom was a powerful South Sea Island native, with all the fierce passions of his race still boiling within him, and not so very long himself redeemed from savagedom; he was not inclined to comprehend the legal quirk now propounded to him, any more than the Papuan chief would be likely to, when it was placed under his notice. He conscientiously believed that the fowl were his property since he had succeeded to all the other effects of his predecessors, and wanted, with all his might, to believe in this side of the question; he knew well that the chief took this view of the matter, so that it was a great strain upon his lately acquired Christian forbearance and meekness to expect him to stand cheerfully by and translate words which gave away what he considered to be his own just and lawful rights.

As we rose to receive the chief and his retinue, I glanced over towards the opposite shore and noticed about a dozen canoes furtively putting off, laden with fighting men, and fearing treachery called Tom's attention to this, upon which he immediately ordered the chief to make them go back, or we would sink them and prevent him returning. When he saw that we were in dead earnest he waved his hand, pointing towards the huts, upon which they all slowly retired.

Now began a long confabulation, during which we who did not know the language were obliged to content ourselves with studying the faces. Nicholas stood quietly behind me, leaning on the barrel of his loaded Winchester, a grim look upon his face, but with watchful eyes. Our chosen representative gave his message, which Tom received with a discontented air and then turned to speak to the chief, who, standing in the centre of the group, did not reply at once, but gazed on the ground with a gloomy brow. Whatever Tom was saying it did not have a conciliating effect upon the chief, from his sullen, abrupt replies.

'Is he translating fairly?' I asked the Greek, who understood the language.

'Yes,' replied Nicholas, 'word for word as he is told, but the native will not own the hens. He says they are Tom's but were under his charge, and that no "Koko" will recompense him for the disgrace brought upon his tribe.'

Another long and excited talk with the same effect and

Tom appears much troubled. 'He wants one of us to be left since he cannot get at the hunter, and gives Tom the choice, so that it is a white man.'

This was becoming momentous, the more so as chancing to look over my shoulder, I saw that while we were all engaged watching the progress of the discussion the native fighting men had taken advantage of our inattention to steal over in their canoes from the village, and now surrounded us, a dark company of armed and threatening savages.

'Look about you, Nick,' I whispered.

'I see,' he replied carelessly, without turning his head. 'Keep cool, or we are in for it.'

'Don't you think we had better let Tom settle the question his own way?' I said to our mouthpiece at this crisis.

'I suppose so,' he muttered turning away. Tom heard, and brightening up once more eagerly continued the conversation with the native. What arguments the teacher used I do not know, but we had the satisfaction before very long of observing the chief look up with a more open expression, while our circle of guards cleared farther from us, and at length, with feelings of relief, we saw the chief hold out his hand, which Tom shook as if ratifying a bargain.

'He will take tobacco for the offence,' observed Tom, turning about, 'and as the hens are mine will allow me to punish the thief my own way, only he must not come to Gilé Gilé any more or he will be cooked.'

'All's well hat ends well.' I now felt at liberty to leave the group and look about me for subjects for my pencil, so I turned about to investigate the place and take some impressions.

I strolled along the beach to where a clump of trees hid the upper portion of the gulf, and getting past these I came upon one of the women the chief had brought, the one with the baby, who was now sitting, with the child lying over her lap, on the sand.

As I paused for a moment to look at them the child moaned as if in great pain, and bending nearer to see what the matter was, I noticed an immense boil on its neck, almost ripe and at its most painful stage.

Feeling that a slight prick would give the little one instant relief, I at once sought by signs to explain to the mother that I could cure it. She regarded me listlessly while I made my pantomimic explanations, and at length, when I thought she understood my intention, I laid down my sketching materials and, producing my pocket-knife, opened the sharpest blade, and knelt down to operate.

I was just in the act of pricking the inflamed part, the mother not objecting, when I heard the voice of Nicholas, who had followed me, shouting 'Look out!' and looking up quickly, felt the imprudence of my interference and my present danger.

A tall, naked savage in the deepest mourning was rushing at me with a large trading sword-knife upraised and ready for action.

He was still about fifteen yards off when I saw him coming, and in another instant I was on my feet facing him, my left hand fumbling in the holster for my revolver. A moment more and I would have been beheaded as neatly as if I had knelt for the purpose.

As I rose the savage brought his run to a walk, and upon my taking a step towards him brought that walk to a full stop; and so we waited, watching each other in eloquent silence.

'Will I shoot him?' cried out the Greek from behind me. 'I have him covered and cannot miss.'

'No, Nick!' I replied. As yet I had never been the cause of bloodshed, and the idea of seeing that fine strong life destroyed gave me a cold chill of horror. 'I will try to manage him without that.'

I continued to walk slowly towards him as I spoke, without turning round, and as he was only watching me, he could not have been aware of his own danger, or how close to death we both were during that past moment. I felt that he had justice on his side, from his point of view, in attacking me, as he evidently thought I was about to kill his child, and that the advance in friendship ought to come from me; therefore, without pulling out my weapon, I drew close to him, watching him keenly while I approached.

As the distance decreased between us he lowered his sword, and folding his arms, waited for me; the Papuan will take an unfair advantage in war, and stab in the dark, but when brought to bay he never flinches or shows the white feather. So with my enemy now: he never swerved as I came up to him, but stood upright, with arms folded and the sword held ready for action under the left elbow.

When I drew near enough we stood face to face, looking at one another much as two dogs might do before beginning the worry. It was then that I began to feel the awkwardness of my position, for I could not speak a word of his language nor he of mine; and as for Nicholas I did not know how far he might be behind, while I dare not turn to see, as I felt the instant I took my eyes off my enemy the stroke would be made. I remembered that at this spot, not six months before, a European had had his head nearly severed from his body even in the act of trading with the natives, and this recollection did not tend to reassure me. I felt afraid—there is no use denying it—the sensation of icy creepings running up and down my backbone, as I stood and looked at his lurid eyes and ash-blackened face; but I don't think I showed the feelings which were freezing my heart

AROMA, NEW GUINEA

up, therefore I suppose this seeming indifference served me the same as true courage.

We stood in this fashion for perhaps three minutes, while I composed my face into a friendly smile and held out my right hand for him to take. No response, except a tighter clutch at his weapon and a deeper scowl; then I tapped him on the right arm to signify that I must have his hand, at which he drew out the sword and intimated that he would not give it to me.

'No, no, not the sword, but your hand,' I motioned as well as I could; of which appeal he showed an utter want of comprehension, as he once more folded his arms and gave me stare for stare.

What was I to do next in order to overcome his savage prejudice? We might continue this position for an indefinite time, and time was an object to me as I wanted to sketch. Suddenly a bright idea flashed across my mind—I would tempt him with koko; so acting on the thought, I dipped my hand into my pouch and brought out a stick of tobacco, which I held out to him, but without avail; he would not unbend, but shut up his lips like a trap and scowled more deeply. Again a moment of thought, while almost unconsciously I brought out my own pipe and began to cut up some tobacco with the open blade of the knife with which I had been about to perform my unfortunate surgical operation, and which I still held in my hand.

I managed to fill my pipe, when the appalling thought flashed upon me, how I was to get it lighted. Smokers all know that it is easy to cut tobacco and stuff it into the bowl of your pipe without withdrawing your eyes from an object; but to take out a match, strike a light and apply it to your pipe, with a wind blowing, without shifting your eyes is an utter impossibility—at least I have never been able to do it.

I dare not put my pipe back unsmoked, for that would show that I was afraid to light it. I dare not take my glance from him to light it, as that would give him the opportunity he was waiting for, to strike; and I could not linger much longer without doing something, for the suspense was becoming insupportable.

At this moment I felt a slight touch at my elbow, and with a swift side glance saw a decrepit old native who had stolen up beside us, and who, seeing me filling my pipe, now held out his own to be similarly treated. I welcomed the interruption like a message of salvation, and taking the pipe from him, began to cut and fill.

I suppose while I was facing my enemy some of the other natives had gathered round, now that truce was concluded with the chief, for before I had supplied the old man three or four pipes were pushed under my nose, all requiring replenishing badly, and held out by brown paws. I could not look at the owners, but spent the next few minutes busily cutting and filling, watching keenly the expression of the face opposite me while I did so.

Gradually, as pipe after pipe was handed back, I saw a shade of regret gather and deepen upon his countenance, while the frown became less ferocious, and I felt that patience would yet win the victory.

Suddenly, before he was aware of my intention, I dipped my hand into the pocket of a net bag which he carried suspended to his waist-cord, and where I knew, if he had a pipe, he would carry it, and without any objection from him beyond a slight gawky shrinking, I found the object of my search and fished out about the rudest and most dilapidated specimen of a native imitation of our pipes that I ever beheld; it was like the rest, empty, and holding it up I made a sign that I would fill it for him.

At this stage a most sheepish look settled upon that

ash-obscured visage, with the faintest shadow of a grin of unbending, at which I felt almost easy. I filled it and tried if it would draw, but finding that it would not I replaced it, and remembering that I had a spare briar-wood in my pocket I produced that, charged it and stuffed it into his mouth before he could object. Not much need for apprehension now—he was unmistakably grinning at his prize.

The old man at my side here made a motion that he wanted me to strike a match and light up all round, upon which I took out my box and again looked towards my enemy. He nodded vehemently to show that he wanted me to light up, upon which I pointed to where the wind was blowing, and signalled for him to hold up his hands together as a shelter. My ruse took splendidly, for up went both his hands as I had directed, and down dropped his sword at my feet, so taking a casual step forward I put my foot, as if by accident, upon the sword-blade, and for the first time I felt safe.

After a few trials, first standing, next both kneeling on the sands face to face, with my knee pressing that dreaded weapon down, while the other natives closed round to keep the wind from us, our pipes were all alight, and then I could afford to breathe.

The danger was over and we were all sitting together, I upon the sword, while my former enemy, now my friend, squatted beside me, an unwashed blackened arm round my neck (for mourners do not indulge in bathing), and the other lovingly patting me on the knee. One of the natives brought my pencil and sketch-book to me, and I began my task with an appreciative and admiring audience surrounding me, passing wondering remarks and exclamations as I proceeded, and pointing from the landscape before us to my pencil notes, with evident signs of recognition.

My guardian angel, Nicholas, stood close by, with his Winchester slung carelessly over his arm and rather a disappointed look on his sunburnt features, as if he was a little sorry that the adventure had ended so tamely. I was not, nor did I attempt any more surgical experiments at Gilé-Gilé.

CHAPTER XLVII

NEW GUINEA

The Return Journey—Teste Island and Mr. Kessick—Surrounding Islands—Lakatoes and South Cape.

I HAVE not taken the reader through the country exactly as I travelled along it myself, preferring to scamper over it quickly, as I like to go over picture galleries, and then return more slowly, lingering over the bits which strike me most.

After leaving East Cape and Milne Gulf, we directed our course to Teste Island, which lies in a south-easterly direction from Samarai or Dinner Island, and about forty miles from the mainland.

Teste Island lies in the centre of a group of islands very singular in their formation, Bell, Cliffy, Boat, and West Islands, all within a mile or two of each other.

Our pilot Nicholas, if he had few virtues to recommend him to the kindly notice of Exeter Hall, at least was thoroughly acquainted with the work which he had taken in hand; he knew the coral reefs as a London cabman knows the streets, and could steer his way as adroitly and as closely to danger, with a bold and steady eye and hand.

Inside the Barrier Reef, from Moresby to the village of Aroma, all is quiet and restful, and much pleasanter to sail or steam along than the stormy waters of the Gulf beyond, if you chance to have a very experienced pilot to guide you; otherwise, I do not know of any more dangerous or uncertain passage. It is as yet very imperfectly charted out, and is filled with coral reefs, or as the sailors term them 'Hummocks,' which jut up to within a foot of the surface, with fathomless intersections, as narrow as lanes, twisting about and terminating in some cases in the most unexpected manner, so that often a vessel has to back out and try another lead.

Where the water is clear, and by day, these threadlike twistings may be easily observed from the deck for many yards in front, the coral, various shades of green, the deep portions intense purple, while fish of every shape and hue dart about over the emerald beds; but as we are continually passing the openings of land streams which wash down the alluvial soil and stir up the sand bars, then the difficulty and dangers are imminent, and the pilot has to be implicitly trusted.

When I passed along this coast, it was at the time that a furious gale was raging outside, so we were either forced to stay at anchor, or risk inside the reefs. Time being an object, we resolved to push on, and feel our way as best we could; twice we stuck fast on sandbanks, both times, fortunately, at low tide, so that a few hours of waiting were our only troubles; four times we tried to get outside, where we thought we saw openings in the surf, but had to 'back' from that awful and thunderous din of waves breaking against the outer wall, not before we could see the white-green sharp teeth waiting to crush us to pieces, while the pillars of snowy froth rose above our masts. It was an appalling moment before the reversing of the propeller conquered the wash, which was sucking us towards that cruel wall, and we watched with bated breath to see which would be master, the sea or our engines.

Then we gave that outside passage up, and trusted to the skill of our pilot.

A hard time he had of it, till we reached Aroma, clinging to the little masthead with bare feet and hand, and waving his orders, with his disengaged arm, to the man at the wheel, while the old skipper sat down helplessly on deck, and bemoaned the open, if rough, sea. 'Give me plenty of searoom, and none of your rat-trap steering,' he grumbled away, while the pilot clung to his perch aloft, and the little steamer picked her steps gingerly along, turning about after the fashion of a cab in a crowded street, while daylight lasted, to come to anchor for the night, and be at it again by dawn. At times some friendly canoes put off from the villages and guided us to them if we wished to visit. Thus we passed along, in sight of scenery the most magnificent in the world, and with aërial effects delicious to the artist, until we reached Aroma, and saw a decided opening, after which the captain took the wheel and dashed out to his favourite element; while we of the tender digestions lay down on our backs and resigned ourselves to the inevitable.

Our captain and Nicholas waged a perpetual war with one another. Not that Nicholas was aggressive, for he behaved in the meekest and most lamblike way, always ready to give up his authority and stand aside whenever the captain insisted upon it, which he did nearly once an hour. It used to make me laugh to see the gentleness with which Nicholas stood aside when ordered to do so, while the captain, in a blind fury, snatched at the wheel and attempted to get out of that coral trap and, sailorlike, make for the open ocean. At such moments Nicholas would fold his arms and lean against the taffrail, with a placid smile upon his thin lips and a sinister gleam in his snaky black eyes. I always knew what would be the result of that resumption of authority, and the conclusion of the struggle for it.

'Breakers ahead!' yelled the man on the look-out, then an ominous crunching at the bows, and the wild cry of the old skipper to the engineers of 'Back her, back her;' after which he would once more give up the post of honour to the wily Greek, and sinking down tailor-fashion on the deck, clutch frantically at his iron-grey curls, moaning at his own impotency.

'Take it, and be ——, you —— pirate! Oh; this —— rat-trap.'

From Samarai to Teste Island required very careful steering, as the sea was fringed with hummocks and reefs; yet Nicholas knew his ground thoroughly, and dashed along at full speed all through the afternoon, shaving gleaming teeth-like edges almost every few minutes, and raising our hair at the dangers we were just missing by an inch or so. When night fell he did not pause, but went on at the same rate, while we leaned over the sides and watched, by the light of the crescent moon and the phosphorescence, the jet-black lanes of deep water, with the silvery gleaming of the wave-covered coral banks on every side of us, the wheel constantly revolving under his strong active wrist, while his dark eyes glared out from the frowning brows like coals of fire.

We run right under the beetling rocks of Cliffy Island, which seem to topple over us like an iceberg about to fall upon us, then over the short stretch of water, and we are anchored at Teste Island.

We are welcomed for the night by Mr. Kessick, one of the most gentlemanly of traders, who lives amongst the natives more like a father or missionary than as a master. The young men of the village sleep at his stores, and obey him with affection, while he also acts as doctor and adviser to the tribes.

The natives all round this quarter have been considered

CATAMARANS AND LAKATOIS

as most savage, treacherous, and remorseless; so that the conversion which Mr. Kessick, with the help of the native teacher, has wrought, is the more to be admired.

Traders amongst savages, although, as a matter of course, they must all be brave and fearless men, are not expected to be particularly refined in their manners or artistic in their tastes, therefore it surprised me all the more to find a modest, refined gentleman, in the true sense of the word, in this Teste Island collector of copra and *bêche-de-mer*, and to see his bungalow ornamented more like a studio than a trader's cabin: native war and fishing implements artistically arranged round the walls, with photographs and woodcuts placed between the trophies. We lay that night on the bamboo beds, while the young natives slept on the floor of the outhouse, lying about in all positions. I think there must have been over sixty of them, of all ages, from four years to twenty, inside that apartment, when we held the candle over the naked bodies and abandoned limbs of these beautifully modelled sleepers. I don't think I ever looked upon a more perfect sight, or one which could have given me a greater respect for their protector, for it showed the utter confidence which the fathers and mothers had in him to trust their children so completely to his charge.

I did not sleep much, for the mosquitoes were very troublesome, and the night oppressively hot, so that I heard Mr. Kessick rise and go out several times—twice to see if the watchers were at their posts, for a raid from the mainland was not an uncommon thing; the other times he went out to give medicine to some of the natives, who were sick with fever. He did all this quietly, without disturbing us, and as a matter of nightly duty.

Next morning I went round the island and made sketches of the surrounding islands and the native village.

Outside Mr. Kessick's bungalow grew a gigantic tamarind

tree, with great limbs and shoots spreading out, and with corrugated trunk. It was used as a shelter for the natives, and was big enough to cover, with its spreading branches and thick leaves, hundreds of them as they sat under it, only a few yards from where the water lapped over the fragments of snowy coral and curiously shaped and varied tinted shells. Inland the soil was very fertile, as all the islands are, and as the native gardens showed.

To the artist, a New Guinea garden is a real treat, but to the lover of method and order a woeful disappointment; a slight scratch of the virgin soil and the dropping in of the seed or shoot comprises the native system upon which the ancient craft is carried out, so that it is from a perfect wilderness of *débris* of palm fronds and banana leaves, left as they wither and drop, that the living vegetation rises. A little space is slightly cleared off, but left in delightful confusion, where the taro or yam is planted, where the mammy apple, or Papuan fruit-tree, spreads out its bulky leaves and massive globes, or the cocoanut, betel palm, or banana waves and drips; up to the knees you wade amongst the dry or drying fronds, used for thatching purposes, or into muddy holes, without warning except for the rich, long, green grasses, or moist sago groves.

Each tree in these gardens has its owner, and is tapu to all others. The family allotments are surrounded by high palisades of twigs, and divided by long, narrow lanes, down which you follow your nude but friendly guide, seeing the luxuriance inside without daring to touch, as the New Guinea owner is conservative in the extreme, and believes thoroughly in the rights of property.

Bell Rock, which lies about five miles distant, is, like Cliffy Island, a most remarkable volcanic formation. It rises like a great bell from the deep waters three or four hundred feet into the air, with upright pillars, steppes, and cavities, while the ledges and tops are covered with foliage. Cliffy Island overhangs very much on one side, while on the other it slopes abruptly down to the water's edge, showing bare cliffs riddled with great caves, inside which countless multitudes of sea birds make their homes and breed undisturbed. Boat Island lies like the great mastless hulk of some war-frigate, with rounded, protruding bow and lofty stern. West Island is grass-covered, with the exception of two solitary trees which stand on the shore side.

Teste Island is about four miles in length, with three high cones in the centre, and slopes gradually down to the sea; it is thickly wooded near the coast and grass-covered on the heights. The native village is a very interesting sight, with the cocoanut trees growing between the houses, and large canoes floating in the cove.

I have given here a group of the ordinary fishing and trading craft of New Guinea, the lakatoes, or larger trading vessels, with thin, swallow-winged sails (generally three in number), being reserved for the longer voyages which the natives take annually to barter their season's stock and lay in provisions for the wet season.

An exciting time it is when the huge village ship takes its departure on the momentous cruise, which means, to those left behind, comfort, wealth, or dreary desolation, as the return is successful or otherwise. The lakatoe, which is the general property of the village, is a vessel measuring fifty, sixty, or a hundred feet, and capable of bearing all the fighting-men of the tribe, who set forth on each of these expeditions armed and prepared to fight to the death for their venture.

They embark about the middle of the dry monsoon with the produce of the year, which they take westward to trade for the sago and rice that they may require. Then there are great preparations, with solemn meetings of the spirit-men to prognosticate their luck; for although the natives of this land are about the least credulous of savages, without veneration or religious tendencies, and ready to mock at the tales the missionary relates, they will not venture out on an important expedition without first consulting the oracles, or spirit-mediums, as to how they are likely to succeed. They hold a solemn conclave and feast, to which some of the seers come, wearing uncouth wooden masks, and crying as if under control; these they believe to be the voices of departed souls telling them what to expect. They have no respect for the masks behind which the medium speaks, as they get them up themselves, and are always willing to sell them for a few sticks of 'koko' (tobacco), which demonstrates that they are not idolaters; they have no form of actual worship, and seem without speculation as to a future, yet they prove their belief in an after-life by the attention that they pay to the spirit-voices.

The bode being favourable, they sail away in their skull- and shell-decorated ships, attended a few miles on the way by the lesser craft, such as are here seen crowding together; then there are wild farewells from the wives, mothers, and old men, who return to wait with anxious hearts for the coming home, while they dash gallantly round the headlands to face the dangers of enemies and the perils of shipwreck, as they steer towards those distant fields.

By-and-by, if all goes well, they return with the wet monsoon—return to gladden the hearts and anxious eyes of those who wait. Then there is feasting and dancing, with new raumas for the young girls, and husbands for those who are ready to wed; but if it is a failure, through disaster or war, then the plumbago is lavishly used, and the women sit with tattered skirts, and mourn the loss of those left behind, and the famine which overhangs their future. Then the girls crouch in gloomy silence or bitterly moan in the darkened chambers, while the young braves shoulder their man-traps and skulk into the woods to watch for the unwary wanderer, and the taro and yams are neglected for the more awful gorges of human flesh—blackening their fame with the notoriety over which we shudder, as we read about the cannibals of New Guinea.

It was upon a calm Sunday forenoon that we reached South Cape, where the mission station founded by the Rev. James Chalmers is situated—a scene of perfect peace and content, with the gong sounding for church, and the many-tinted garments of the natives, who were appearing and disappearing between the trees and scrub, on their way to church. Of course it is only on high days and holidays that these striking-looking garments are put on, and as the haberdashery stock is limited, they take them by turn, and the sermon by instalments, which accounted for our seeing about two-thirds of the natives sitting around, in a state of nudity, outside the church, when we got ashore. They were waiting until their friends inside had enough of it, so that they might also be able to dress and have their share.

The native is not very devout as a rule, but he has an inquiring mind, and likes to try experiments with the new faith and the unaccustomed costume. He is also very industrious, as we saw by the indications, while passing along, of terraces and gardens leading right to the summits of the lofty and abruptly-rising hills. The natives here are comparatively peaceful now to what they were on the arrival of the first missionary, and are becoming used to the sight of white faces and the *advantages* of civilisation.

The romantic aspect of South Cape recompenses us for the more Australian appearance of the hills farther west. Here we begin to find rocky cliffs and overhanging leafage, which dips and repeats itself in the calm waters, ever increasing in loveliness as we sail farther towards the east.

CHAPTER XLVIII

MISSIONARIES AND TRADERS

The Rev. James Chalmers and his Work—Samarai—Jerry's Swim—Kerepuna—Dressed and Undressed Savages—Currie, Guise, and the *Pall Mall Gazette.*

THE Rev. James Chalmers, who was absent from New Guinea while I was there, but whom I met in London and compared notes with, is one of the most enterprising and fearless of explorers. With the exception of Samuel Macfarlane, LL.D., who was the missionary pioneer of this land, no white man is more respected and loved by the natives of New Guinea. He has a great liking for, and trust in, the natural honesty and goodness of the savage, and thinks no more of setting out upon a long expedition to unknown districts with only his pipe and stock of tobacco, than another man would of taking a morning stroll. He carries no firearms or weapons, and trusts entirely to Providence for his provisions; so he has succeeded where more cautious or timid men would have failed, and his name as your friend is enough to ensure safety almost all over the land.

'Tamate,' as they call him, does not attempt the impossible or seek to revolutionise them too suddenly. He goes amongst them, laughs, and amuses them, establishes a station, lives with them for some time until he has won their confidence, and then leaves amongst them native teachers to finish what he has begun. Personally, I think he has the fewest prejudices and the least bigotry of any missionary that I have ever met anywhere, and if the matter rested with him to decide, he would gladly welcome and extend the right hand of fellowship to any missionary who came to civilise the natives, no matter to what sect he might belong, Roman Catholic or Protestant. He is bigoted only upon one point, in which I also join entirely with him—to protect strictly the claims, rights, and persons of the natives.

It was at South Cape he had the affliction to lose his brave and noble partner, Mrs. Chalmers, and here they had some of their hardest and most dangerous experiences before they overcame, by kindness and patience, the animosity of the savages.

South Cape is a perfect garden of loveliness, with all the islands lying closely about, like the islands and headlands of one of our Scottish lakes, the lofty peaks of the North Foreland rearing above the trees 1,800 feet, and dotted all over with the terraces and gardens of the natives. Palm, Stacy, Heath, and Samarai, or Dinner Islands, cluster closely together, and open one on to the other, almost like the bends of a wide river.

Yet, although beautiful, there are dangerous episodes often occurring in these straits, for atrocious murders by natives are by no means a thing of the past. On Heath Island we passed the empty house of a trader who had been killed about six months previous to our coming. In fact, as we sail along close to the land, it is necessary to take watch and watch about each night, so that we may not be surprised, and so share the fate of many of our predecessors.

Samarai is a delicious island, which has been made even more perfect by cultivation. The missionaries have

BELL AND CLIFFY ISLANDS, NEW GUINEA

planted a fine palm-tree avenue along the sands, through which you may walk in deep shadow to the station, with the feathery fronds of the cocoanut and betel trees waving and meeting high above your head.

The night we reached Samarai I went through this palm grove with one of the traders there, a Russian, to see some birds of Paradise and curios which he had preserved. The night was hot, and as we had to wade ashore from our dinghy we wore only our pyjamas and went barefoot— a silent march over the loose sand in the inky darkness, with now and again a soft satiny body touching us, as a naked native glided past. No words were spoken; we could feel a light, warm breath on our faces, and, as we put out our hands, the smooth skin.

Inside the store-room we found the single men and male children all lying about asleep, as at Teste Island, with arms and legs tossed over one another as they had flung themselves down — here a stalwart young man crushing full weight upon the tender limbs of a little boy who did not appear to be disturbed by the load, or, in another place, one little fellow making a pillow of another's breast or stomach.

The box where the trader kept his birds was at the other end of the apartment, and it astonished me to see the careless way in which he walked over these nude sleepers. Planting his foot on a head, or a body, or limb, he calmly strode upon them without considering his steps in the least, or disturbing them much. The sleeper merely gave a grunt when the weight was removed, and half turned himself, but without waking up. It was the most Spartan and apathetic exhibition I had ever witnessed.

That night, when we got back to the ship and were having a smoke with the trader, after settling for our purchases, we were startled by the apparition of a dripping wet, wild-looking little object, who had scrambled up the sides of the steamer, and appeared before us with only a red rag tied round his waist.

It was one of the trader's mates, a very tiny man, half Mexican, half Frenchman, who had lived so long with savages that it was hard to decide what he was, his skin was so thoroughly baked from exposure to the sun. He had swum from the island, a distance of about two and a half miles, past the reefs, through water infested with sharks, and had come to purchase from us a rifle, disdaining the aid of any of the canoes, several of which were then lying alongside of us, with the natives aboard.

'How the devil did you come, Jerry?' asked Nicholas, who knew the little man well.

'By de water, of course; you didn't tink I could fly, did you?'

'But the sharks?' I asked.

'De shark be good—God-dam,' answered the little man contemptuously, as he shook the water out of his long, matted hair.

We showed him some of our new rifles and Winchesters, and after we had bargained as to price, he dived his dirty paw into his soaking waistband and produced what had been a roll of bank notes when he left shore, but was now a handful of soft pulp, perfectly useless to any one, as he squashed them up in his fist, and flung them with an oath from him against the cabin panels, where they stuck like a pat of clay.

'Dere goes eighty pounds,' he shouted, with a wild laugh. 'Gi' me the gun on tick till to-morrow morning.'

We handed him the gun, and he prepared to go off with it as he had come, fish-fashion, when Nicholas caught him by the nape of the neck, saying gruffly :

'No Jerry, my boy, you don't wet that 'ere gun until you have paid for it,' and lifting him clean up, as one might do a kitten, pitched him carelessly into one of the canoes.

A couple of yells followed his descent, one from the startled native, who had been sitting dozing inside when the butt end of the rifle struck him, and one from Jerry, as he landed across a paddle on the small of his back.

'Oh, you ugly black Greek pirate! let me at you'—and Jerry once more scrambled up the sides, on vengeance bent, to be met, as his head appeared, with an open-handed smack from Nicholas, which landed him once more in the bottom of the canoe, where he lay perfectly quiet. The native paddled him ashore, while our pilot rejoined us sedately and as if nothing out of the ordinary had occurred to disturb his equanimity.

After leaving South Cape we sail along the coast towards Kerepuna, passing Arangoni Bay, Mayri, Table, Baxter and Cloudy Bays, with the Owen Stanley Ranges for ever on our right—Mount Thompson 6,900 feet high, Mount Simpson 9,972, Suckling 11,228, and the other peaks ranging from 7,000, to Mount Owen Stanley 13,205 feet above the sea, majestic mountains with rugged, upstanding peaks floating softly blue amongst and about the snowy clouds, with bold, lofty hills between, and great yawning valleys, and fearful precipices over which glittering waterfalls pour like silvery threads in the distance.

Then, after getting past the native towns of Dedele and Domara, we get into the districts of Aroma and Loyatupu, and come to Hood Lagoon and the great town of Kerepuna.

Kerepuna may well be called the capital of New Guinea, or rather of that portion under the English protection, in comparison with the other towns, such as Hula, Aroma, &c. It is a city, having streets and lanes where the houses face one another, with their broad platforms in front and a vast confusion of piles and posts all about.

Although built upon the shore, it is above high-water mark, and from the sea the backs of the houses only are to be seen, with the rows of canoes and mat-protected lakatoes. Inland, the streets lead to the gardens, where all who are able work from sunrise to sunset two days out of every three, it being the custom to have two rest-days every six, on which they lounge about and receive or pay visits to the other friendly tribes. On these rest-days the town presents a very animated appearance, with shell-adorned warriors practising their spear-throwing, or women chattering and laughing merrily; while others who follow the sea, ply their trading vessels or lakatoes about the translucent waters.

On working-days the sick or mourners only are to be seen about the streets, with the occasional pet pig or dog sniffing about the palm-leaf covered and highly flavoured remains of some departed relative. Yet the Tapu-house and its tall spire always looks festive with the many fluttering streamers fringing its sides. The people of Kerepuna are magnificent specimens of savage health, strength, and beauty. Indeed, I have never seen any human beings as tall as one or two that I saw here, the chieftain particularly, who was a perfect giant in stature, with very light, copper-coloured skin, and splendidly proportioned. I saw also here one of the native men with a complexion as fair as any European, which I believe is not an uncommon sight amongst the Papuans; his appearance struck me as very disagreeable amongst his more richly-toned companions: he looked so *naked* and out of place, whereas the brown skins never gave one this impression of nudity. A native dressed is a native spoilt, as I afterwards realised at Hula, where Kama held his court in florid-coloured pyjamas and bandana hat. After all, it is only we Europeans with our colourless, glaring skin who cannot afford to go without covering.

Some time ago in the pages of the *Pall Mall Gazette* were published some articles on New Guinea, in which the names of two Europeans, Guise and Currie, were mentioned as having, by their immorality, rendered themselves obnoxious to the natives of Hula. I am happy to say that I am in a position to state that these *Pall Mall Gazette* charges are utterly unfounded, so far as the natives of Hula are concerned.

It seems a pity, when sweeping charges of this description are made, and the victims are too far away to contradict them and prove their falseness, while by mentioning the names the friends at home are made to writhe impotently, that there is not a more careful investigation made than appears to have been made in the present case.

Messrs. Guise and Currie, a few years ago, went over to New Guinea from Australia, prompted partly by an English spirit of adventure, and partly by the hope of making themselves useful to Government. Failing in the latter hope, of getting employment, they settled down in Hula, the only Englishmen not connected with the mission society who had ventured to take up their residence with the natives. That they may have aroused the jealousy of the missionaries by daring to settle down, as it were, upon their preserves without asking and obtaining their permission, I will allow; and that the representatives of Government were biassed enough to regard with suspicion their staying, without apparent occupation or purpose, in this uncivilised portion of the globe, I will also admit; but that the natives of Hula objected to their presence, as stated, I must emphatically contradict, as I must also the gross charges made against these two gentlemen, of being the cause of immorality and dissatisfaction amongst the natives.

Before Messrs. Guise and Currie took up their abode at Hula, the mission officials at Moresby had left on the ground one of their South Sea Island teachers, with one Kama as his assistant. Kama hitherto had been considered a convert amongst the natives of New Guinea. A native of Hula, they educated him at Moresby, and when they considered him sufficiently prepared, sent him down with the islander to see what he could do amongst his own people.

The Papuan differs very greatly from the more impressionable South Sea Islander in his credence in the spiritual; he is open to conviction on things material, but having no religious tendencies, or credulity in tenets which he cannot test, will only listen so long as the things taught are a novelty, and openly derides them when they cease to amuse. This is the secret of the non-success of the missionary in making many real converts of the natives of New Guinea. With an idolater it becomes easy work to transform him into a Christian, as the soil is so far already prepared; and that he may be devout and sacrificing in his new faith stands to reason, considering the utter, unquestioning belief he had in the old creed. But the Papuan is a materialist in the strictest sense of the word and, beyond a little coquetting with spirit-mediums at odd times, as much out of sport as for instruction, laughs openly at all forms or indefinite promises.

Kama had learnt to sing hymns and to read the Motu Testament, but the payment he was to receive as assistant teacher was the chief motive of his acceptance of the post, and very shortly, finding that it was not what he expected, he threw off the mask of religion, and bringing the vices which he had learnt, along with the hymns, home to his simpler relatives, gave to Hula the name for immorality which it at present bears, and which has been put to the account of the two plucky young Englishmen, Guise and Currie.

That Kama has brought this disgrace upon his kinsmen may be proved by the fact that he was discharged for dishonesty and immorality, although I could see no mention of this missionary convert in the account given in the pages of the *Pall Mall*; and as he still lives at Hula, plying his evil trade, although no longer in the employment of the missionary, I had ample chances of investigation while I was there. Hula is the only village in New Guinea against which any charge of immorality can be laid. It is not bad, in comparison with other places in the South Seas or in more civilised portions of the globe, but for New Guinea I do admit that it is; yet Kama I hold to be the sole cause, not Messrs. Guise and Currie.

When I was in Hula I mentioned the two names supposed to be obnoxious, and was warmly received in consequence by the natives; they asked me eagerly if Guise and Currie were not coming back. 'They were very good, and we liked them much,' the natives all said.

When the Government representatives banished the young men from the land, they could not possibly have then laid the charge that their presence was obnoxious to the natives, as they were forced to use stratagem to get them away from the tribe without being themselves molested, and the two gentlemen went of their own accord, otherwise the war-sloop would not have ventured to drag them from their allies. Also, if they had been unwelcome to the natives, Government would not have been troubled in the matter except to avenge their murder, as the natives generally kill and cook first, and complain afterwards; but the fact that the young men were permitted to stay for two years amongst the tribes, is the strongest evidence that they were welcome guests, without the additional evidence which my own experience enables me to render to the good names of these two plucky young Englishmen who have been so grossly maligned.

Mr. Guise told me a good story about Currie, which shows the mettle of the man. When they first settled amongst the natives, they were viewed with much suspicion, and several attempts were made to kill them, which, happily, they turned aside without damage to themselves or bloodshed.

On one occasion the natives came *en masse*, with their spears and weapons, to attack the strangers. Currie, looking out, saw them coming along the sands, and without waiting to pick up anything to defend himself, or even his hat, rushed out to meet them bareheaded, and putting down his head like a goat, ran it right against the stomach of the chief, bowling him and a couple of those behind him over with the one blow. Whether it was this unusual mode of fighting or the face of Guise, who stood laughing at the door of their hut, which impressed the natives most, he could not say, but they made no more attempts at violence, and heartily joined in the laugh and made friends. The Papuan has a keen sense of humour, and enjoys a practical joke hugely, as I have found out often in my intercourse with him.

Guise I met at Yorke Island, where he was waiting for his time of banishment to be past. Poor Currie had gone to Japan in search of adventure, and there met his doom in the shape of the poisoned blowpipe. The news of his death came home about a month after this calumny had been published in the *Pall Mall*.

As for Kama, the renegade Christian Papuan, when I mentioned his notorious name to my friend Mr. Chalmers, he quite agreed with me that he was the very worst man in New Guinea, and that no crime was too vile for him to commit.

HOUSES AND HUTS, NEW GUINEA

CHAPTER XLIX

KEREPUNA

A Big Man—Mourners—Hula—Coast Scenery—Port Moresby Elevara and Hanuabada.

When I landed at Kerepuna, the big man who stood leaning on the huge branch of a cotton tree, lazily watching the coming ashore of the strangers, waited until I had come close to him, and then, with a good-natured smile upon his good-looking but massive features, took me up by catching hold of my waist-belt, and, hoisting me upon his broad shoulder, strolled off leisurely to his own part of the town, followed by a crowd of laughing natives, male and female, and giving me almost a bird's-eye view of the surrounding landscape.

He was playing a merry joke for the benefit of his people, and they appreciated seeing the white man perched like an ape upon the shoulders of their great chief. But he did not intend any harm; for after parading me through all the streets, he deposited me very tenderly on the platform of the tapu house, and patted me gently and encouragingly on the back, as I straightway pulled out my sketch-book and began to draw the *city*.

Kerepuna is divided into five tribes and villages, each tribe having its own tapu house, or great meeting-place. The spires of these tapu houses shoot high over the house-tops, with ribbons of grass and palm fronds waving from them.

While I was sketching at a corner of one of the streets, I saw a man come along curiously adorned. His body had been blackened with plumbago and ashes, which was the native sign of mourning, and round his neck and waist were hung the entire bones of a human body, skull and all complete, with pieces of the decayed flesh still adhering to them. On one side swung a female rauma, or petticoat, and altogether he was heavily laden.

As he came nearer to me, with the wind blowing from him, the aroma could only be compared to that of a dissecting-room during the very hot weather, when most of the students are away on their holidays, and only a few enthusiastic ones left to take care of the long-kept 'subjects.'

It was very appalling, and made me for a moment cling to the posts of the platform behind me, while I gasped for breath; then, motioning him to go to leeward, I recovered myself in time to prevent a faint.

He was a widower, and the relics which he carried were all that remained of his deceased spouse, over whose loss he was at present mourning. According to custom he had watched beside her grave while she decomposed, picking out the bones as they loosened from their ligaments, and making a necklace and waistband of them. He had not washed since she passed away, anointing himself instead with the putrefying flesh, as it became 'resolved,' according to the immortal bard, 'into dew.'

'What love,' I thought, as I regarded him, 'this man must have had for his wife to be able to endure this kind of mourning!'

Then he became friendly, and, as all Papuans do when they like a man, wanted to embrace me. For a time I dodged him as politely as I could, for I did not wish to hurt his already wounded affections. But as he became more demonstrative in his attentions, I incontinently fled up one street and down another, with the afflicted one after me, and all the bones of his wife rattling along with him. I rushed in an easterly direction, for the wind was coming from the east.

These burial customs are the one and only objectionable ceremony amongst the Papuans, for cannibalism is merely a matter of education, like the vegetarianism of the Buddhists, or our half-way habits of beef-eating, and therefore should not be regarded as objectionable excepting to anti-flesh-devourers.

At another place I passed a low covering of palm-leaves erected to shade the three widows of one chief, who had died about six months before. His body, or what remained of it, lay underneath them, with only a plank or two between them and it, and they had not stirred from the spot since it was buried, nor would they until he was thoroughly decomposed. The tribe brought cooked yams to them once a day. I believe, in a case like this, they tossed up as to who was to possess the skull when it was ready for lifting, dividing equally the other bones as they could get them, meantime smearing one another with the awful moisture of mortality as it *thawed*. I observed, however much their sorrow may have been, that they were not too greatly engrossed to notice me, for as I passed three blackened arms and hands were pushed out from the sides, with an action about the moving fingers unmistakable to one who has experienced the crook of a waiter's expectant fingers. I placed a stick of tobacco in each bereaved paw, and passed on my way.

There was one comely youth, of about sixteen years of age, who kept closely by my side all the day, with the most perfect face and figure I ever looked upon. The limbs were slender, but beautifully rounded, with long graceful lines, and he had a magnificent head of hair, carefully tended. They told me that he was a great scoundrel, and he was handsome enough for anything. I cannot say much of the women of New Guinea, because they were all very shy, except at Moresby and Hula, so that I had not much opportunity of observing them very closely. Those I did see were all little women, but well made when young, with small feet and hands, and pleasant laughing faces. At Hula I did see some bouncing and rather forward hussies, but these were the pupils of Kama, and were not to be taken as samples of the women of the nation, who, as a rule, smile when a stranger approaches, and afterwards run away like startled fawns.

Hula lies about twenty miles from Kerepuna, and is built, like Tapusuli, in the sea, a mile or thereabouts from the shore, raised on high piles. The people occupy themselves fishing and begging 'koko,' from the traders and man-of-war sloops. They have been somewhat spoilt by their free intercourse with the Europeans, and are by far the most mendacious we met.

Indeed, it is extremely difficult to drive a bargain for curios along the coast where H.M. sloops have gone. The people are surfeited with tobacco and the decided advantages which they enjoy under our protection, while the slight meed of justice doled out to them for their many massacres has given them the idea that we are not men, but women in disguise; they say they have no longer any cause to fear the white fellow, as he does not revenge his wrongs, so they have learnt to despise us, and, I hear, have raised a native song, which they now sing, having the chorus of—

> Poor white fellow is a woman, not a man,
> Very good to eat, but no good at fighting.

This ditty is now chanted throughout the land, and what the 'Marseillaise' did for France during the Reign of Terror it seems to be doing here—directly tending to place the lives of Europeans at the mercy of savages who perpetrate their atrocities under the protection of a foreign Government.

The houses are raised on higher piles than at Moresby, and placed farther out to sea. Like the gondolas in the waterways of Venice, the canoes, catamarans and lakatoes are constantly on the move, and although the distant reef breaks the full force of the water outside, there is always a sense of motion, light and life, here. The coast-line is flat, and densely wooded with crotons, mangroves, and fruit-trees, with distant ranges of mountains to be seen when ships approach.

Kama, whom we met here, is, in spite of his black-guardism, a very merry dog, who will take his well-thumbed hymn-book, and sing hymns which he learnt at Port Moresby with a comic drawl and upturned eyes, while he cheats the visitor at trade. His history has yet to be written, and also his final doom when his simple-minded countrymen find him thoroughly out; he is very artful, and, as yet, has managed to hoodwink them completely. He is also very adroit, for when, after a few dark hints and suggestions, he gathered that we were after curios and legitimate trade only, he became preternaturally upright and moral in his conversation, driving away the bevy of fair girls from his doorway with a great display of sternness. It was only through Nicholas that we gathered the full extent of his depravity, Nicholas being our pilot and guide in more ways than through the coral hummocks.

Between Pyramid Point, Bootless Bay, and Kapa-kapa, we get a very distinct view of the Astrolabe Ranges looming up in front of the more distant Owen Stanley, which can only be seen from the sea, like Adam's Peak at Ceylon, on the very rare occasions at dawn when the atmosphere is free from clouds.

A coast-line full of bays and promontories, with the ridges of cone-shaped or ruggedly indented mountains piling one above the other, and softened with the curtains of mist rolling upward from the deep hollows and valleys.

Along the shores at times we can see columns of smoke rising behind the lines of mangroves and other trees, where the natives are burning out the kangaroos; or, again, a lakatoe, with its fantastically-shaped mat-sail, skurrying westward on a trading expedition from Kerepuna or other distant villages to Moresby or Motu-motu.

These ranges are densely wooded with forest, broken up with vast precipices of sheer inaccessible rock. As yet the explorer has been unable to penetrate far, or do much of discovery, owing to the exhausting work of having to cut, through virgin undergrowth, each foot of the passage, and the difficulties in the way both natural and from the timidity or unwillingness of the inland tribes. To penetrate the interior of New Guinea successfully an expedition must be large, plentifully provided with money, leisure and provisions, for it can only be carried out by patience, perseverance and time. Thus far explorers have gone out inadequately furnished, and so have been forced to abandon their projects at the threshold.

A peaceful sight is Port Moresby at early morning, with the warm fumes of the hill-hidden sun mellowing the mist overhead, giving rosy gleams to the night clouds melting swiftly out of sight, the land breeze lulling down, and a general sense of waiting for that supreme moment when the disc of light may appear and banish rest.

Far in distance trembling ether, faintly blue and misty grey,
Filled with undulations softened, and mild lights that sunny play:
Shifting from the mid infinite, striking on the upturned sides
Of the crowding herd of cloudlets that along the blue plain rides.

In the middle distance mellow, with its purple and its brown,
Bathed in shadow broad and simple, from the darken'd flanks
    thrown down:
Forests, fields, and lanes partaking of the dreamy morning rest,
With each local tint appearing only to the eye in quest.

In the foreground, starting boldly, blades of grass and lichen cold,
Crimson dockens, snowy daisies, with their rounded breasts of
    gold—
Tangled tufts of blooming heather, thistles, buttercups, and bells,
Waft away to indistinctness middle space and further fells.

On shore, the dews lie heavy on spider-webs and croton leaves, making the grasses on the side of Mount Pullen moistly grey and the hut tops to glisten white. Two schooners are lying at anchor; the canoes are creeping out softly, some with sails set to catch the sea wind when it comes, but at present being paddled like the sailless catamarans which are carrying wares out of Basilisk Bay. I notice one canoe occupied by girls only. As they wave their hands in passing, I recognise one young lady who has been disobedient to the desire of her stern parent, and who is now being sent to a neighbouring tribe for punishment. She will not consent to marry the young man her father has chosen, but fixes her affections where her sire disapproves, so she has been banished for a time. I hope the change may do them all good.

Mount Pullen rears up behind the native township of Hanuabada, the few European cabins and the mission station where Mr. and Mrs. Lawes teach the native children to speak English and sing hymns They are very apt at some things, these children, and the stranger can hardly realise that he is in the only land on the face of the globe as yet unexplored, when he is greeted by a chorus of 'Rule Britannia,' 'Wait till the clouds roll by,' and 'Abraham,' from one of the canoes of juveniles rowing past. Next to the mission house, the store erected for the convenience of the few residents by the enterprising firm of Messrs. Burns, Philp & Co., with the house of the store-manager, Mr. Andrew Goldie, naturalist and explorer, greet us; then the shanty raised by Mr. Cuthbertson and his surveying party, and the abode of the brothers Hunter, employed as interpreters, farther on; then the little Government Bungalow, where the resident magistrate, Captain Musgrave, prolongs existence by settling the nice points of native grievances, and which is occasionally honoured by the genial presence of His Excellency the Hon. John Douglas.

This comprises the European element of Port Moresby, with the exception of an occasional trader who chances to put up, or the carpenter and assistant who are busy putting up the first house of the new city, 'Granville,' planned out eastward of Moresby. This house represents the first, and strongest point of law, a jail; as yet there are no jailors and no criminals, but these, with the steady advance of civilisation, will come in good time. The site of the new city is well chosen and ought to be healthy, being to the windward side of the native villages, by which forethought the present Governor shows his good common sense, the native burial customs more than the climate or soil being the principal cause of the present unhealthiness of Port Moresby.

A little over ten years ago, a voyage to New Guinea meant literally the taking of a man's life in his hand, and risking it. All the tribes are not cannibals, but in those days they were all murderers—that is, they tried to kill whoever landed upon their coast; in parts they killed them through

THE GARDENS OF HULA

an instinctive hatred and distrust of strangers, in other parts they killed them because they wanted their flesh to devour.

To-day a stranger may travel from the Dutch boundary on the one side to the German boundary on the other with safety, if he does not go with the intention of wronging the natives or infringing on any of their rights. Personally, I travelled over the coast between these bounderies, and without exception was, in every village where the missionaries' names were known, treated with respect and friendship.

I found that they all, whether redeemed from their evil customs or still in a savage state, liked the missionary at Motumotu or Gilé-gilé, as also in the head-quarters, Moresby. If I had space I could fill many pages describing instances of the noble devotion and self-sacrifice displayed by the coloured teachers whom I met at the different stations—great simple hearts who live a life of purity and tenderness, reflecting, every hour of the day, the noble example and instructions of their white leaders. I think on the whole I felt closer to God in the company of these South Sea Island exiles with their little Papuan huts, watching them go about their daily duties in the midst of those savage sons of Nature, than I have felt before or since; their faith was faith unvarnished and utter, their patience sublime to heroism.

Great men, noble martyrs, they go to New Guinea to lay down their lives for the cause of their Master, as their instructors have taught them by precept and practice, and the result has been wonderful considering the time.

The Papuan is a born artist; he likes to decorate himself and all that he has about him, and he has the true antique instinct for lines and colour. Hence he values the limbs which God has given him, too much to hide them under costume of any sort, and walks in the sun nude, with skin like satin (when in health), clean-cut and statuesque, and like man before his fall, in perfect unconsciousness of anything wrong in his nudity.

He does not require clothes, so he does not wear them; and singular to relate, after the strangeness of the first sight, we do not seem to notice anything odd about his lack of covering. It is all so natural, so unconcerned, that we also could almost drop into the general fashion, only for the glaring inconsistency and whiteness of our skins, which look out of place alongside those beautiful bronze statues.

But although he despises dress, he spares no pains to improve upon Nature according to his lights and tradition. His hair is frizzed, and embellished with flowers and feathers; he wears rings—finger-rings, earrings and nose-bars, armlets and necklaces, in fact decks himself up like the exquisite male birds around him, relieving the dark masses with bright touches so that there may be no sense of monotony. But in these ornaments, as in the colours with which he sometimes paints himself, there is nothing garish or discordant; the Papuan decked up and painted is a picture of unity and harmony.

The woman has her grass petticoat and her tattooed breast which looks like a tight-fitting jersey; the husband is too jealous to allow her to be as he is himself. He alone ordains to be beautiful like the male bird; she is for him only, and not to be looked upon, hence she is dressed.

I have two raumas, or petticoats, before me, the under one of two colours, dusky red and low-toned yellow, the upper one, broad grey and dun-tinted reed stripes. I never saw a gaudy colour all the time I was in New Guinea.

Out of about two-dozen carved arrows which I have, there are not two alike in the design, yet all are lovely and quaint, showing in each line the decorative translation of a natural object.

Their hair-combs and lime-spoons show the same loving, tender work over which time has not been an object. So also their pipes or bau-baus, and lime calabashes, designs worked out without knives, with bits of sharpened shells, or firebrands, infinite labour, with observation and intellect, guiding the crafty hands, producing results which I regard with great hope for their future, if their white brothers will only be content to lead them onwards.

A pleasant and picturesque place to look at is the native village of Elevara, whether you take your stand on the verandah of the Mission House, and so overlook it and the crescent-shaped bay beyond, broken only by gentle ripples, till the eye wanders to the white foam-fringes which reveal the coral reefs outside, with the dark blue line which shows the trembling waters of the tempestuous gulf, or whether you take your seat in one of the little canoes and paddle, or get paddled, a short distance from the shore, and so view it from the sea.

A picturesque spot to sketch from a distance; although like its sister village, Hanuabada, or Naples, and a number of other places of beauty, it is best seen at a little distance, and with the wind blowing from you, particularly if there happen to be many mourners about, as there are generally, and as there were at the time I visited New Guinea. At such times, to walk with impunity through the villages, I would advise travellers who are at all sensitive as to smell, to carry with them a few cloves, as medical students do. This preventive may help them along, and by chewing, take the keen edge off the perfume about.

The natives of Elevara, who are of a different tribe to, although friendly with, their neighbours, occupy themselves principally in fishing. They barter the fish to friendly tribes inland. The other coast tribe are gardeners and earthenware-pot makers. As a rule, these tribes are very industrious, the villages by day being nearly deserted, except by the old men cutting canoes, the old women making and firing their pots, the children tumbling about the sands, playing at spear-throwing, or wading through the shallow waters, and the mothers looking after their children, the young pigs and puppy dogs, nursing them all impartially and by turns.

As at Kerepuna and other places, here and there you will see some hideous-looking figures, mourners smeared with ashes and plumbago, like darky minstrels, squatting upon the plank and palm-leaf covered mounds under which decays the relative they have lost, and from which wafts the pestilent odour.

Elevara lies directly under the Port Moresby Mission Station, and nestles at the base of an abrupt rock which juts out from the shore. At low tide you can walk through it to Hanuabada and along the coast dry-footed; but at high tide, the piles upon which the houses are built lie two or three feet under water, and, with the setting sun going down behind the rock and the huts in sombre shadow, it is most impressive, a purple haze mantling the distant hills and bluffs, the foliage broad and indefinite in masses on the rock above, the canoes half submerged in the waves, and the natives housed—for they go to bed, with the birds, at sundown. There is a solemn silence and repose suitable to the glory of that golden hour. So the sun goes down, and we know that night is upon us by reason of our myriads of visitors, the lively mosquitoes.

CHAPTER L

PORT MORESBY

A Parting at Port Moresby—Mr. Lawes and Father Vergus, the French Missionary—Laws of Permit—Andrew Goldie and his Journal—A Pretty Sunday-school Story.

WE parted with our pilot Nicholas at Port Moresby. One of the traders had died there while we were east, and left his vessel; so the Governor, the Honourable John Douglas, kindly offered the Greek his choice, either to take the vessel over to Cooktown to the widow who lived there, for a certain sum, or else go as a banished man in the Government sloop to Thursday Island.

The Government had long wanted to catch the wily one on the hop, that they might proceed against him, but without success; he was too much for them always. But at last Nemesis caught him up. He had taken the fever during his last visit, and spent all his money and provisions feeding himself and his men; and so, instead of proceeding on his voyage, he had been forced to sell his vessel to Government in order to be able to pay his debts. We had come upon him at the evil moment when his fortunes were at low ebb, and now that we were done with him, he was offered these alternatives, the former of which he promptly accepted.

'What will you do when you get to Cooktown?' asked our captain before they parted.

'Marry the widow, and come back again with the vessel; it will be mine then, you know,' replied Nicholas, calmly. He accepted his bad fortune philosophically, yet planned out the future like a Napoleon, whom he somewhat resembled in features.

'But I thought you had half a dozen native wives already, Nick.'

'That don't matter. I haven't got a white one yet.'

So we parted from our worthy pilot, and saw him sail out of the harbour. He was to me a most interesting study. I also said good-bye here to General Ronald MacIvor, the hero of 'Under Thirteen Flags.' He had come over from Queensland as the guest of Mr. Douglas, and was then staying with Mr. Andrew Goldie, the naturalist, at the stores of Messrs Burns, Philp & Co., as the Bungalow was hardly large enough to entertain him. He has a commanding figure, and a keen Caledonian eye; but the foe was unworthy of his steel, for he is a man born for the thunder of war, not the slow duty of an explorer. We spent some pleasant days and nights together, the General and I, out in Port Moresby, and I found him, like Nicholas, a more than ordinarily interesting study.

I met him in London after his and my own return. One day I had gone into the International Club to wait for a friend; while sitting in the lobby I heard a manly voice, which I thought I recognised, talking about New Guinea.

The subject interested me as much as the man, so I smoked on and listened to all his adventures on that savage soil.

Presently my friend entered, and coming up, said:

'Hallo, Nisbet! Ah! MacIvor, how are you? By the way, you ought to know one another.'

The General turned about and looked at me. Any one

who is at all intimate with the General knows that he must be emphatic or nothing.

'Good God, Nisbet, is that you?'

'Yes, General.'

'Have you been long here?'

'For the last half-hour, General.'

'Then damn it, you have heard me tell what I did in New Guinea, and can vouch for its accuracy. Isn't it all true?'

'As Gospel, General!'

'Gentlemen, you hear that now, and Nisbet was there at the time. Perhaps someone present didn't believe me a few moments ago?'

The General and I shook hands warmly, as travellers who had been long parted. Good, brave warrior, may a war break out somewhere soon, that you may have a chance once again to be Generalissimo, and so be able to fulfil that old promise of yours, of appointing me on your staff as war correspondent!

I paid one visit, in as much state as my very limited wardrobe could command, to the Mission House, and Mr. and Mrs. Lawes, who were at home on my return visit to Moresby. I had only one clean shirt, and my visit to the Mission House used it up, so that I was forced to refuse an invitation to dinner at the Government Bungalow the next day; although, as genial John Douglas said when I afterwards met him at Thursday Island, that would not have mattered; still, when one goes to visit the King or his representative, one ought to be able to raise a moderately clean collar for the occasion.

Mr. Lawes is the State Missionary of New Guinea, as Mr. Chalmers is the working missionary. He and Mrs. Lawes had been for a sail round the coast when I arrived the first time, so that I did not see them then, but I had taken the liberty of using their verandah for sketching purposes, which, I trust, when they learnt, they forgave me for doing.

Mr. Lawes is a remarkably good-looking man of the Persian type. Mrs. Lawes has the appearance of an active and energetic woman, one who would not permit much sentiment to stand in the way of what she considered her rights. I fancy that I came with a little prejudice against Mr. Lawes, for I had been to Yule Island, and seen there three of the noblest and most self-sacrificing men I had ever seen in my life before, who for the cause of Christianity had been compelled to steal into the land (over which Mr. Lawes ruled supreme) like thieves, because they were Roman Catholics; and as this kind of bigotry in the nineteenth century makes me turn sick with contempt, as it also would if a Roman Catholic clergyman prevented a Protestant minister from trying to convert savages to civilisation, I was naturally disgusted at the narrow and foolish policy of this autocrat of Port Moresby.

Let me try to give, as I understand it, a fair and impartial record of the case in point. Of course I never attempt to appeal to sectarians, as no man can do such a thing and hope to come out of the argument with *éclat*. I write now for the men and women who seek to follow the teachings of Jesus Christ, as He taught them, broadly and simply, without paying any heed to the particular bias of any school.

Mr. Lawes, as the representative of the missionary society, being first on the field, made rules and regulations, which the Queensland Governor sanctioned and endorsed— that no one should be permitted to land on New Guinea soil without a special permit, which is framed somewhat after the order of a Russian permit and passport. As I had to fill up this permit and sign to the autocratic conditions,

I speak from experience. At the time I did so I had not visited the land, yet I thought that, as a free-born subject, I had never signed any conditions which gave away my freedom of action so utterly, or degraded me more in my own purity and self-respect. One of the conditions I remember, was that I was not to speak to a native woman while on New Guinea, as if females of New Guinea could not take care of themselves, or the men who visited that quarter of the globe could not behave like men. This is what I felt at the time, but when I went to the land and saw how completely the visitor was under the control of the authorities, and how much this power could be abused by those in office, then I felt for the first time in my life like a Russian serf.

Of course, all through these humiliating reflections ran the stinging thought that I had no right as a British subject to sign those conditions—that I ought to have torn up that iniquitous sheet and, after trampling upon the shreds, gone over, and as a protest, landed in spite of the prohibition of those half-dozen representatives. That is what I ought to have done as a Scotchman, and what I feel ashamed to this hour that I did not do; but then I had made myself a slave already in other quarters, so that for the year 1886 my life and the hours were not my own to waste on patriotic sentiment; and thus weakly, for the sake of peace and time, I yielded and signed the permit-sheet of foolish and tyrannical conditions. After doing so I felt as if I had drifted back to the year 1212 before John had signed the Magna Charta, and poetically I felt satisfied that it was Machiavellian if nothing else.

It appears that Father Stanislaus Vergus, of the Sacred Heart of Jesus Order, asked for a permit to go to New Guinea in order to propagate the religion of Jesus Christ amongst the natives. The Government Representative at Thursday

Island was not in any way averse to this, but the Rev. Mr. Lawes, as the authorised representative of the religion of Jesus Christ on benighted New Guinea, put his veto upon all such rival aid in the good cause, and determined that the natives were either to have Protestantism or else spiritually starve.

From his point of view, as a staunch disciple of Martin Luther and John Knox, I dare say he was quite right to resist, to the bitter end, what is termed the growing influence of the Scarlet Woman of Babylon, but from mine as a humanitarian, I thought him at the time, and still consider him, too absolute and mediæval in his notions for both modern Christianity and the real benefit of the Papuan race, which must be after all the motive which induces Messrs. Lawes and Chalmers, &c., as well as Fr. Stanislaus and his brethren, to leave the security and comfort of home to suffer privations, fevers, and risk their lives amongst the savages. And so, honouring them all alike for their noble self-sacrifice, it makes me the more enraged that such a trifling blur should have stood in the way of my complete admiration, and the more anxious to wipe it away as quickly as possible.

Fr. Stanislaus, when the permit to land on New Guinea was refused to him on account of his religion, resolved to land with his two companions on Yule Island, which lies at the entrance to Hall Sound, where the prohibitive law was not supposed to extend, it being off the mainland.

This was about the most likely island along the coast for a man to qualify as a martyr upon, for it was the most unhealthy of all. The natives, also, were considered dangerous, particularly since the Italian naturalist D'Albertis had lived there; indeed, a mission station which had been established there once upon a time had to be abandoned as no teacher could live upon it.

This was the poor island which Fr. Stanislaus fixed upon to begin his work in, and which no one surely would have grudged to him, seeing that it had been relinquished as hopeless, by the opposition mission.

He bought a crazy little craft from one of the traders. This was in such a fearful state of decay that, as the trader informed me, no one but a madman would have ventured in it outside the reefs. Then, with his two companions, and one young fellow of his own faith to act as pilot—his sole qualification for the post being that he had once before visited the coast—he set out upon that stormy sea to cross a gulf, pretty nearly always in as great a state of turmoil as the Bay of Biscay. 'And by Saul! they did it too,' said the trader to me when recounting the adventure. 'How they did it the Lord only knows, for they knew no more of steering or managing a craft than an inland baby! They sailed that 'ere old cobble right over the gulf, storms and all, and all that lay between them and eternity in two or three places of her bottom was the three coats of white paint which I pitched into the bargain. Some of the holes you might almost put your head through. Those of course I covered with a bit of tarpaulin, but the small ones got hidden up with the paint. I tell you what, when I heard that these French priests had landed all safe on Yule Island, instead of foundering, which they oughter have done according to nature, it made my flesh creep and my hair start up, for it seemed to me a clear sign that there was a God arter all and that He was taking care of them.'

They had been about eight months established upon their mission station when I landed at Yule Island. I was met by the Fathers, who showed me over the place, for they had succeeded in winning the confidence of the natives, and held service in a little chapel between the two native villages of Morni-Cherné and Riora-Aremma. Like Mr. Chalmers further east, they contented themselves, for the present, with interesting the tribes without trying to make converts.[1]

They were not, however, left to their own devices long at Yule Island, for when Mr. Lawes heard that they had stolen this march upon him, he at once packed off four South Sea Island teachers, with their wives and children, to the old abandoned station, so that they might counteract the *baneful influence* which had crept into the land. This would have been all very well from his side of the question, only that in his haste to plant his men in the field he forgot to provision them properly, the consequence being that Fr. Vergus had to administer the necessities of life to these poor rivals, otherwise they and their families would have died of starvation.

On the day we anchored at Hall Sound, Fr. Vergus and one of his companions were rowed aboard by the four South Sea Island rivals, which surprised and gratified me very greatly to see them living in such unity together. I asked them for an explanation, to which they replied :—

'Massa Lawe he sent us here, but he no send any food ; Massa Vergus come to us and feed us. Massa Lawe may be right, but our bellies say no ; Massa Vergus may be wrong, but all same he save our lives, therefore we like Massa Vergus best, and serve him first ; Massa Lawe come along afterwards when he sends us food.'

I do not attempt to make any charge against Mr. Lawes of culpable neglect of these teachers ; it may have been that provisions were scarce at Port Moresby at the time, so that he could not help them. According to what I witnessed myself in other parts, these native teachers have often pri-

[1] For further account of missionaries at Yule Island, see 'The Land of the Hibiscus Blossom,' chap. xxii.

vations of this kind to endure. Mr. Andrew Goldie, who is one of the early pioneers of New Guinea, confirms me in this opinion, as the following quotation from his Journal, which he kindly gave me permission to publish, will prove: —

'May 25, 1882.—Up to this date, he is at Dinner Island, where he has heard from the native teacher of a cannibal massacre; the teacher had witnessed the cutting up of a man, and also when he came to the place of sacrifice which was at Milne Bay had seen one with his hands cut off but still alive, crying piteously) 'it is eight months since a missionary vessel paid the teachers a visit. We had brought them stores from the head mission quarters at Port Moresby, which consisted only of one bag of rice for each of them, a few beads, fish-hooks, knives, and trade hatchets. The teachers, in their letters, were informed that the mission stores had nothing else to send them, yet before I left Moresby I had offered the missionaries half a ton of flour, six casks of beef, and what tea and sugar I could spare. But these they refused for reasons best known to themselves, although at the same time they did not hesitate to borrow the same kind of stores for their own private use. I learnt from Tom (a native teacher), at Dinner Island, that H.M.S. 'Beagle' had been there a week before, and the captain had asked him if he was in want of biscuits, beef or any other stores, but that he replied in the negative, although he was literally in want of everything. I am aware that these native teachers have instructions to make no complaints to any of H.M. ships. These instructions are only too well carried out, as they have not courage to brave the white missionaries' wrath, which seems to them terrible, and tell the truth.

'Poor fellows and helpless women! Already over fifty of them are laid in New Guinea graves, fruit of gross neglect and literal starvation! At one time seventeen new arrivals died within a period of four months, yet still they come; we expect a fresh batch, although by this time they ought to know what kind of fate is in store for them.

'I put some questions to the teacher concerning the fever, if he had it, &c.; he said "Yes."

'Do you take quinine?' I had seen a bottle of it standing. "Oh, that belongs to Chalmers." I told him to use it, no matter to whom it belonged, but he said he did not know how to use it. I then took it, got acid from the ship and mixed up a brandy-bottle full, leaving some acid to dissolve the rest, instructing him how to use it. I do think by this time these teachers ought to know how to use fever medicine, for when one is attacked you cannot mistake the symptoms for any other disease; a few doses of quinine, if taken in time, will soon put you right, but if not taken at once, periodical attacks occur which are hard to shake off. I left the teacher all the supplies and stores which we could spare, viz., two bags of flour, one bag of rice, two bottles of Liebig's essence of beef, tea, sugar, and a dozen of trade hatchets.'

Mr. Andrew Goldie, in 1879, made a most successful exploring voyage round the coast in his vessel the 'Alice Meade,' besides many other voyages, being well received by all the tribes. He is one of the best authorities on New Guinea, having discovered and named much of it, and is thoroughly acquainted with native manners and customs.

He lives now at Port Moresby, and is the New Guinea manager of Messrs. Burn, Philp & Co.'s stores there, that enterprising Sydney firm being invariably kind and helpful to all explorers. To their kindness alone I am indebted that I was able to go so far round the island, and at so little comparative expense to myself, otherwise my pecuniary losses would have been very serious, or my efforts sadly crippled, as the firm which I then represented repudiated all expenses over and above what I had stipulated for before leaving England; so that I only lost about seventy, instead of three or four hundred pounds sterling, for the sake of risking my life amongst the savages.

Andrew Goldie gave me a great deal of information while I was at Port Moresby, and is one of the most modest and retiring of men. He is a confirmed bachelor, and does not encourage any of the 'female persuasion' about his place, which fact has been one of the causes of his great success amongst the natives; a most moral, good-living, peace-loving, yet fearless man, from whose lips I never heard either a coarse word or anything at all approaching an oath—which is the more remarkable in a land where the language is apt to be flowery, if anything.

I was very greatly amused one day, while in Tasmania, to read in a missionary record the following tale of savage life. I am sorry to add that this story was related by Mr. L wes, or at least printed in his name; it was called 'How a Sabbath Breaker was Rebuked.' 'There was a man who kept a store at Port Moresby' (Andrew Goldie is the only man who keeps a store at Port Moresby, so that he might as well have mentioned his name—at least it would have been the most manly way) 'who used to curse and blaspheme awfully, and work all the Lord's Day driving in nails, &c., while the native service was going on. One Sunday, one of the native teachers, who was a strong Christian, physically as well as morally, went up to this Sabbath-breaker and said to him: "How is it that you, a white man, dare to break the Sabbath by working and cursing, while we try to teach the New Guinea men how to keep it holy?" And this blasphemer seeing that the teacher was a strong man, respected him, and laid down his hammer so that it was heard no more at Port Moresby.'

As a missionary yarn this is extremely pretty, but it is too personal considering that it is all a fabrication. In the first place, Mr. Goldie is a Scotchman, and as much a believer in the Sunday as Mr. Lawes himself, also he never swears; in the second place, if he had felt inclined to drive in nails on the Lord's Day, and any ignorant South Sea Islander had attempted to interfere with him, I am afraid that this coloured man would not have been able to conduct services for the next month or six weeks after, for Mr. Andrew Goldie, although a very patient man, is also a powerfully built man and one whom I would not like to cheek up to.

After I arrived in England, and during the time that the Rev. Mr. Lawes was lecturing in Brisbane, one of the papers of that city published what was supposed to be a letter of mine, running down the missionaries. It was used as a quotation from a Scottish paper as if from a letter of mine there, and after some remarks on my injustice to these self-sacrificing men, asked me, Did I think that I would have lived to tell the tale of New Guinea if it had not been for them?

My attention being attracted to this charge, I wrote to the Scottish paper in question, and got a direct contradiction from it as to this supposed letter. With this contradiction I went to the head-quarters of the missionary society, and offered to give the lie direct to that Brisbane paper, and also demanded the name of my traducer; but I was informed that it was too late for me to contradict the words now that they were published, and my offer was declined.

I now beg to give the lie to that newspaper, and trust that they may reprint this with the name of my traducer, so that I may be able to tell him what I think of darkstabbing tendencies. I will also say that I endorse entirely what the Brisbane newspaper said, that but for the civilis-

MORNE-CHERNE

ing efforts of the missionaries and traders who had been before me, I do not think that I would have come back from New Guinea to tell the tale ; and to my predecessors I am grateful accordingly, not forgetting the careful watch which our Greek pilot Nicholas kept over me with his Winchester while I was in the land.

CHAPTER LI

FAREWELL TO NEW GUINEA

The Islands of Torres Straits—Thursday Island, and once more towards Brisbane.

SAILING westward from Moresby to Motu-Motu we get a good view, from near the native villages of Oriapu and Jokea, of Mount Yule rearing up behind to a height of about 10,046 feet, as nearly as has yet been judged. Mount Yule is a peculiarly rich hunting-ground for the naturalist, botanist, and geologist, Mr. Edelfelt—a plucky young naturalist explorer whom I met at Thursday Island, making his second trip for the purpose of exploring this mountain—informed me. He was accompanied by his wife, and intended settling, for a time, at Motu-Motu.

Mount Yule is rugged in outline, and as the sea is unprotected about here, rough weather is by no means a phenomenon, for, like the Bay of Biscay, the Papuan Gulf is unrestful, and with strong sun-heated monsoons blowing the ship along and raising the waves till they tumble things about and break along the decks.

As the traveller proceeds inland, he will come across deserted villages, with the houses falling to pieces, significant tokens of the fierce wars waged by the hostile tribes, and the sweeping effects of fever. Some of the houses are raised six and eight feet above the ridges on which they are built, others are perched high between the forked limbs of trees, and are reached by long, roughly-fashioned ladders. In many of those tree-houses he will see sun-dried corpses, grimly waiting, the sole tenants of the deserted homestead. These tree-houses are consecrated to the dead in time of peace, and are used as a place of refuge for the women and children in time of war; they look odd and unsafe at first sight, to the stranger, but after a time he gets used to them and can appreciate their utility amongst a nation where spears and arrows are still the principal weapons. One man on such a height, protected by the twisted tree limbs, has it in his power to annoy an enemy and escape himself; it takes a long time for a stone axe to cut down a tree, while it is much easier and more effective to pitch down a spear than to throw one upwards.

At Motu-Motu, a splendid native town and the direct highway to Mount Yule, we reached the limit of our westward journey. Here we lay for one night before crossing the Gulf and leaving the land where we had experienced so much in such a short time.

We are now returning by Bramble Bay, the Neve Group, Darnley, York, and other islands which stud the Torres Straits, and where the copra traders and missionaries pretty equally divide the field.

In these islands, as in New Guinea, the rarest of orchids and varieties of crotons grow; there are over twenty varieties on the volcanic island of Darnley, with beautiful blue, green and dark winged butterflies of gigantic size lighting up the dark moist shadows.

We have been a pleasant company through the voyage, and now that the captain has left strange waters he is once more in his element. Although moving a little languidly about the deck, he has steadily refused my medicine, viz., two grains of quinine three times daily in whisky, and I fear that he has caught the fever; but my friend Mr. Vivian

Bowden is all right and active, as he has been all along, and the men on board, white and dark, seem glad to be getting back to fresh beef once more.

The sheep we were taking over were the worst off, as we had run short of fodder for the poor animals, so that they had to fast until we reached Moresby; yet we had always been fortunate with our fishing, and got some splendid fish each day as we passed along. All we had to do was to trail a line with a hook at the end without any bait; the fish came and hooked themselves on without any temptation, and delicious eating they were.

I think Darnley Island is the most lavishly fertile of the Torres Straits group, and the natives have some of the most curious customs. They embalm or rather dry their dead, fixing them for that purpose to ladders and setting them in the sun, extracting the moisture from the body by tapping the heels and, most horrible practice of all, catching the 'juice' in vessels as it drips and drinking it.

Two or three native teachers are placed here, with their wives and children, and seem to lead a happy enough life, for the natives are fairly accustomed to strangers by this time; yet I saw one poor young wife dying while I was there. It was a sad parting between husband and wife, for both were well aware that he would have short time to mourn for her, three months being the limit allowed for his remembrance, as after that time of waiting he must marry another wife, who will be forwarded to him from the islands by his missionary masters.

The wives are mostly the first victims to the climate of New Guinea, but Goldie told me a strange story of one young Kanaka woman who had outlived all the husbands provided for her, and was still free, young, and attractive.

Murray Island is the station which Mr. McFarlane

established—its old name was Meer—and it has a cone of about 750 feet in height, an extinct volcano. There are two other islands lying close to this one, Meer and Dower Islands, the latter 605 feet high and very bald looking.

There is a fine Papuan Institute at Murray Island, which Mr. McFarlane describes fully in his work 'Among the Cannibals.' Here they have succeeded in training the natives of the western districts from Kiwai, Mibu and the Fly River, not only in the English language but in many useful trades, particularly joinery, blacksmith and ship-building work. They have already built a ship, which is one of the prettiest round the straits from Murray Island; the trees were felled, sawn, and dressed by the native converts in their own workshop under the superintendence of Mr. Robert Bruce, a Glasgow ship-builder.

Mr. McFarlane believes, as I do, in the future possibility of the Papuan reaching as high a state of civilisation as the Maori has reached, if not higher; for he makes an intelligent and apt scholar, and does things more from conviction than by imitation.

York Island is low-lying but well timbered, and the natives here, like those on the other islands, are all industrious, working for the traders who settle amongst them. They give their work and he looks after their larder, keeping the entire tribe—old men, women and children—and they all live in great harmony, working cheerfully when wanted by their easy-going guest, who does not bother them as to hours or quantity.

One business they engage upon is preparing copra—that is, they sell to the trader the produce of their cocoanut gardens, cutting out the fruit in small pieces and drying it in the sun, after which it is packed into bags and sent away to make oilcake.

The other trade is with *bêche-de-mer*, a black sea-slug

which they fish for, and after drying in the sun, smoke in firing sheds and then send to the Chinese market, where it is much prized in the making of soup. As I have fully described nearly all the islands of the Torres Straits and the copra and *bêche-de-mer* processes in my book 'The Land of the Hibiscus Blossom,' I need not repeat them here.

We lived like City aldermen after leaving York Island, as they had caught a large turtle there which we bought from them, so that it was turtle soup for dinner and turtle steak for breakfast and supper after that, until we grew so completely surfeited with it that even to this day I can hardly hear the name of turtle soup mentioned without a shudder.

It is singular what strange thoughts possess people at times and the odic influence one man's thoughts may exercise upon another. One night, as we were steaming along towards home with the most lovely tropical moon shining above and the half-formed coral islands gleaming like silver bands on the darkly luminous ocean around, I lay with my friend Vivian Bowden on deck, smoking and looking dreamily outward. We had both been for a long time silent, when suddenly he said:

'Hullo, Nisbet! thinking?'

'Yes,' I replied.

'So was I, and I bet you a drink that you cannot guess what my thoughts were about on this balmy night—have a try.'

'You were thinking how you could wolf up a beefsteak, underdone, with a pint of stout,' I replied solemnly.

'By Jove! so I was, but how did you know?'

'Because I was thinking upon exactly the same thing.' We had not tasted fresh beef for over a month, and somehow the loveliness of my surroundings suggested the subject, so that the silver rays of the moon reminded me of nothing at the moment more entrancing than a silver grill and a juicy beefsteak sputtering upon it.

Thursday Island was as we had left it, with the pearl-fishery owners striving their hardest to keep their own divers attached to them by extra kindness, or seeking to bribe someone else's diver from him; for this is the principal worry of the owners, how to be able to keep a good man. And all the while these Kanaka masters of their employers strut about with lordly independence and flourish their bank notes in careless unconcern.

It takes a man of great nerve and experience to be a good diver, as he must generally stay in his bathing-dresses, under the water, for about six hours at a stretch. I laughed at an illustration which Cassell's 'Picturesque Australasia' gave of my subject, 'The Pearl-Divers and their Work.' They had some *naked* divers scrambling for shells, and as I hadn't the opportunity of pointing out the great mistake before the book left the Press, I had just to grin and bear it.

No pearl-diver ever goes down in those shark-crowded waters without his diving suit. They screw him into this costume and load him down with heavy weights, so that he becomes helpless in their hands, above water. Then they lift him up and drop him overboard, letting him down gently with a rope, pumping the fresh air into his helmet all the while. When he gets to the bottom he gives them the signal and goes on gathering the shells, the boat above following the direction he is taking below.

No Kanaka diver will trust a white man to stand and work the air-pump; it must be his own bosom friend, for his life depends entirely upon how it is done. Too much air is as bad almost as too little, and if anything goes wrong with the air-pipe, a sudden twist or accidental turn, it means a sudden and horrible death to him. This is their main danger, for the sharks, although they may be attracted round by the smell of the bolt-grease in the helmet, are generally too frightened at the strange looking apparition to come very near. Still there are dangers enough in the occupation for their owners not to grudge them 60*l*. per month and other chances.

In spite of the scarcity of ladies, fashion runs very high and very pure in colour at Thursday Island. In the morning they visit one another in white trousers, coloured sashes, well starched shirts, and Chinese silk coats, for refreshments and cigars. In the evening they knock about, still for refreshments and cigars, in tropic naval full dress, white trousers, vest, and well starched shirts, finished off by white linen monkey-jackets. They are very generous with what they have in the larder, but sometimes they run short of fresh provisions, and then they have to fall back on tinned meat. I never heard, however, of an instance where they had run out of tobacco or whisky; they are all fine young fellows and good comrades with each other.

McNaulty used to kill a bullock sometimes. When this was done the islanders and surrounding stations immediately got up parties, breakfasts, dinners and supper feasts, in the different houses, and so ate it up before the heat could spoil it. I was at one of these convivial gatherings one night, where they treated me so very well that I could hardly hold my head up the next morning. I fancy that I dined the day after on a soda and a cinder.

When a man gets tipsy, or otherwise misbehaves himself, Mr. Milman, the Government Resident there in place of Mr. Douglas, has a very wise way of punishing him: for the first offence one day's hard labour, without pay, on the roads; for the second offence, two days, and so on. The Kanakas, Malays, and Chinamen don't like it half so well as imprisonment, and seldom repeat the offence.

We had a very amusing Malay waiter at the hotel. His

FROM MURRAY ISLAND, TORRES STRAITS

way of describing things was exceedingly funny and much garnished; he would utter the most horrible oaths with such an unconscious air that no one could have the heart to correct him.

When I first got there, a very ill-natured billy-goat used to occupy the back verandah, and any one going out in the dark that way was almost sure to be butted over at the most unexpected moment. 'Billy' was a very old favourite with the landlord, so that the visitors had just to endure the affliction as best they could.

One day, however, we had roast mutton for dinner, a little tough but very palatable, for the cook was a Chinaman, and Chinamen are wonderful cooks as well as gardeners.

After dinner the Malay waiter asked me how I liked dat d——d mutton for dinner, and when I said 'first rate,' he brightened up and grew confidential:

'You know dat dam ole billy-goat dat allays butt, butts at everyone?'

'Yes! too well.'

'Dat dam billy-goat will no trouble any fellow any more in dis hotel—he am de roast mutton.'

The landlord had been short of provisions for his lodgers and had been forced to sacrifice his favourite!

One night while we were all sitting at supper, a young fellow came staggering in very much the worse for his day's visiting, and sat down opposite to me. He commenced to glare and throw out very insulting remarks; he had reached the quarrelsome stage in his cups.

I stood it as long as I could, but at last had to retort, upon which he started up and demanded instant satisfaction.

The weapons fixed upon were revolvers, and the ground the moonlit sands outside. I went upstairs for my weapon, while he staggered out to find his.

Then I came down to the verandah, where I found him

waiting for me without his 'barker'; his mood had changed while I was preparing upstairs, and he was now all love and friendship. I was glad of this, for I don't like either shooting or being shot, so that instead of a duel we all had a drink first and a song afterwards.

He sang to us, and I never heard a more perfect or more carefully-trained tenor voice anywhere; it was a delightful ending to a quarrel.

What a host of incident was crammed into that ten days' wait for the Brisbane steamer at Thursday Island. I worked hard all day and enjoyed my evenings with these fine fellows; it was here I finished off, amongst other drawings, that full-page illustration of 'Mount Owen Stanley from the sea,' which I was charmed to observe bore another artist's name on the cover instead of mine when it appeared in print. I am always pleased to see such evidences of honesty—it redeems poor humanity so much in my estimation. I found that my *nom de plume* on this occasion was 'Charles Wilkinson'; but I had many more artistic *aliases* throughout the work, 'Picturesque Australasia,' which tickled my fancy very greatly, and made me think what a funny fellow the art editor must be in his own quiet way.

But the hour of parting had come; one fine morning the 'Alexandra' steamed through the outside reefs into the harbour. She had got a new propeller at Townsville, and was now upon her return journey from Normantown to Brisbane.

I took our poor old skipper down with me to Townsville, where his wife lived. As I expected, he had caught the New Guinea fever, which reduced him in two days' time to a complete skeleton. He put himself under my medical charge at last, so all the way down I dosed him with quinine—he was getting better when I sent him ashore, yet even then he could hardly walk; it would be months before he became his old burly self again.

A friendly shake of the hand with those genial wellwishers at Thursday Island—kindly John Douglas, Mr. Milman, Vivian Bowden, McNaulty, and all the others--and we were once more off on our long journey southward.

CHAPTER LII

ABOUT A VEXING QUESTION

To Men and Women who may wish to Emigrate—Where they should go—South and Western Australia—Queensland.

In England, where only the specially favoured by fortune can afford to live with any degree of comfort, or without the constant worry which small incomes bring to people, the question will for ever crop up, 'Cannot we cure this misery in some way or other?' Then visions of Australasia will float vaguely before the mind; but these, without the necessary knowledge of where best to go, will be apt to end as they began, in airy wishes.

The best man or woman to emigrate always is the one who has been left a couple or three thousand pounds. With this sum in England he is in a worse position than the workman or even the pauper—indeed, the true-born pauper and the wealthy aristocrat are the only two classes to be envied in England; all the intermediate classes are merely gradations of self-importance, foolish envy, and undeniable misery.

In a new land, when such a man goes out with his little capital and the strict determination to cast dignity to the dogs and put out his own hand, the moment he takes possession of his land he has leapt to the same social level as his aristocratic landlord at home, and may leave his successors as wealthy, if he likes. Yet while I would like to see as many small capitalists go out to Australia as possible, I look mainly to the workmen and labourers who are here crowded and worked like wild beasts in other lands, but without a hundredth part of the liberty of action that the wild beast has, to form the true backbone of the countries which I am now going to describe in a brief way, so that you may know where to be able to live, instead of taking up the yoke of starvation and slavery.

Let me premise my remarks by telling you plainly, that you will not have to work a whit less hard than you are forced to do in England. Possibly for the first year you may have to labour harder and endure *nearly* as much in the shape of privation. I say *nearly*, because not having the crushing winters to endure which you have here, it is not possible for you to suffer quite so much, even at the very lowest ebb of your fortunes, as you are compelled to suffer for six months every year of your lives in England.

Still, after witnessing, as I did, the true nobility and Spartan endurance of that great army of dock strikers and the devotion of their women in London in 1889, I am not in the least degree afraid to speak out plainly to such Englishmen. If they carry that spirit with them to Australia, the first difficulty in their way will disappear like ' snow from a dyke-side before the sun,' and it is only the first months which are likely to daunt their hearts.

Now all the difference between your hard labour here and your hard labour there lies in this:—In England you must go on working, from the first hour you go into the battle until death releases you, without bettering your condition one iota. You are living only on sufferance, for nothing here belongs to you. It is not your native land, although you were unfortunate enough to be born and dragged up in it, any more than the plantation around was the native land of the negro slave who chanced to be born there in chains. In Australia, it may be your native land, for you are landlords of the allotment you purchase, and every year that you labour adds to your own wealth and freedom, instead of making some rich idler richer.

I should like to see England yielded up entirely to its real owners and left altogether to them, and all the workmen and labourers, man-servants and maid-servants, clear out to their own heritage, and so let the lords and their sons labour upon their own lands. If this great time ever comes, then we will see England divided into small lots and put up for sale, and free selectors invited over to take their choice. And so it should be.

I read in the pages of the *Pall Mall* of February 18th, 1890, of a thousand men and women going about destitute in Sydney, which may be true, and will only bear out exactly what I have written in earlier pages. These thousand men and women have no right to be in Sydney, with all those hundreds of thousands of square miles of land lying north and west idly waiting for them and you to occupy and live upon them.

In the Northern Territory of South Australia the area is 523,600 square miles, or 335,116,800 acres, much of it vast rolling downs, wide, well-grassed plains, rich alluvial flats, large navigable rivers, and metalliferous areas exceptionally rich in gold, tin, copper and silver. The principal port, north in the Gulf of Carpentaria, is Darwin, the main inland rivers being the Macarthur, Roper, Summers, Hodgson, Robinson, Goyder Inlet, the three Alligator Rivers, Adelaide, Daly, and Victoria—all great waterways which fertilise the ground!

In this vast area there are to be found waste lands, as there are everywhere, with rocky and sterile ranges, yet no worse than the land round about Sydney was in the year that the first shipload of convicts landed upon it.

ABOUT A VEXING QUESTION

I quote here from the notes given by the Hon. I. L. Parsons, the Government Resident in the Northern Territory:

'It is estimated that there are between 4,000 and 5,000 Chinese, a sprinkling of Malays and Cingalese, and large tribes of aboriginals who at present claim the country according to their tribal boundaries; the white population is about 2,000. The mean temperature all the year round is about 75° and the thermometer is never lower than 58°, the atmosphere is heavy and steamy in the wet season, and dry, parching, and malarial in the dry season, so that until one gets acclimatised he must guard against malaria with its fever and ague; this of course, as in all tropical countries, can only be rectified by working the earth, draining, clearing and cultivation. I believe the present difficulty with the land lies in that it cannot be purchased without the consent of the Imperial Government, the conditions of which are subject to alteration according as may be considered fit; but these laws must very soon be altered.

'The Chinese population are at present cultivating rice and sugar-cane on the banks of some of the rivers. There are thousands of square miles of good sugar-growing land on these banks, also parts where coffee, millet, tapioca and all varieties of tropical products may be cultivated throughout this Northern Territory, from 26 parallel south latitude right up to the Indian Ocean.

'The land laws are liberal in the extreme; pastoral blocks of land not exceeding 400 square miles can be leased for twenty-five years at a rental of 6d. per square mile for the first seven years and 2s. 6d. per square mile for the remainder of the term; while 1,280 acres can be selected, of the agricultural land, on credit, at a rental of 6d. per acre, with a right of purchase at 12s. 6d. per acre, and any lessee who *bonâ fide* cultivates 640 acres with tropical products during the first five years of his lease is relieved from further payment of either rent or purchase money, and is entitled to a grant of the 1,280 acres in fee simple; any area in excess can be purchased at auction at the upset price of 12s. 6d. per acre. At the present time there are open for selection or cash sale 240,000 acres.'

I must not forget to add that the great overland Adelaide telegraph line has opened up the land from Adelaide to Palmerston, as it cuts right through its centre for the entire length, over 1,800 miles.

Captain Carrington, who in 1884 explored in the Government steamship 'Palmerston,' has given a good account of the rivers and the soil about them. He steamed up the Macarthur for twelve miles, his ship drawing 11 ft. 3 in.; beyond that distance smaller vessels are required. The Victoria River, he reports, is navigable for vessels of the largest class for fifty miles from the sea; the Daly is two miles wide at its entrance; the South Alligator river can be navigated for sixty miles; East Alligator for fifty miles; the West Alligator for twenty-two miles; the Adelaide for eighty miles; and the others, Roper, Goyder, Liverpool, and King are all good navigable waters, with splendid soil on both sides, easily worked and highly productive, although some portions are at present densely fringed with mangroves.

All that the man with small capital, such as I have mentioned, requires to do, is to fix upon a site as near one of the rivers as he can get, and purchase it upon the working lease. The poor man who has no capital, but who has sinews instead, should get as near to the rich selector as possible, and do sufficient work for him to keep himself while he is clearing the land which he has bought on the credit system. To all I would say, get as far north as you possibly can get, and away from the cities and townships; plan out new towns for yourselves, and the Govern-

MOUNT YULE, NEW GUINEA

ment will aid you where and when it can. No one need starve on the land, and although, perhaps, for a time, you may have to go about your work in rags, that is no hardship in a country where no one will heed such a trifle or think the less of you for it. Imitate the aboriginals as far as you can; hunt and fish for your daily food until you can once more become a white man, which, if you work with a purpose, will not be long.

Western Australia covers an area of 1,000,000 square miles—that is, about eight times the size of Great Britain and Ireland.

The population at present may be roughly estimated at 42,488, of which there are 7,000 more males than females. Nearly a third are located in the towns of Perth and Fremantle, where wages are very good; yet I still must give the warning—do not cluster or stay in the towns. Clear out to the bush for land of your own.

The country is divided into six divisions, viz.:—South-West, Gascoyne, North-West, Kimberley, Eucla, and the Eastern.

The South-West division is where the population is mostly centred and the land already largely occupied, although not nearly all taken up; where not cleared it is heavily timbered, and when cleared, highly productive. It is about the extent of France, and grows grain and fruits of pretty nearly all kinds, the vine, particularly, being very thriving, and the grapes very large where cultivated.

Farm labourers are much in demand; their wages range from 15s. to 20s. per week with board and lodging.

One of the largest rivers of Australia, the Murchison, runs through the lower part of this division of Gascoyne for over 100 miles from near Port Gregory; the land about this river is good. The other rivers are the Gascoyne and Lyons, which run into Sharks Bay; the land away from the rivers is rich in minerals and is good pasture.

The North-Western division is watered by the Ashburn from Exmouth Gulf, Fortesque, Yule, Shaw, and other rivers, with good alluvial land on either side; the coast line is low and covered with mangroves. It is chiefly pasture land.

The Kimberley division, lately made famous by its gold fields, is tropical and similar in character to the northern territory of South Australia. It covers 134,000 square miles.

The Eucla division is as yet not much known, but from its locality in the Bight and latitude it should be found to be somewhat similar to the upper portions of New South Wales.

The Eastern division is as yet marked 'desert,' that is, it has not been tried; personally, I always feel tempted to try the desert portions of Australia from the wealth that has been discovered in other portions which were a few years ago so termed on the map.

The conditions of getting land in Western Australia are:—100 to 1,000 acres may be obtained by any one over eighteen years of age at not less than 10s. per acre, payable over twenty years: the purchaser must fence in the whole of the land (one-tenth of it in two years), spend an amount on improvements, in addition to the fencing, equal to the purchase money; reside on the land, or if not resident he must pay double instalments of purchase money. If he fulfils these conditions within the twenty years the land becomes his own; if not, it is forfeited.

It is twenty years since I sojourned in New Zealand, and then only in the Northern Island, therefore I am not going to describe its beauties here. It deserves to have a special book written about it, which I trust, at some not far distant date, I shall be able to do. Indeed, I hope to be able to go over once more, and this time more thoroughly, Australasia and the South Sea Islands, and to give some vivid pictures of each particular locality, more especially those unoccupied portions of Queensland, South and Western Australia, and then afterwards on the return journey be able to come back, recruit myself, and freshen my eyes with the richly-toned emerald foliage of this exceedingly picturesque land, New Zealand.

It may well be called the land of mountain, valley and flood, and even though one of its many strange beauties, the Geysers, with the Pink and White Terraces, has disappeared, and what was once a rare scene of loveliness has now become a dreary waste through that awful upheaval, still it has enough attractions left to lure the traveller fully 16,000 miles to look upon them.

I am doubly fortunate in that I once beheld the terrace and hot springs at Rotomahana, and managed to escape by almost a miracle being there at the moment of the eruption. Now I don't feel as if I'd like to look upon the lake of mud and the awful fissures which were once such a fairy picture.

However, in this chapter I am not describing the beauties of the country, but its advantages and utility to emigrants.

New Zealand is the place of all places for Highlanders, Welshmen, Irishmen or Cumberland farmers to settle upon. They will find both mountains and valleys enough to satisfy them, with gloomy passes, deep lakes, lofty waterfalls, mist, rain, cool weather and all that goes to make up their idea of Paradise. It is as if all the tit-bits of Scotland, Cumberland, Wales, and the Emerald Isle had been carted off to a southern latitude and planted down there, with suggestions besides of the blue Danube, Switzerland and the Rhine mysteries over all.

At the present time New Zealand is rather heavily taxed, as it is deeply in debt compared with some of the other colonies; yet there is no portion of it, north or south, where a man may not live well and thrive in spite of the burden which he must help to bear. Land, where it can be sold, is sold at low prices to settlers, although a great portion still belongs to the original owners, the Maoris; in such cases it has to be leased at the rate of about 4d. per acre, but this, if the holder stays, may become his at any time, as these lands are constantly coming into the market.

Assisted passages are still given to emigrants, who are advised not to rush into farming for themselves all at once. Let them wait a year or two and look about while working at anything that turns up, and so get accustomed to prices of things and colonial customs. There are always coming into the market second-hand farms and selections where the old owner may have got tired of the locality and wants to shift, which seems a kind of chronic state with many of the settlers. New Zealand is of all the colonies the one with the most hopeful future, and the best climate for Englishmen although it has not the extent of Australia.

For the man who wants to live a quiet, peaceful life, free from excitement, and to make a homestead as nearly approaching his ideal of what English homes might be if he could become a perpetual landlord, New Zealand is the place to go to. He will not become wealthy so quickly as he might in some parts of Australia, but he ought to get contentment and freedom, and his family will certainly gain health and happiness.

But if he wants an active life, with plenty of excitement and the prospect of a speedy return for his labour—that is, to make and leave a fortune behind him—I would advise him to fix upon Australia—the lower portions of the Western or Southern parts.

If again climate is not so much the consideration, or if he would like to live the tropical life of a planter, which has its many fascinations, independent of the attractions and certainty of wealth, then let him fix his mind upon upper Queensland, the northern territory of South Australia or the Kimberley end of Western Australia; there he will find all his desires gratified in rich foliage and luscious fruits, with an ardent sun for ever blazing overhead.

One thing all will get wherever they fix upon—light and sunshine. When they leave the English Channel they may say good-bye to fogs, famine, caste, contumely, and all the special horrors and miseries incidental to good old, used-up England.

CHAPTER LIII

TASMANIA

Prisons and Prisoners—Hobart—To Launceston—Bischoff Tin Mine —A Launceston Sage—To Sea.

I FOUND a great bundle of letters waiting for me at Melbourne when I got there. They had been forwarded from Queensland, and as the agent had written on the backs of them: 'To be returned if not called for in three months' time,' I suppose he gave me that limit, if I was not eaten by the cannibals.

I had hardly time to glance over them, however, before I was once more on the way to Tasmania, that garden of Australia. My editor wanted a few sketches of that island, and of the Alps, since he could not send me to New Zealand. Orders had arrived that it was not to be done, enough photographs having been obtained to serve the purpose. I think that I could almost have foregone the beauties of Tasmania and the grandeur of the Victorian Alps for a rush once more over Maori-land; but 1 am a very good soldier when under orders, so off I started to make the most of the six weeks still at my disposal.

Tasmania is about one-sixth part smaller than Ireland, and a little larger than Ceylon. I don't exactly know why Ireland and Ceylon should be clubbed together by way of comparing size, unless it be that both islands are considered to be gems in their way, Ireland as the Emerald of Britain and Ceylon as the Pearl of India. Tasmania may be termed the Ruby of Australia in commemoration of the blood which has been shed there in past times; now it is as sleepy as a cat gorged with mice.

A wild and rugged coast all the way round from the Furneaux Group in Bass Strait to Hobart—an historical coast where almost every promontory and bay has been the scene of a tragedy, for Van Diemen's Land is more renowned and remembered as a place of horror than even as a health resort, beautiful and healthy as it undoubtedly is.

I did not think so much of the gardens, orchards and lovely women I was to see there, as of the olden convicts, to whom this land meant Hell. My mind was so morbid about it, that the whole place seemed to reek of abominations and cruelties, and the echoes to be filled with the ringing of fetters and chains. Marcus Clark and his awful, realistic story, 'His Natural Life,' must be held accountable for this state of my mind.

I wanted to see the prisons and ancient prisoners more than the picturesque Cape Pillar; and also to visit Port Arthur, Hell's Gates and Sarah Island, and look on the horrible convict jailors and the victims driven mad by their awful torturings; before I left the land I saw the grim originals of this weird romance and felt satisfied.

Hobart is a beautiful place, in spite of its evil reputation, with Mount Wellington rising up behind it, its top covered with snow. After New Guinea I could hardly stand the cold. Although people were saying it was a nice warm day, I felt the wind piercing as it blew up from Storm Bay and ruffled the fresh waters of the Derwent.

In the olden days the most refractory criminals were sent from Sydney to Hobart, and there the blackest amongst them were picked out and consigned to Port

Arthur. After Port Arthur no man or woman wanted or was fit to live; I think even the devils in Hell drew the line at passengers from Port Arthur—they had a special limbo of their own prepared, where they might be kept apart and so not be able to contaminate the fallen angels.

I got a warning from the friend who met me at Hobart that it was not considered 'good form' while in Tasmania to say anything about transportation, as one never knew whose feelings he might be wounding by alluding to the subject; so I took care to be always on my guard.

They were all most hospitable and kind to me whilst at Hobart; too kind indeed seeing that I had such a short time to spend amongst them, for they could not get to understand that I must work hard. Time was made for slaves, not authors and artists, they said, as they poured invitations in upon me all day long which I was forced to decline, being a slave. They told me to take my time and do the thing well, for I could not see their island under three months at least, gave me long notices in their papers, and made me an honorary member of their clubs; in fact, they so covered me with attentions that I was forced at last to take time by the forelock, and abscond from their midst, else, I think, I would never have got away at all.

And yet I would have liked to have stayed there for a long time, for the town is so cleanly and quiet and its surroundings so rural and homelike, with hedgerows of hawthorns, and gardens of apples, pears and cherries, and so much to be seen all round. The natives are so civil and so scrupulously honest in their habits that no one ever thinks of locking their street-doors at night; housebreaking and stealing are crimes unknown. As they told me, there was no use stealing at Hobart, as there wasn't a single receiver or even pawnbroker in the place, whom they could

WHITE TERRACE, NEW ZEALAND

take the goods to. This is one of their proud boasts in this city founded by housebreakers and felons.

I paid a visit to Mrs. L. A. Meredith, the aged authoress of many Tasmanian books. I admired her really very fine flower painting and the great botanical knowledge which these drawings revealed. She has written some works both in prose and verse which will not let her be forgotten by her grateful countrymen. I trust she has quite recovered from the bad mood she was in the night I spent at her house, and has long ago forgiven the stranger who had only admiration for her, and tried to do his best with her dearly-loved country.

I received great assistance from Mr. Justin Brown, who showed me some of the oldest newspapers and re:ords of the town, also from Mr. Morton, curator of the museum there, an old New Guinea explorer; and indeed by all I was treated much better than I deserved.

I have also to apologise to Miss Mitchel of ——, who kindly sent and gave me the use of her sketches of the west coast, not only because some of them were not used, but also because, like many of my own works, the sketches which were accepted and used were not only unacknowledged in 'Picturesque Australasia,' but appeared with other artists' names upon them. I trust this lady will free me from all blame in this matter, as I wrote her name on each of the drawings, with full instructions to the printer, when I sent them home. Why they appeared in the form which they did is one of the mysteries of the art department, over which I had no control.

The town of Hobart forms nearly a square in shape and is built on a number of hills, so that there is a good deal of stiff climbing to be done going over it. It covers over 1,270 acres, and has a population of about 28,648 inhabitants. It is well endowed with churches and charitable institutions, and has, for its size, few public-houses. The ladies predominate—I suppose because the young men mostly all go to seek their fortunes elsewhere; they are all healthy and nearly all pretty, and welcome eagerly the advent of single young men. Hobart in this respect resembles a well conducted seminary where good wives are being educated for sensible men, who ought to visit the country once in their lifetime at any rate; they will be difficult to please if they go away without becoming Benedicts.

The Cascades is the place where the insane convicts are kept. Most of these are relics of the olden times; nearly the whole of them have been made imbecile by the cat and other tortures inflicted upon them. It is a soul-depressing place to go through; one of the idiots there, named Roland Rooney, had received as a single sentence 15,000 lashes of the cat. The worst of the convict-floggers, also insane now, was dying when I saw him—a grave-looking, long-faced, melancholy man who might have passed for a revival preacher. Rooney's back was so tanned by repeated floggings that when this extraordinarily severe sentence was passed on him he laughingly said, 'Give me a chew of tobacco, gov'ner, and make it another extra thousand.'

Before leaving Hobart I went up Mount Wellington, which overlooks the city, 4,166 feet, had a splendid view of the surrounding country from the 'ploughed field,' and saw some magnificent bush scenery on the way up; I also drove along the Huon River and Brown's River, where the trees surpassed even those in the mighty forests of Gippsland.

The railway line from Hobart to Launceston is one succession of splendid pictures of mountain scenery, with a great number of townships on the way both to right and left, all filled with the history of early struggles of the pioneers—wars with natives before they were exterminated, and bloody bushrangers before peace settled down so completely over the land. I passed Jerusalem, Jericho, Oatlands, Tunbridge, Ross, Campbelltown, Cleveland, Epping Forest, Evandale, St. Leonards, and lastly Launceston on the beautiful Tamar.

Launceston is 133 miles from Hobart by rail, and about forty miles from the mouth of the river Tamar, and lies in a valley enclosed on three sides by mountains known as Windmill and Cataract Hills, where the rivers North and South Esk join.

A short distance from the town lie the Cora Linn, Devil's Punchbowl, and the Cataracts, where the scenery is really grand in the extreme, with the river foaming over the rocks and rushing along the deep gorge towards the Tamar.

I went to the Cataracts with the governor of the gaol at Launceston and my landlord, and afterwards over the gaol and invalid depôt. Judges and governors of gaols have now an easy time of it in Tasmania. There were only three prisoners at Launceston Prison when I was there, and these had been the only ones for a month past; one a shoemaker and Salvationist who had been tripped up by the arch-enemy in the shape of a bottle of rum, and the other two very small boys who had been caught robbing an orchard. This prison was a model of cleanliness and comfort, so much so that I wondered there were no more applicants for its friendly shelter.

But that it had not been always so I had ample proof of in the rows of heavy ankle-chains hanging about, some of them weighing from fifty-six to seventy-five pounds—a heavy load for a man to carry about all day while working on the roads.

How these criminals ever made their escape it would be hard to tell; a gang would be making a road when suddenly one would break away and run for it. Mr. Foster told me of one incident where the man had scrambled up a ten-foot wall during the daylight with heavy chains upon him, and rushed up the sides of the Cataract rocks with the soldiers' bullets playing about him; several struck him, for they traced him by his blood afterwards into the bush where he managed to evade them. He was absent about ten days and then returned to give himself up, with the chains about him still and his prison clothes in rags. He had not dared to show himself anywhere, and there was no chance of getting from the island, so he came back to his punishment a living skeleton, not having tasted food the whole time. They fed him, cured his wounds, and, when well enough, gave him the lash; that little escapade of his would take from him his chance of a ticket-of-leave.

At Hobart Gaol I saw a convict with a most fantastic dress of bright red and yellow; he was an habitual prison-breaker, so he was dressed in this gay fool's costume that he might be the more readily noticed.

In the depôt I saw many old convicts spending the remainder of their lives in clover after the hard lives they had gone through in their early days; they had everything they desired, and could go and come as they liked. The prison at Launceston is no longer a place of punishment, but home, sweet home.

Of course I could not go all over Tasmania while I was there. I went to St. Mary's Pass, a wildly romantic place, and to Mount Bischoff and Waratah, the wonderful tin mountain of Tasmania, which has done more to enrich the country than any other discovery, and where the supply seems inexhaustible. Mr. Birchell, of Messrs. Walsh Brothers & Birchell, publishers, took me over the tin-smelting works, and showed me the men melting the raw material and pouring it into the moulds like gleaming silver.

But where I could not get to about the island Colonel Aitkenson, editor of the *Launceston Examiner*, and who is one of the best of photographic artists, very kindly gave me photographs of, with permission to use as I required.

My landlord at the private house where I put up was a very wonderful man. He had retired from business with plenty of money to keep him, but spent a good deal of it in building a house like a hydropathic establishment, as large as a barracks, on one of the most perfect sites of the town, where, from one of the upper verandahs—for there are three tiers right round this magnificent house—the visitors may look over the River Tamar winding and twisting along the distant green plains for nearly the whole forty miles.

They were all young men located here as lodgers, for Mr. Foster was very particular whom he accepted as his guests. I was compelled to report myself thoroughly before he consented to receive me and my hold-all, but after I had satisfied him he treated me like a son; we were all brothers in that establishment, and splendidly coddled up for a reasonable fee. Mrs. Foster made the finest pickled onions in the world; they were like an exquisite fruit, so that I longed for supper hour to taste them again. She gave me a recipe, and I am seriously thinking of starting on a large scale as a pickled-onion manufacturer, for if I can only turn them out like Mrs. Foster, then Mrs. Lazenby may retire as soon as she likes.

If ever any of my readers visit Launceston, let them hunt up Mr. Foster of —— and try to get into his charmed home-circle. If they do, they may congratulate themselves on two things: first, the comforts they will enjoy; secondly, the respectability of which this enjoyment is a sure voucher. Whatever your sisters may say about you at home, you are a moral young man if Mr. Foster takes you into his comfortable boarding-house.

There is another establishment at Launceston which is well worthy of a visit, Ackerman's Exhibition, Hiring Depôt, and Bathing Establishment, which has the motto, 'The Poetry of Science, and Music of Motion.'

I did not see any hiring or bathing apartments while I was there, but I found the philosopher at home amongst his discoveries and mechanical toys. I expect the bathing was a gentle lure to draw visitors inside to be enlightened upon scientific mysteries, for during the half-hour I passed listening to his explanations of the conic sections, and watching the perpetual motions, earthquakes and submarine explosions where the earth was made to record her own vibrations, the crystallisation with polarised light, and evidences of things unseen, I saw nothing of it.

He was intensely in earnest this aged sage, and impressed me with that if with nothing else; also his charge puzzled me considerably. It was 2s. per half-hour for a single person, but if married only 1s. I got my half-hour of the wisdom of the spheres for a shilling. He asked me to look at an animal with a thousand heads through the microscope, and promised me a new hat if I could capture one. I gave it up, and after getting as much of the wonders of organic and mystical Nature explained to me as I could take in by means of little wooden dolls, I departed as gratified as if I had been to a lecture at one of the young men's mutual improvement associations. His artificial rainbows did not strike me, however, so greatly as did his description 'the Moon in full dress paying her respects to Jupiter'; as a metaphor that line sent me away deeply pondering.

The population of Launceston is 17,715, and the area of the town 8,840 acres; it possesses a free library containing nearly 11,000 volumes.

After seeing all that there was to be seen at Launceston, I once more took the train for Circular Head, after which I returned to Formby, Port Frederick, whence the steamer sailed for Port Phillip. A rush past ploughed fields and distant mountains, then we steamed out past Formby Beacon and House Top into a very rough sea. The old Bay of Biscay sensation was on me once more, so that I had to shut up my note-book and hasten down to my berth; my next appearance was at Yarra Wharf.

CHAPTER LIV

THE AUSTRALIAN ALPS

Feathertop, Baldy—Razor Back—The Dargo—Omeo—Kosciusko—
The Murray Gates—Drive to Bairnsdale and End.

I COULD not have ended my long journey in a better way than I did when I wound up by taking the Alps, although I must confess it was undeniably hard work; it was like ending a book with a grand climax. All the rest of the scenery (leaving out Peter Botte and the Owen Stanley ranges) seemed like lesser incidents leading up to the big scene of all, which is brought before the spectator with a bang and left at that for him to digest.

I took the train to Beechworth Junction, by Kilmore, Tallarook, Mangalore, and Benalla. How well I remember a long tramp which I had once to Kilmore, when all the stock-in-trade which I had to carry me along was Boucicault's song of 'Pat Molloy!' Yet I found it carried me very well along, as most of my entertainers were Irishmen; however it is a story which must be reserved for my next book, 'Tales of an Australian Tramp,' as it properly belongs to that nomadic order.

From Beechworth I went to Myrtleford and stopped the night at the comfortable little hotel there. I would like to have said 'slept that night at Myrtleford,' but as a quartz-crushing machine was in full work at about ten feet distance from my bedroom, the walls of which were

VICTORIAN ALPS: MOUNT KOSCIUSKO

composed of weather-boards, sleeping was an utter impossibility.

What a most infernal din those heavy stampers made as they pounded the quartz lumps into fine powder! It felt as if my head was under them and they were grinding my thick skull into dust in their vain attempts to extract gold out of my worn-out brains. I say vainly attempting, for how could these senseless steel crushers get out of my brains what I have tried for years to get without succeeding? Every instant throughout that long dark night I sprang up with a fearsome start as the stampers came down, with my heart responding, in wild thuds, to each of those thunderous smashes.

'You could not sleep much last night I fear,' said my kindly hostess as she spread the table for breakfast and observed my wearied appearance.

'Does any one ever sleep in Myrtleford?' I asked her, amazed that she should think such a feat at all possible.

'Oh yes, we always are able to sleep while the machine is working. It is only on the Sunday nights that our rest is at all broken; the unaccustomed stillness when it is not working disturbs us.'

From Myrtleford I drove by coach to the mountain-surrounded township of Bright. The driver was a Dane, weather-beaten and sun-tanned, with a keen blue eye and a fund of racy stories. By the way, I noticed a singular colonial habit while I was going by train, that I did not exactly admire, the 'jumping' of seats. Once I was in a crowded train, where some of the passengers had to stand; a lady opposite to me was sitting with her wraps on, and getting wearied she got up to lean for a moment out of the window, leaving her wraps on the seat; immediately a young man who had been standing, stepped over, pitched the wraps to the floor, and sat down; and the strange part about it was that neither the lady nor any of the other passengers seemed to think it unusual, or that he ought to have been kicked outside; she merely picked up her wraps and stood holding them in her hand, but showed great surprise when I rose up and offered her my seat. However, this happened in a third-class compartment, and the young man was a lout who mistook unmanly vulgarity for independence, and I only saw it occur once. As a rule the roughest colonial is a gentleman, although the law of 'jumping' is considered as one of the colonial rights, and not to be disputed when it has been successfully accomplished.

I passed the Buffalo Ranges, rugged and grand, with the Bogong, where live and breed in perfect freedom large droves of wild horses who have never known a shoe or a saddle. They are magnificent and ferocious beasts, who have been foaled from wild mothers and untamed grandmothers, and through living constantly upon the mountains have almost changed their original natures and become like panthers in their spring and sureness of grip as well as their untamable savageness. As yet none of them have been caught alive, for no trained horse can take the heights or wild leaps over gorges that they can; sometimes they are seen bounding along the mountain tops from rock to rock, like the chamois of Switzerland, with their long manes and tails flying far behind them. The Houyhnhnm is here seen in his full perfection and wonderful grace; he is descended originally, many generations back, from stray horses that have wandered and lost themselves in the mountains.

I passed lovely bends of the Ovens River with lofty waterfalls, such as the Eurobin, falling and splashing over the rugged precipices and getting lost to sight amongst the giant gums and ferns, and then I came to a Chinese town, with its Joss-house and all complete.

Artful fellows these Chinamen are, and great favourites

with the colonial girls. They are not allowed to bring Celestial houris with them, so they have to get white wives, and as they are invariably model husbands, being gentle, easy, generous and complaisant, they get the very pick of the bevy. When a Chinaman lands in the Colony he at once begins to save up his money in order to *buy* an English girl, and after saving enough, he goes to the father and mother and gives them a good lump-sum down to be allowed to court their daughter; few of the girls say No to their suitor, as he lets them do what they like after the wedding, and never interferes with them or exhibits any disagreeable jealousy. One night I sat in the pit of a theatre with a smiling John, who was perfectly oily with satisfaction and pride because his pretty wife was enjoying herself in the dress-circle with a crowd of young mashers.

'Dat my wife,' observed he proudly to me, as he pointed up to where the fair one sat, dressed in the most expensive silks and overloaded with bangles and gold chains, ' and all de swells am friends of Maly's.'

It was nothing to John that Mary ignored the presence of her lord and master in the pit; enough that she was the most extravagantly-dressed and best-attended woman in the theatre. He had none of the nature of the 'dog in the manger' in him.

From Bright I drove to Harrietville on the post-cart, getting in the twilight rare glimpses of hill scenery with the sparkling river rushing along pure and fresh. Next day the laborious portion of the journey began— the mountain journey on horseback.

There was a maidservant at Allan's hotel who startled me very much. She was middle-aged, tall and gaunt, with hard features and a morose air of gloomy mystery which filled me with apprehension.

When she entered to lay my supper and arrange the

fire, she would come over to my side with a teacup or plate in her hand (for she ushered the articles in separately), and in a sibilant, hoarse whisper begin to tell me something, but what it was I never could quite gather, as, before she had well begun, her smart mistress would bounce in after her crying, 'Look alive there, Jane!' Then she would put her finger warningly to her thin lips and utter the one sound 'Hush!' lay down the cup and disappear for the next article.

Whatever did the woman mean? Was I in a den of bandits who were only waiting for the hour of sleep to enter my bedroom by some trap-door and cut my throat? I asked her nervously to tell me several times as she hovered near, but the communications were always cut short. I could only gather such disjointed sentences as ' To-night when all is quiet '—' I know your room '—' Look out.'

I did not feel happy, but I had a task to perform before I could get to bed, a preparation against the morrow, so having finished my tea, I stole out quietly to a little tailor's shop in the silent township and laid in a stock of needles and thread, also some sheets of cotton wadding. After Deniliquin experiences in the saddle, I resolved to prepare myself against all emergencies, so by the light of my candle I did a bit of artful tailoring in the seclusion of my bedroom, after carefully locking my door; then with a sigh of relief I covered myself up and fell asleep. No fell tragedy happened that night at the hotel, so next morning after a hearty breakfast and a walk round Harrietville, with its creek of delicious ice-cold water, valleys and extensive scenery, I mounted the old black horse assigned to me, and with my guide began the ascent to Feathertop, and the snowy Alps.

Mr. Gallacher was the name of my guide, the mountain mail man. He had a weekly round of the hills, winter and summer, of about 160 miles, all up and down tremendous mountains. In summer when it was clear it was comparatively easy, for he could then ride over his ground, but in the winter, when the snow was heavy and drifting, he had to walk over Feathertop and Razor Back, sleeping out in the cold where best he could, and walking along fearful ridges of frozen snow with nothing underneath for 2,000 feet or more.

He told me as we went up that he once conveyed a father and two sons over Razor Back when it was covered with snow. He had great difficulty in keeping the young fellows to the solid narrow track, for seeing a broad level surface of hard snow they would not believe him when he told them that it was only a thin outstanding ice-shelf over a fearful abyss. But when they got over the dangerous ledge, and he gained a point of the journey where they could see it, then as the father looked at the three or four thousand feet of clear drop, and that awful bending narrow shelf of ice and snow protruding over it, along which they had passed in their unconsciousness, he fell back in a dead faint. Razor Back is 6,300 feet high, with only a very narrow edge along the top of the vast precipices. Gallacher does his winter journey in snowshoes.

About a mile from Harrietville a little woman met us, on horseback, with her riding-habit wet through to the waist. She had just come over Feathertop and reported that the snow in some places was up to her horse's neck, but that it was rapidly melting. She was a farmer's wife and rode this dangerous journey alone, going down to Bright for some groceries she was short of at home. This is the land of unconscious heroes and heroines;—the roadway had been impassable for some weeks before this, but she could no longer wait for the provision cart or want her cup of tea, so she had coolly braved the dangers of the way.

Feathertop is 6,303 feet high, Bogong 6,508, Buffalo 5,645, Hotham 6,100, Baldy 4,625.

It is a stiff climb up the track for those 3,000 feet, from the mountain town of Harrietville to the hospice, with deep gutters and great yawning valleys spreading out, and from where the mountain sides slope up like house-roofs, forests covered at the bottom and gradually thinning up to dead wood and finally rocks, grass, and patches of snow. Feathertop was almost clear, but on Razor Back and Baldy the snow still lay in square patches and ribbon like stripes of glistening white.

William Bonstead, the landlord of the hospice, received us with a roaring wood fire, for we were cold, and it is always sharp at the hospice; then after a rest we were once more in the saddle and on our descent into the valley of the Dargo, down, down without a pause, along narrow ledges with fearful precipices below us. We passed in the space of two or three hours, from the height of winter weather to torrid summer.

My horse was as surefooted as a goat, yet I shivered sometimes as he stumbled over the loose stones when descending these narrow ledges and I heard the stones rattle over the edge and strike with a faint far-off sound against the rocks below. At one part my waterproof dropped from my saddle and fluttered down for hundreds of feet without interruption, until it looked like an amber-coloured butterfly against the blue haze of the tree tops upon which it had finally rested.

The Dargo was a pretty, swiftly-rushing stream just then, but sometimes, as I saw by the high-water mark on its banks, it becomes a great and roaring flood, bearing along everything in its impetuous force.

That night we slept in an old deserted woodman's hut at a place in the valley called Mayford. Gallacher was an expert bushman, therefore he soon had a blazing fire and a boiling billy of tea, while I lay back helpless. Now that I was off my horse, it was ten thousand times worse than walking, still not nearly so bad as it might have been, thanks to that midnight ceremony which had taken place with the cotton wadding at Harrietville.

Next morning I said farewell to Gallacher the mailman. He directed me on my way to Omeo from where I could get to the highest of the Alps, Mount Kosciusko on the New South Wales side, and which is 12,000 feet high.

It was a plain track that my guide pointed out, and plain directions which he gave me before he rode away on his lonely round, yet I lost my road utterly within an hour after leaving him, and but for Bob, my sagacious old horse, my whitened skeleton might have been riding still amongst these grand mountain passes while my horse grazed on peacefully. But he had been on the journey before and knew his way, so that after I grew tired out with racking my brains and exercising my own judgment, I flung the reins on his neck and let him go as he liked, which was the very best thing that I could have done, for he brought me to Omeo as the night fell.

All about the region of Kosciusko is wildly romantic in the extreme, the mountain itself with its snow-covered sharp peaks—for it is seldom bare, the Cobboras, Gibbos and other points rising high above the forests—precipices, and gorges through which rapid rivers and streams rush. It is all a wild climb over boulders, piled-up rocks, snow-covered peaks, tangled valleys, up and down a country of wild and savage grandeur, right on through deep fissures with great precipices rising up, till I come to that mighty chasm called the Murray Gates.

Here daylight is nearly always shut out from the spectator by those 3,000 feet of perpendicular cliffs, while the Murray runs quietly along over the pebbles and past the boulders at their feet, a moderately sized stream, but soon to be fed by the many hill tributaries until it swells into a mighty river.

A wonderfully impressive scene of solitude and greatness —as I stand outside my temporary camp, looking up to that little strip of evening sky overhead, the full moon smiles over the fissure and repeats its silver lustre in the ripples of the stream at my feet; I am not quite alone, since that familiar moon looks down upon me in this vast abyss, yet, but for that silver circle, how unutterably and morbidly lonely it would have been!

From Omeo to Bruthen I go by stage coach, a drive to be remembered long afterwards, for our driver is courageous and in a hurry to get over the ground, his horses are fresh and full of mettle, but the road is of the roughest description. After many stops and topplings over, at which times we have to get out and help the wheels out of the deep ruts; after our insides are nearly jolted out, and after repeated walks up the hills, we arrive at our journey's end wearied and grateful for any small mercies which may be bestowed upon us.

Along by the High Ranges, Mount Elizabeth, and Fainting Range with its cuttings, cliffs, and gorges, past bullock drays slowly and painfully toiling along, we jump and jostle, now two or three feet into the air, now banging against one another, or what is worse after my long ride, landing full upon the hard seat again before we can take any precaution to break the fall. On we go without a pause down the Tambo Valley and over Monkey Creek, bringing behind us volumes of choking dust.

Parrots are plentiful here, also the beautiful lyre birds; I hear the Bell bird once again and at one part we crush over the gliding body of a large black snake; then past Lucknow we rush, covering it up with that dense dust-cloud; past lonely patches of bush, trailing honeysuckle, and reedy marshes where stupid green frogs sit croaking and waiting to be devoured by the watchful snakes, past Bruthen, and so once more into Bairnsdale. My travels for the present are over, and now I may have a bit of a rest.

THE END.

www.ingramcontent.com/pod-product-compliance
Lightning Source LLC
Chambersburg PA
CBHW032047220426
43664CB00008B/898